In Continuity

Austin Warren

The Last Essays of Austin Warren

Books by Austin Warren

Alexander Pope as Critic and Humanist (1929)

The Elder Henry James (1934)

Nathaniel Hawthorne: Representative Selections (editor) (1934)

Richard Crashaw: A Study in Baroque Sensibility (1939)

Literary Scholarship: Its Aims and Methods (with Norman Foerster, J. C. McGalliard, René Wellek, W. L. Schramm) (1941)

Rage for Order: Essays in Criticism (1948)

Theory of Literature (with René Wellek) (1949)

New England Saints (1956)

The New England Conscience (1966)

They Will Remain: Poems by Susan Pendleton (editor) (1966)

Connections (1970)

Teacher and Critic: Essays by and about Austin Warren (edited by Myron Simon and Harvey Gross) (1976)

Becoming What One Is, 1899–1936 (1995)

In Continuity: The Last Essays of Austin Warren (introduced and edited by George A. Panichas) (1996)

In Continuity

AUSTIN WARREN

THE LAST ESSAYS OF AUSTIN WARREN

Introduced and edited by
George A. Panichas

MERCER UNIVERSITY PRESS
Macon, Georgia 1996

ISBN 0-86554-501-4

PR
99
.W34
1996

In Continuity:
The Last Essays of Austin Warren
Introduced and edited by George A. Panichas

Copyright © 1996
Mercer University Press, Macon, Georgia 31210-3960 USA
All rights reserved.

Printed in the United States of America.
The paper used in this publication meets the minimum requirements
of American National Standard for Information Sciences—permanence
of Paper for Printed Library Materials, ANSI Z39.48-1984.

Library of Congress Cataloging-in-Publication Data

Warren, Austin, 1899–
    In continuity : the last essays of Austin Warren / Austin
Warren ; introduced and edited by George A. Panichas
    xxv+ 200 pp.   6x9"
    Includes bibliographical references.
    ISBN 0-86554-501-4
    1. English literature—History and criticism.   2. American
poetry—20th century—History and criticism.   I. Panichas,
George Andrew.   II. Title.
PR99.W34   1996
820.9—dc20
                                                    96-2407
                                                    CIP

To

With the drawing of this love and the voice of this calling

We shall not cease from exploration
And the end of all our exploring
Will be to arrive where we started
And know the place for the first time.

—T. S. Eliot, *Little Gidding* (1943)

"Obey the voice at eve obeyed at prime . . ."

—Ralph Waldo Emerson, "Terminus"

Contents

Introduction

I.

The essays found in the following pages, composed in the 1970s and early 1980s, are the last that Austin Warren (1899–1986) wrote in a long and distinguished career as an American man of letters. Disabling illnesses in the years immediately preceding his death, however, prevented him from fulfilling his plan to publish in his lifetime a book containing his late literary criticism. He had hoped to join this book to his two earlier books of practical criticism, *Rage for Order: Essays in Criticism* (1948) and *Connections* (1970). As in his other books, the essays here assembled were first published in various quarterly reviews and, in a few instances, as contributions to books.

In his critical writings Warren never failed to disclose sincerity and integrity of purpose. Partisan and polemical approaches he found unacceptable. Equally unacceptable were ideological preconceptions, which he condemned as leading to critical conformity. Throughout his career as a professor of English in leading universities, he came also to disdain more and more what he perceived as the decadent tendencies of the academy. He himself remained steadfast in his refusal to belong to any one academic coterie or critical camp, insisting that he be his own man and not part of what Henry James once decried as the "associational process." Intellectually and spiritually, Warren sought to maintain his independence even in and despite the isolation that allegiance to critical principles can often impose.

Any cursory glance at Warren's critical essays will show an absence of anger, or haughtiness, or impatience, or pride, or vindictiveness. A wonderful openness of spirit, of a friendly and unaffected general intelligence, of a steady even-temperedness identify the main sources of his critical powers and efforts and also account for this good influence. But at the very same time these irenic and magnanimous qualities, which no doubt also conduce a particular temperament, must not be seen as harboring or inciting an excessive prudence, or safeness, or timidity. Rather they were the qualities of a critic who not only discerned his own rage for order but also confessed his constant need for an inner check. He had no fear at all of both confronting and voicing those felt truths that emerge from the rigors of a critic's quest for value:

> But to write and publish at all can be considered an act of aggression; and the more modest, tentative, and exploratory a man is, the more (appearing in public, there to conduct his self-education) he finds it necessary to don some armor—of belligerence or extreme courtesy, or both.

As a university teacher of literature, of "culture" or the humanities, from 1920 to 1968, and as a writer of books ("not as a means of professional advancement" but rather as "an indispensable instrument of self-definition and intellectual clarification"), Warren aspired most to the virtues of measure and humility. These are precisely the virtues that were to nourish his critical achievement, as well as to endow it with the insight and wisdom that Warren's famous Harvard teacher, "my old master," Irving Babbitt, affixed as the highest goals of the critic. Indeed, it can be said that, among the major American teachers in our time, Warren was an exemplary servant of the critical spirit, possessing what other critics so often lacked, freedom from sectarian vehemence, and the gift of fusing the dignity of literature and the dignity of critical thinking.

Warren belongs to that critical line of classical humanism that begins with Matthew Arnold and continues with Babbitt, Paul Elmer More, and T. S. Eliot, whose critical ideas and texts he assimilated and ramified. From Arnold he no doubt acquired a deep appreciation of disinterestedness and flexibility as the chief ingredients of expounding one's critical concerns and sympathies in their breadth and depth. In particular, he embraced Arnold's own confidence in the humanities, the liberal and humane arts that Warren stalwartly honored in his teaching and criticism.

From Babbitt he learned his greatest spiritual lessons— "that in my classical humanism (with its Eastern equivalent in the humanism of Confucius) and my Catholic-orientated religion (with its Eastern equivalent in Buddhism), I was heir to great, to perennial traditions." To be sure, Warren did transcend the dogmatic and didactic bias that characterized Babbitt's contributions to the republic of arts and letters. But from Babbitt he derived his greatest critical lesson, a profound understanding of the interpretation of values, which Babbitt summed up on the first page of his penultimate *Democracy and Leadership* (1924) and which Warren was fond of quoting:

> When studied with any degree of thoroughness, the economic problem will be found to run into the political problem, the political problem in turn into the philosophical problem, and the philosophical problem itself to be almost indissolubly bound up at last with the religious problem.

No other words better confirm for Warren the internal values that the critic as man of letters should subscribe to. If, as Warren averred, he came in time to feel closer to Eliot than to Babbitt and More, "finding him more literary, more 'aesthetic,' than either," it was Babbitt who transmitted to him first principles of criticism that were to remain irreversible in influence and importance. Stuart P. Sherman's words of tribute to Babbitt—"He had given you theses about literature, about life, which you would spend a lifetime in verifying"—found genuine enactment in Warren's life and thought.

From his great masters of modern criticism Warren learned well lessons that stayed him and gave him the inspiration that he needed to climb the critical ladder. He was their catechumen without at the same time being a mere enthusiast or slavish sectary. From the beginning his critical writings disclosed that the critical principles, the lessons, that Warren had learned also gave him a creative critical courage. The true "cost of discipleship," as Dietrich Bonhoeffer reminds us, dictates a transcendent discipline and a greater heroism. Criticism, too, must have its "costly grace," if the work of the critic is to develop viable and authentic distinctions.

Never failing to show his "loyalty to earlier admirations," Warren went on to define his own critical perspective and make his own critical connections, which came to underline his critical independence, if not uniqueness. His intellectual eclecticism, in this respect, was always a disciplined one; and reverence, he emphatically disclosed, must ultimately translate into something higher, as the critic makes his ascent, "transcending by including." He firmly believed that "the critic needs both reverence and courage of judgment." At the same time he emphasized that "the critic must judge for himself, and then be possessed of the final courage to utter his judgment."

In Warren we view the critic as seeker who ascends to become "the man of letters in the modern world," to use here the title of Allen Tate's 1952 essay. Warren frequently returned to this essay, and it is not difficult to understand his admiration for it when one considers Tate's fervent depiction of the man of letters in strenuous contention with a world of increasing fragmentation, found especially in the

> . . . illiberal specializations . . . in which means are divorced from ends, action from sensibility, matter from mind, society from the individual, religion from moral agency, love from lust, poetry from thought, communion from experience, and mankind in the community from men in the crowd.

Warren's critical writings, in their parts and in their whole, embody uncompromising resistance to and rejection of all those divorcements that give rise to "a vulgar contemporaneity" and erode "the values and the virtues of 'Culture' and 'Tradition.' " Indeed, Warren affirms the role of the modern man of letters who understands the full meaning and demands of his critical responsibility:

> He stands for man's recognition of his dual citizenship in church and state, society visible and invisible, for man's recognition that all we are we owe; that we do not, and cannot, begin *ab ovo* and *de novo* but are heirs to a great inheritance of tradition and wisdom, represented in the West by our joint indebtedness to the Greek philosophers, the Hebrew prophets, and the Christian saints.

The cornerstone of Warren's achievement, what defined his critical perspective, stamped its essential character, mobilized its conscience, in short, what gave it both moral energy and spiritual vision, was his generalism. "As a literary critic," he asserts, "I have no 'method,' no specialty, but am what is called, in another discipline, a 'general practitioner.' " His admirations and loyalties, the sum of what he owed to his mentors, ancestors, and kinsmen, in whom he discerned a deep metaphysical heroism that infused their calling and vocation, provided him with paradigms that he sought to preserve and yet also advance in a modern world of rapid, at times even reckless change, when what Joseph

Conrad termed "the endangered stability of things" becomes an acute and pervasive problem.

At the heart of this change, affecting as it did culture and society, Warren found an increasing and imperious presence of the specialized attitude leading inevitably to the very destruction of the world as an organic whole. He confronted this attitude in his essays, in his books, which he shaped with diligent care and with precisely that "spiritual discipline" that he associated with the task of "confronting disorder in one's self and in the world . . . [and] of facing existentially, as a total human being living in time, the responsibility of vision and choice." For Warren this responsibility was to center in the critic's responsibility as a generalist "who seeks to reclaim the ancient, the primitive, freedom of scope."

Warren's generalism was neither unfocused nor uncentered. It had an inherent order of discipline that gave his criticism authoritative identity and guidance. "The final necessity for the critic," Warren states, "is, ideally, space and time for withdrawal, for critical distancing; absorption, withdrawal, often repeated, are constantly procedures of criticism." His writings were to emerge from these procedures that not only the creative artist but also the creative critic honors and that can yield to each the highest degree of accomplishment. Warren's writings in their totality— whether in the form of a review, or a review essay, or an essay, or prefatory comments, or, finally, a book—emerged from a sustained, inclusive process of critical thought wrought by painstaking contemplation.

From his earliest theological writings in the 1920s and 1930s in two Swedenborgian periodicals, *The New-Church Messenger* and the *New-Church Review*, the devotional element in Warren's writings was pronounced. There is, in fact, something toughly ascetic about his essays in the search for a purity of exposition and a sincerity of commentation. One cannot fail to discern in them the critic as seeker who rises above himself through complete adherence to his critical vocation. His essays register a transcendent search for order:

> . . . if there be a *universe*, and not a chaos or a pluralism, then a man must set himself resolutely in search of its order, and must construct, for himself at least, a tentative hierarchy of values in that smaller world

(presumably representative of the larger cosmos) in which he lives and functions.

Criticism, for Warren, thus signifies a "serious call"; the critic's task is to reconcile self-definition and self-discipline in ways that bring directly to mind Ralph Waldo Emerson's declaration that "each man and woman is born with an aptitude to do something impossible to any other." Criticism, Warren also showed, was no mere academic activity; "the business of criticism" was clearly a phrase that he rejected as intimating a crassly secular pursuit. In the ascending character of their composition and structure his writings have the quality of interiority that eludes many modern critics. For Warren the creative imagination and "the experience of literature" affirm the life of the soul. This affirmation, written and unwritten, was to give his voice its special tone and his thought its special quality.

In his achievement we discern an astonishing confluence of the art of criticism and the witness of criticism. In effect each piece of writing was for Warren a spiritual exercise which demands the utmost effort of concentration and meditation and which, in James's words, exalts a critic "who has knelt through his long vigil and who has the piety of his office." A celebratory seriousness, it can be said, was to emerge from such an effort. Few modern critics were to excel Warren in his open celebration of great ideas, great writers, great souls. Literary greatness for him meant spiritual greatness, that is, the kind of greatness that gives us guidance and helps to orient us toward the good, or, as Plato puts it, "to make us grow wings to overcome gravity."

II.

As a critic Warren was to be intensely aware of his spiritual responsibilities, finding and determining the value of a work of art which testifies to some spiritual reality a writer himself may not have consciously discerned; and also defining as fully and honestly as he can the poet's spiritual cosmos in terms of the literary structure which corresponds to it. This is not to claim, of course, that Warren was essentially a religious critic, for he eschewed an exclusive category that limited his understanding and elucidation of literary texts. For the religious faculty Warren had much feeling; in temper and sympathy he was of an integral religious disposition without at the same time being possessed by fixed views that restricted critical exploration and discoveries. He had too much reverence for literary texts, for the mystery of the word, to allow them to be used for proselytizing purposes. He was a critic rather than an evangel of the religious imagination. How does the critic reconcile valuation and celebration? That was the challenge that Warren grappled with in his writings. The poets, novelists, critics, and thinkers who evinced his admiration were those who struggled with "ultimate religious questions about ultimate values." Their spiritual quests became, in a deep sense, his own, as he so acutely demonstrated in his two companion books of "culture history,"—the "disguised autobiography" of a "latter-day Transcendentalist," as Warren's friend Glauco Cambon observed—*New England Saints* (1956) and *The New England Conscience* (1966).

From beginning to end Warren remained a Christian humanist who sought to reconcile, in word and work, the tensive values of human existence. His own critical view of inner and outer tensions made him unusually aware of the interplay of the tensions of existence in their undiminishing power. "I belong, like Tillich," he admitted, "with those whose lot it is to live 'on the boundary,' with those who are 'torn between.' " His critical interpretations emerged from a thoroughly disciplined and exacting consciousness of the constant encounter of the physical and the metaphysical.

If he saw himself as a Christian humanist continuing in the footsteps of the Christian Platonists of Alexandria and the Cambridge Platonists of the English seventeenth century, of Anglican Bishops Jeremy Taylor (1613–1667) and Charles Gore (1853–1932), and of Baron von Hügel (1852–1925)—whose writings he did not cease to study—he also saw himself as a Christian realist sensitively attuned to the human condition in all of its problematic facets. He shunned illusion and reverie in any guise, intellectual or spiritual. He remained suspicious of all institutional forms, especially in religion and education, "for I am at ease only on the periphery of both," he insisted. And yet in that periphery he found the critical latitude to be his own man and to effect a mediation between his skepticism concerning the nature of institutions and also his "steady faith in the importance of continuity."

Warren wanted connection, not separation; *sophrosynē*, not rashness; order, not chaos. But above and beyond these wants he was a critic who practiced the courage of discrimination that transcends bias in spirit and in aim. Living in an age of cruel disarray, he particularly sought for the renewal of the virtue of order as a form of moral life within both the individual and the community. With "Mr. Pope"—"the moral poet of all civilization," Lord Byron wrote—he could fully fathom the meaning of the words, "Order is Heav'n's first law." His critical heroes, his saints, were those capable of teaching one "attention, concentration, the scrupulous analysis of one's own mental and affective state." For Warren criticism was in effect an exercise in self-courage and self-discipline. The critic cannot be passive or complacent or shrinking in his recognition and defense of fundamentals:

> It indeed takes courage to face, in one's own silent thought, in one's speech, in one's letters and in one's published writings, this ceaseless and fatiguing discrimination—never to allow oneself to slip into easy compliance with the currently accepted compromised standards of one's neighborhood, one's university (academics are not noted for their courage), one's inherited nation, one's church or religion. There can be no relaxation of the critical spirit, no unbending of the bow; and no sphere is exempt from its operation. . . .

Reconciliation is a sacred thread in Warren's Christian humanism. The act of reconciliation, embodying for him a tempering and ordering of human tensions, brings one closer to harmony and proportion. To Warren the reconciliation of religion and culture was of especial importance, and he was assiduous in explaining and defining his perception of the checks or balances he deemed essential to the process of union. "Christian Humanism is the combination of religion and culture, of learning and spirituality," he wrote. "This proper balance—I better say— is ideal, difficult, and precarious." Spiritual religion, he went on to argue, is the more fundamental of the two, but he also insisted that culture served as a check on religion. Without religion culture can become, for the gentleman, urbane, but superficial; and if it is "the culture of the professors" it simply becomes "intelligence without commitment or moral responsibility." Without culture religion can become fanatical, bigoted, obscure: "Religion stands in need simultaneously of some restraint by culture and some relief from it." Warren's Christian humanism defined his critical humanism, its beliefs and criteria, with the characteristic precision and honesty that identified his perspective as a whole. An exemplar of what he reverentially named a "literary priesthood," he abjured the "tradition of infidelity," as C. S. Lewis saliently described it, which many other modern critics eagerly embraced.

Warren composed nothing without showing or demanding care, conviction, seriousness. No literary pomp, no pretense, no pose, no falsity could betray his method of writing. "It is impossible to name his style without naming his character: they are one thing," is a statement that could be said of Warren as it was said of Emerson by John Jay Chapman, another, if forgotten, New England Saint. The power of words was to fill Warren with the fear and trembling that inhere in the responsibilities of the critic. No less than the manifest accent of his own New England speech—crisp, austere, precise, lucid, measured, unhurried—his written language attains its equivalent discipline of style, enduring in construction, absolute in meaning, unstinting in integrity. "Style is not disjunct from substance: it is considered substance rendered expression." So Warren wrote, or, better, insisted, his words reminding us, too, that his own style emerged not so much from his critical thought but from his character and conscience. Ultimately Warren's is that transcendent style of which Alfred North Whitehead speaks as the ultimate morality of mind.

A lifelong member of the academic community, Warren was not always at ease with academics and the orthodoxies and conformities they tend to create and expect of each other. "But then," he wrote to one of his epistolary friends, "all my life I have found the company of literary people, especially poets and poet-critics, much more congenial than the company of academics; for literary people have convictions, views, and tastes—in other words, life, while (as you bitterly know) academic people have none of these, and so are 'dead.' " A gentle, courteous man, Warren did not wantonly initiate conflicts or animosities with his colleagues in the professoriate. Decorum and civility were virtues he practiced patiently and scrupulously. Adversarial situations he found contrary to his sense of *douceur*. Of academics, as of authors of whose work he disapproved, or from whom he strongly dissented, he chiefly practiced what he called "the rhetoric of silence." Clearly he had his own work to do, his own character and talents to explore, his own values to impart as teacher and critic: "Integrity is the best—and almost the only gift—we can hope to transmit to the young."

The quest for transcendence requires a greater courage on the part of the teacher as critic "in multiplying sharp distinctions" and putting these "distinctions into the service of the character and will," to quote here words from Babbitt, whom Warren honored as "an enlightener and an enlarger." The academic marketplace was not for him. The teacher, no less than the critic, must try to go "beyond personalism" and attain a form of "decreation," as Simone Weil, whose writings Warren studied and admired, uses that word. "With the man of integrity," he wrote in his Journals, "his whole being takes incarnation in his every act, his every paragraph. He is always representative." In this connection, too, Warren recognized a peculiarly cleft quality in himself that unveiled in his avoidance of polemics and confrontation. "Mine is an irenic spirit, and talent. . . . In me, from the start, have existed an artist (or at least an aesthete) along with a moralist (sternnest in self-judgment)," he confessed. This self-dichotomy he never entirely resolved, choosing as he did to err, if necessary, on the side of kindness and magnanimity.

Himself a native New Englander, Warren could speak as forthrightly to others, to his students and readers, as did his "New England Saints," "my spiritual ancestors and kinsmen," "to whom reality was the spiritual life, whose spiritual integrity was their calling and vocation"—Archbishop Fénelon, The Reverend Edward Taylor, Charles Eliot Norton, Irving Babbitt, John Brooks Wheelwright. He wore the mantle of prudence with distinction. Yet he could also speak with thorny simplicity and directness when axiomatic truths were in question. He always had a reservoir of fundamental goodness, kindliness, unselfishness; he possessed, too, a quick and warm sense of humor. Behind his manly candor there was redemptive decision, and behind his rectitude, deep affectionateness and compassion. Nowhere are all these humane qualities better illustrated, or illuminated, than in the following paragraph from a letter to a younger academic, and friend, with whom he had had an acrimonious exchange:

I deeply regret that ill-advised and bad-spirited letter I wrote you (an evil spirit entered me and spoke through me). But I cannot *wholly* regret it, for it served as a warning to me and as the occasion for searching self-examination, which, though painful, had, as you suggest, its own form of purgation. *But* I wounded you who stood in no need of further wounding, *from a friend, too*, so I ask your forgiveness.

The moral sense of responsibility shapes Warren's prose and heightens his critical substance. An abstinent quality appears in the leanness of his prose and in the sinewy forces of his critical thinking: "Civilization as we understand it may fail; let us, at least, not fail it." "Civilization is the art of the complete consciousness, in the individual and in society." In his words and thought we hear "the call" to moral responsibility. No excess, no undue softness, no crooked line, no sentimentalism, no false aplomb enfeeble the vigor and centrality of his writing. His composition is also his construction, each as much a keystone as the other, both built to be permanent, the one empowering the other, each depending on the other and each holding the other as a companion in common pursuit of order and understanding. Yet in the very sturdiness of his verbal constructs and judgments there are also some wonderfully subtle and supple, even poetic, notes, never reaching too high or too low, demanding patient attention, trust, lest one lose sight of the whole circumference of the critical presentation.

The symmetry of Warren's language and thought; the potency and resonance of his creative intelligence; the felicity and judiciousness of his probings: these are the major properties undergirding and overarching his critical achievement, which at the maximum point of its value and insight is inclusively moral, conveying as it does, as it must, honesty of concern and purpose. In whatever subject he chose to write about—and the conceptual grasp and sweep of his literary interest in lives and letters was rich and comprehensive—he depicts his humanism, forging it with *Serenitas Conscientiae* in the hard face of the crisis of modernity, with its fragmentations, its impieties, its "Terrible Presences"—"Where do they come from? Those whom we so much dread," to recall a line from W. H. Auden.

III.

In 1970 Warren moved to Providence, Rhode Island, where he lived during the remaining sixteen years of his life in retirement. After thirty years of university teaching in Iowa and Michigan he gladly returned to his ancestral New England. The New England that he knew and loved, it should be added, was not the New England of Mary E. Wilkins Freeman, and of rural life in eastern Massachusetts, as some of Warren's early commentators assumed, but rather the New England of Boston, and of Massachusetts north of Boston—Waltham, Stow, Littleton, Lincoln, Fitchburg, Ashburnham—as well as of Connecticut, from Middletown to Willimantic. Indeed, Hebron was the Connecticut village in which he and his Wesleyan University friend Benjamin Bissell established St. Peter's School of Liberal Humane Studies, an intellectual and cultural community patterned after Little Gidding and Alcott's Concord School of Philosophy. This "creative enterprise"—in the years 1923–1931—marked, as Warren wrote, "my first critical effort at finding my vocation."

His house in Providence, located at 90 Oriole Avenue, close to Brown University, which awarded Warren an honorary Litt.D. in 1974, quintessentialized both order in place and order in time. Ancient, stately, and commodious, it was a house in which intellect and spirit, dignity and serenity, wisdom and insight cohered with a beautiful quiescence that his many visitors—pupils, friends, auditors, colleagues—found restorative. For Warren this house aided the double rhythm of reflection and com-position that he saw as being indispensable in his determination to effect connections and continuities as a literary critic and man of letters. The loving support of his wife Antonia, a former medical doctor and a woman of broad intellectual and humanistic interests and independent judgment, as well as a gifted writer of short stories, helped immensely to create and sustain those domestic, everyday conditions that play their due role in the unrelenting procession of one's works and days.

His Providence years gave him much happiness and free time to devote himself uninterruptedly to a life of meditation and to "the truths of the inner life." The writings found in this book were the extraordinary offshoots of this happiness and this meditation, and they reflect unflag-ging concern with the intellectual life and the spiritual life. Indeed, Warren's Providence years were a period of rededication, with Warren as emeritus teacher and humanist critic continuing his quest for value: "We have to do our work, our thing, *ohne Hast, ohne Rast. . . .*"

The same sensitive but robust quality that stamped his earlier writings stamps his last writings. At the same time a more contemplative temper distinguishes the last writings that make up this volume. In them we observe what More calls "a steady growth in Grace." There is no pretension here, no pontificating, no oracular bent. To the end humility remained a constant virtue in Warren's work and thought. He was ever aware of the tensive task of combining the eagle and the dove, never an easy or a necessarily successful task for any critic. Confronting the neoclassical with the baroque, the aesthetic with the moral, was for him a battle that he kept on fighting.

For Warren this battle was a form of invisible warfare, one in which the critic fights to regain a spiritual center and to achieve conditions of criticism that go beyond purely evaluative interpretation and also beyond the contraries of thesis and antithesis and the indigenous strife they foster. To raise criticism to a higher metaphysical level by recovering the ancient precept that the visionary artist is a teacher who can help make men and women better in their cities by overcoming the hubris that destroys the city was an aim that encompassed Warren's aspirations. This aim is central to identifying his critical humanism. It also signals axiomatic qualities that further identify Warren as a Christian humanist who builds bridges between faith and knowledge. Here, also, his long-lasting admiration of Saint Clement of Alexandria, one of the Old Fathers of the Church who struggled to integrate Christian beliefs and ancient Greek principles of *paideia*, has a distinctive relevance. Clement's statement, "When a man is reminded of the better, of necessity he repents the worse," has a distinct echo in Warren's critical purposes.

In his last writings there is no parade of high morality, though moral effort is decidedly one of his impelling criteria. The critical orientation of these writings is toward the Good, the True, and the Beautiful. His critical perceptions convey confidence, encouragement, affirmation, spiritual joy and buoyancy. Yet these last writings do not belong, either necessarily or qualitatively, to a late or even final phase of Warren's achievement. Rather they disclose a line of continuity in his humanistic interests and thought, not monolithic but pliant. Proportion was the final object, Warren believed; his search for order was simultaneously his search for proportion. He instinctively admired "the human voice in its middle register." The even and poised quality of his critical explorations and thought, already evident in early books like *Alexander Pope as Critic and Humanist* (1929), *The Elder Henry James* (1934), and *Richard Crashaw: A Study in Baroque Sensibility* (1939), prevails in his last essays. If the state of contemplation now radiates their intelligence and grace, a feeling of confidence empowers their content and facilitates the serenity and the assurance that emerge from a combined sense of control and moral discovery. Inevitably the right word and the right accent conflate to give rise to Warren's apprehension of right order.

Warren's realization of his vocation as a man of letters in the modern world perhaps reaches an apex in these essays. In them we find the critic who is at peace with himself and with the world; who knows fully the value of his values; who communicates these with surety, perseverance, urbanity—and with what might best be called an unselfconscious humility that lies at the heart of his critical calling. Warren imposes no arbitrary standards in these essays but instead allows his standards to record the fullness of his acceptances and affirmations. In these essays, above all, we hear the voice of a humanist teacher and a friendly critic and not of a literary magistrate. The tone is honorific, celebratory, confessional, always respectful of T. S. Eliot's admonition, in *East Coker*, that "The only wisdom we can hope to acquire / Is the wisdom of humility: humility is endless."

Some of the essays are the fit occasion to express "gratitude" to a writer like Lewis Carroll, whose books Warren cherished, or to pay "homage" and "tribute" to great poet-critics like Allen Tate and T. S. Eliot and spiritual heroes and saints like William Law, to all of whom he was naturally attracted for their paradigms of honesty and faith, and for a legacy that continues "to challenge and to bless." Other essays contain his "pondering" of a writer like Walter Pater, who has a unique ability to teach one "attention, concentration, the scrupulous analysis of one's own mental and affective states." Still other essays are written in the form of what Warren speaks of as a "revisitation" of major poets like Robert Herrick, Robert Frost, and W. H. Auden, who have long meant much to him. In his old age, then, he was to reexamine, rethink, rejudge, and reflect on their achievement, as well as on their character, and often in the context of what Warren calls a "psychograph," in which "the proportion of stylistic analysis to biographical, or biographical to ideological, will be found to vary from essay to essay," chiefly for the purpose of delineating the "spiritual cosmos" of the particular writer he is reconsidering. And still other essays are written in the form of "personal and private visions" in which Warren concerns himself with ultimate spiritual values and conditions—the love of art, the love of knowledge, the love of man, the love of God.

Behind these last essays is a formidable man of mature thought, a *spoudaios*, who gratefully avers that his "religious faith and faith in writing, and writing have kept me going"—"with the steadiness of his first zeal," to use here Emerson's phrase. The last twenty years of his life were to see seismic changes in the cultural and spiritual life of the country. "I regret that we live in such a barbarous age, which grows steadily more barbarous," he wrote in a letter dated July 31, 1976. It was a situation which, understandably, made him apprehensive of the state of the humanities. In the midst of this anxiety he could hardly escape the "bleak and black state of depression" that so often affects refined and introspective writers and fills them with feelings of lassitude and doubt. Still he labored on with the characteristic patience and devotion of "a contemplative worker who had faith in his 'inner working.' " "And through whatever masks we speak," he wrote, "it is a living soul in search of verbal incarnation which is sent into the world. . . ."

Doubtlessly Warren did experience much personal satisfaction during his retired years in Providence, free from the burdens of his "oral teaching" as a university professor—a New England "apostle to the midwest," as he described himself. But at the same time he felt keenly his own isolation in a society and culture increasingly hostile to the humanistic spirit to which he remained faithful and to which the essays in this book testify so eloquently. Yet his inner resources were "the fruit of the Spirit." And with those selfsame New England martyrs and saints he so deeply revered and with whose aspirations he equated many of his own, he refused to give in to the Kingdom of Enmity. Had he not, after all, been the pupil of one whose whole life was an act of courage and the memory of whom was deeply rooted in his heart and soul? Of that recollected person, Warren was to write: "To mention his name once more, Babbitt, in his noble isolation, so fortified my youth that his example still strengthens [me] in my isolation."

In the happiness of his Providence years Warren conquered his isolation, even as in his isolation he moulded the spiritual happiness that sustained the equanimity and the wisdom that grace the writings included in this book and that define their critical spectrum. One cannot read any one of these writings without being aware somehow of Warren's rising above inner and outer ambivalences in the process of "becoming what one is." A critical transcendence, even resolution, characterizes the tone and the ethos of these writings, their steadiness of purpose, their quality of insight, their energy of intuitive intelligence. His mastery of English prose, and of his own prose style (with its aphoristic vigor and distinction always in arresting evidence), punctuates his undiminishing reverence for and responsibility to the *logos*. The sapiential thrust of these writings deepens their critical outlook, gives them significance not of the little day but of the longer time. A perfectionist not only in the aesthetic but also in the spiritual sense, Warren sought to bind the two in order to consummate their totality of value—the value of valuing, in short.

Invariably Warren reveals a life in search not of administrative principles of criticism but of sensibility of principles, of humane values and their proper place in the great triune of life, literature, and thought. To the end a quiet but persevering fortitude was to guide him in his "thinking, striving, and writing"; and to the end he persevered in his allegiance to the supreme task of "pushing things up to their first principles," to use here the words of another of his strong admirations, John Henry Newman. Never one to exalt himself or his work, he had originally captioned the manuscript containing his last writings simply as "Literary Essays of 1970–1980's." The task remains for his readers, indeed, his votaries, to assess their intrinsic worth and the critical nature of their completeness and fullness. This task, however, must first begin with the recognition of an interior visionary quality that makes these more than simply literary essays. And in them he speaks more than as simply a literary critic.

Warren's critical vision can perhaps best be described as a syncretistic vision that discerns at once things visible and invisible; and that knits together the gifts and excellences of the teacher of literature, of the scholar who has been assigned the fact, and the critic, the value, and, finally, of the teacher as critic who reaches toward the center and participates "in that archetypal balance which is not compromise but tension and balance." The attainment of this mediation illumines his critical essays as these render his search for principles of order. "We need definition of ends and standards," he declares. "We need to have literature correlated with the other arts, and with metaphysics, and with life. And, in needing these, we are but avowing our need of the critic." All these needs, it can be said, are met and integrated in his last writings.

Constant and consistent, as the essays in this book attest to, is both his concern for "first and last things" and his pursuit of "an honest facing and ordering for my own inner voices." His criticism here, as always, proceeds dialectically, in continuity. "Whether theoretical or practical," writes Warren, "the best criticism is, however, nearer the catechetical than the expository. The best criticism is that of the critic asking himself questions he finds hard to answer, and giving the most honest (even if tentative or uncertain or negative) answers he can." It is the *honnête homme*—widely read, philosophic in temperament and attitude, and ever aware of the whole intellectual and spiritual life of society—who speaks to us in these essays.

In this "age of criticism" there have been too few good and wise men to whose texts we can turn for inspiration and guidance. "The wise man," Warren reminds us, "looks down at the earth with one eye and up to heaven with the other; yet his vision is single." We now see a severe contraction of the frontiers of criticism as literary theorists and ideologues increasingly set out to regiment moral, intellectual, and cultural life. Doctrinaire, destructive attitudes much distort the literary and critical situation of our time, and thus much reduce both the critical sense and the larger interests of humanity. Against such usurpers and usurpations Austin Warren took his stand, striving no less bravely than Emerson's "great men" "to exact good faith, reality and a purpose; and first, last, midst and without end, to honor every truth by use."

George A. Panichas

A Spiritual Chronicle

I.

I find it ever harder to write or speak on an abstract or theoretical subject —those subjects being (if within my competence) literary or spiritual— without an autobiographical approach, without making my own identity clear by defining where I stand, what I have at stake, and how I came to believe as I do. The kind of vision at which such subjects aim cannot be had without initial commitment; and presumably the objectivity of which they are ultimately capable is a sum total and synthesis of competent and committed personal and private visions.

I am ethnically Anglo-Saxon Protestant (ethnically Protestant, not spiritually). Born in 1899, I was reared a Methodist. In my high school days, I was a Fundamentalist—indeed, what would now be called a "Jesus freak," though, unlike current varieties, I did not set up on my own: I remained within my sect and respected the clergy even though I thought my father's half-witted hired man holier than any of them. The gospel hymns were my treasury and delight.

While I was a Latin major at Wesleyan, I became a Swedenborgian, and a member of the Church of the New Jerusalem founded to promulgate the "heavenly doctrines" of Swedenborg. My period in this church introduced me to mysticism, allegory and symbolism, exegesis of Scripture, and comparative religion. It made a Christian Platonist out of me and a Christian Gnostic—that is, one who distinguishes the esoteric wisdom of the Church accessible to "knowers," spiritual intellectuals, from the superstitious and legalistic or magical practices associated with popular Catholicism or the moralism of popular Protestantism.

In my twenties I became, by conviction and confirmation, a communicant of the Episcopal Church, the American version of the Anglican Church (that is, the now worldwide Church of England); and my allegiance, however qualified, was to the Anglo-Catholic party in the Anglican Church, that party which holds the whole Anglican Church to be, by historic succession of bishops and by its creeds and sacraments, an integral part of the Catholic Church, the other integral parts being the Roman Catholic Church and the Eastern Orthodox (Greek and Russian).

1

In my forties I was influenced for a time by Kierkegaard; but I rejected his influence after a while as tending to make me proud of my psychological complexion and as putting the claims of religion in so exacting a fashion as to make it impossible to be "saved." He was, I found, even more rigorous than the William Law who wrote that *Serious Call to a Devout and Holy Life*, which had so impressed Dr. Johnson before me. I turned back to the Christian Humanism, coupled with Quietist mysticism, of Fénelon, the seventeenth-century Roman Catholic archbishop who, of all single spiritual guides, has most quieted my soul, steadied my course, and ministered to irenic wisdom.

Also in my forties I was much influenced by Aldous Huxley's *Perennial Philosophy*, an anthology of passages from the saints and mystics of all the "higher religions"—including Eckhart, St. Bernard, St. Francis of Sales, Fénelon, and Law as well as Hindus, Buddhists, and Sufis—together with an illuminating commentary by the anthologizer. It is Huxley's contention (and I think he demonstrates it) that within all the "higher religions" there is contained a yet "higher," an esoteric, religion. For some reasons (partly, I should think, "personal"), Huxley, on the basis of this, became Vedantist (an esoteric follower of the Hindu religion), while I (like Dom Aelred Graham, in his *Zen Catholicism*) have concluded that, as the highest spirituality is found also, even if not always on the surface, in the Catholic Christian tradition, there is no good reason for a Westerner reared in the Christian tradition to reject his own heritage for that of an alien culture.

The spiritual experiences of my fifties were three: I had five or six years of close association with the Eastern Orthodox Church in its Greek form: without leaving the Episcopal Church—indeed, with the permission of my Anglican confessor, I did my regular Sunday duty at the Greek church. I studied the liturgy, continued and developed my interest in Orthodox iconology, and much profited from reading such nineteenth- and twentieth-century Russian spiritual writers as Soloviev, Berdyaev, Bulgakoff, and Lossky. Then I suffered (and was enriched by) a severe psychic breakdown—a relief and release and emancipation. And, lastly, I had a number of periods of close association with a community of Anglican Benedictine monks and their Prior, a man of tenderness and holy wisdom.

In these last decades I have also managed what, for a convert to Anglicanism or Roman Catholicism, is difficult: an ecumenism which includes a sympathetic recognition of the genuine spiritual values of orthodox Protestantism—especially in my own ancestral Methodism and in the ancestral religion of New England, the Calvinist tradition of Cotton Mather and, most of all, of Jonathan Edwards and his disciples, the Protestant Scholastics, as I have called them. Wesley, the preacher of "heart religion" and holiness, and Edwards, the philosophical theologian, have taken their place with Origen, Andrewes, Fénelon, and von Hügel among my "saints."[1]

From 1920 to 1968 I was a university teacher of English, or (as I preferred to say) of literature, of (shall I say) of "culture" or the humanities, of whatever I knew and hoped, by verbal discourse or dialogue or sheer osmosis, I could impart to the young. For most of my life, I practiced in three forms: I gave public lectures, taught seminars and other small groups (esoteric instruction), and privately educated those who sought me out as one who could, as the Friends say, "speak to their condition." And I wrote books, not as means of professional advancement, or even, primarily, as a part of my professional obligation (though I do indeed old-fashionedly consider "research" or close critical study eventuating in writing and publication as well-nigh obligatory parts of the academic's life). I wrote: subjectively, because I found it for me an indispensable instrument of self-definition and intellectual clarification, a method of therapy and of salvation, and objectively, on the relation of religion (Roman Catholic, Anglican, and Protestant) to the arts (specifically poetry) and to culture.

Both in religion and in education I managed to stay within their respective established and institutional forms, the university and the church. I say "managed to"; for I am at ease only on the periphery of both. I have not been able to function well as a committee member, a party worker, a vestryman; and I do not wish to be an administrator (*Nolo episcopari*). But I am not so ungrateful as to hold administrators in contempt. To them I owe, at minimum, gratitude for providing a

---

[1]For irenic views of the spiritual values in Protestantism written by converts, cf. Ronald Knox, *Enthusiasm* (1950), especially for its tribute to John Wesley, and Louis Bouyer, *Orthodox Spirituality and Protestant and Anglican Spirituality* (1969).

framework within which public libraries can be collected, classrooms and sanctuaries can be built, and I and others like me can lead a relatively contemplative life, sharing their time between their own prayers and studies and the direction of the studies of the young or the maintenance of the public worship of God.

I have outlined my own spiritual chronicle as a preliminary to my reflections on the current situation in university and church, the religious situation of today, and the spiritual plight of the young.

I belong, like Tillich, with those men whose lot it is to live "on the boundary," with those who are "torn between." I have myself stayed within church, university, and (I may add) state partly out of skepticism (the evils of institutions are inherent in the nature of institutions, and are not to be abolished by substituting a new set of institutions: institutions are, for mankind, a necessary evil) and partly out of steady faith in the importance of continuity. These reasons probably mark me by intellectual constitution as a conservative, even though a liberal conservative.

But, throughout my adult life, I have understood and sympathized with the young, have either taken their side or attempted to mediate between it and the administration, the powerful elders. I still instinctively feel for the critical and rebellious young; but the present situation is difficult for me to face. The tension between the establishments and their young critics is more extreme than any I have known. I try hard to sympathize with the young; but they seem to me so unlovely, so intolerant, so opinionated, so ungenerous. I dislike their conformist dress, which caricatures that of the really poor. I dislike their limited vocabulary, their designed or feigned inarticulateness. I dislike their economic dependence on the very parents who they despise. I find them inimical to any culture save their own limited and provincial sub- and counter-culture, and arrogant in their ignorance of history.

Undoubtedly what irritates me most in the current young is their sense of uniqueness and their pride in it. I was, in my time, a strange, and odd young man, who fitted ill with my college contemporaries preparing for careers in business, who was disdainful of the American ethnically Protestant middle class in which I was reared, and disdainful of the American identification of progress with technology, of civilization with modern comforts and big business. But it was a joy to me to discover, in the classes of Irving Babbitt at Harvard, that I was an oddity only to provincial eyes, that in my classical humanism (with its Eastern equivalent in the humanism of Confucius) and my Catholic-orientated religion (with its Eastern equivalent in Buddhism), I was heir to great, to perennial, traditions.

And so that remarkable man Emerson (though mostly on the side of the Future, not of History) had pleasure in pointing out, to the conservatives of his time, that the Transcendentalism of New England in the 1840s was substantially identical with the "way of thinking [which], falling on Roman days, made Stoic philosophers . . . , on superstitious times, made prophets and apostles; on popish times, made protestants and monks . . . ; on prelatical times, made Puritans and Quakers. . . ."

If (as it is a commonplace to remark) our period has its frightening analogies to the breakdown of the Roman empire, with its welfare program of bread and circuses, its threatenment from without, its corruption and decadence within, its influx of Eastern religions and its disputations between rival brands of existential philosophy, it belongs more immediately, especially as it concerns our intellectuals and our young, to the sequence which began with the Industrial movement and *its* counter-statement in the form of the Romantic movement, German, French, English, and American. And most immediately it reminds one of the American 1830s and 1840s—the period of Transcendentalism and the Reform movement. It reminds us of Transcendentalism with its self-reliance (the "self" ambiguous between the idiosyncratic self and the Hindu True Self or Atman), its appeal to the "higher laws," its turning to the Sacred Books of the East; and it reminds us of the many-sided Abolitionist movement, into which went the most spiritually intense energy of the period's activists, and of the Utopian Socialism exemplified in Brook Farm and the Perfectionism of Oneida.

Four lectures that Emerson gave at Boston in 1841 and 1842—"Man the Reformer," "Lecture on the Times," "The Conservative," and "The Transcendentalist"—all speak with remarkable aptness (or "relevance") to our own times. (He makes a better, a more philosophic, case for conservatism than most conservatives could make.)

Emerson speaks, with especial insight and tenderness, of his younger contemporaries (such, presumably, as Charles Newcomb, a picturesque member of Brook Farm), those who most closely resemble the "loafers" and "inviters of their souls" among our hippies. There were, then, too, those who, in Paul Goodman's phrase, "grew up absurd," finding no proper work—those who, rather than accept work they could not find worth doing, did none—who (as Emerson says in "The Transcendentalist") "feel the disproportion between their faculties and the work offered them; they prefer to ramble in the country and perish of ennui to the degradation of such charities and such ambitions as the city can propose to them." They are lonely; yet they will make no concessions to adult and conformist society; they are "the most exacting and extortionate critics. They prolong their childhood in this wise: of doing nothing, but making immense demands on all the gladiators in the lists of action and fame." They have looked at the pursuits of their elders and found none to satisfy: "from the liberal professions to the coarsest manual labor, and from the courtesies of the academy and the college to the conventions of the cotillion room and the morning call, there is [they find] a spirit of cowardly compromise and seeming which implies a frightful scepticism, a life without love, and an activity without aim." So they idle; so they wait, critical, expectant.

What became of Emerson's young and not-so-young friends as they grew older? As Emerson himself asks, what has become of the young idealists of yesteryear? The utopian communities, all save those which (like that of the Shakers) were founded upon a definitely religious basis, came to an end in a relatively short time, as the communes of today will presumably do. But I am aware of no former members of Brook Farm, the most articulate, best-documented of the communities, who were not, after they returned to that outside world which the called "civilization," proud of having once had, in their youth, the idealism to engage in so utopian, so model-making, a venture. Some few drifted off into vacuity and day-dreaming; but most of them managed some honorable substitute fulfillment of their aspirations: they became Roman Catholics (Father Hecker, the founder of the Paulists, was a Brook Farmer); they became musicians or artists or writers or editors; most of the women made appropriate marriages: Margaret Fuller, their feminist ally though never literal member, became a journalist, a feminist, a valiant worker for the Italian Revolutionary Mazzini, and finally a mother and a martyr.

The situation of the young in our time, of the spiritual questers among them at least, is not totally unique. Certainly there is a difference between the *now* crisis and other crises—most clearly, a quantitative one.

The disaffected young—chiefly university students or university dropouts or their allies—are far more numerous than ever before. There are far more wandering hippies than, in the Middle Ages, there were Wandering Scholars; and their travels take them to more remote places; they are, at least so far as capitalist countries go, international. Whenever the Industrial Revolution has had time enough to succeed, it has brought such material advantages to the middle class that many of the sons of that class find its good things not finally good, only "status symbols." While the poor of the industrialized capitalist countries and the poor of the Third World are in need of the necessities of life, while the blacks, having the necessities, want automobiles and color TV—those who have "had all these things from their youth up," the relatively rich young rulers, find they still lack something, something to give significance to their lives.

To these ultimate questions about ultimate values there are, so far as I know, no new answers. We know of the "relatively rich" for whom it is so difficult to choose objects for Christmas exchange, who "have everything." We can envisage as possible some remote time when all the people of all the world will "have everything" and many will still be unsatisfied.

The finer spirits in any age will have to betake themselves to values which are neither material goods, nor status symbols, nor means to ends; they will have to aim at activities, or states of being, which are ends in themselves. They will have to aim at a self-fulfillment which is (differentially viewed) a self-forgetfulness, a life-saving which is a life-losing. These values, which are ends in themselves, remain: the love of art (esthetic contemplation), the love of knowledge (science), the love of wisdom (philosophy), the love of man (philanthropy), and the love of God (religion).

Sooner or later the disaffected young idealists will have to rejoin society, rejoin the human race. If they have reason to reject the standards, faulty indeed, of their parents, the middle-class America in which they grew up, let them remember that they have grandparents and great-grandparents and ancestors. They are "encompassed about by a cloud of witnesses" and a "choir Invisible" of martyrs, saints, and sages, even in the spiritual history of America. Every family of minds has its own heroic progenitors.

II.

It is sad to find the young limited to a vulgar contemporaneity. Perhaps their immediate elders are partly to blame for this limitation. Reading a recent theological book like *Soundings* (1962), a symposium of modern-minded Anglican clergy, I am shocked to find scarcely a philosophical or theological work cited published more than a decade before the date of the book—and nothing before Barth, Bultmann, and Bonhoeffer. One could find some plausibility to this contemporaneity were one in the world of the physical or even the social sciences: but, in the humanities and even more in religion, there are truths which do not change from generation to generation, or from century to century. With relief, I turn to Dom Hubert van Zeller's *Approach to Monasticism* (1960) and discover that St. Benedict and St. Bernard are referred to with as much respect as Thomas Merton, the recently deceased admirable American Cistercian, or to Père Louis Bouyer's *Introduction to Spirituality* (1961), in which all the classical names of Eastern as well as Western ascetic and mystic thought are seriously cited.

When genuine young idealists rejoin the human race, they will find the traditional alternative paths or ways open to them. They can live "in the world, but not of it." And that is the way for most men. But that, the modern and Protestant and secular answer, is not the only one. The Catholic Church, Catholic Christendom, offers as rich and varied a series of lifestyles as can be found. It is full of ways and of models for secular or quasi-secular imitation. Think of the religious who work as Christian Brothers, of the nuns who work in hospitals, of the friars—the Franciscans, the Dominicans and the Cistercians (or Trappists)—these out of Western Christendom. Then think of the monks of the Eastern church, who follow, at Mount Athos and at Mount Sinai and elsewhere, the Rule of St. Basil. Think of those who live in monasteries and "would have an abbot rule them"; and then the more primitive types, those who live the idiorhythmic life of the *skete*, the tiny community gathered around their spiritual father, and, finally, the hermits (traditionally, in the East, the most spiritually advanced). Another William James might write a humanistic *Varieties of Monastic Experience*.

Jacob Needleman, a young professor of philosophy at San Francisco State College who has studied the "new religions" (chiefly Indian,

Japanese, and Tibetan) of the California young, and who has wisely meditated on his observation of these cults, has this to say: "it is an indication of our twentieth-century American idea of religion that monasticism is by and large considered on the fringe, as secondary to church religion. Of course, this is a complete reversal of the historical relationship between Church and monastery, where the latter was the source of the life of the former."

The monasteries are at the present moment having their difficulties in recruiting novices; but one Benedictine has recently—I think with justice—prophesied that within the next twenty years many of the hippies will be knocking for admission to the monasteries. Only, adds the same Benedictine, the monasteries "better be genuine"—not relaxed, or modernized, or adapted, or otherwise made easy.

The lack of instruction in the spiritual life and methods for attaining it is a shortcoming of the Christian Church as it exists today. Like Dom Aelred Graham, Mr. Needleman finds the Church failing the spiritually minded young by not giving them, as the Zen Buddhists do, or as Vedanta does, systematic training in meditation and prayer—even in physical posture as a preparatory spiritual discipline. He remarks upon the "absence in [our contemporary religious forms] of practical technique, method, and discipline. Various rituals, prayers, services, and the like, no longer function as a part of the mechanics of the religious process, but mainly as an emotional lift. . . ." They "help to preserve the quality of life we lead rather than transform it." The young have "heard exhortations, commandments, prescriptions by the basketful, but nobody was telling them how to be able to follow them."

Suppose a physician read aloud, or the patients read to each other, some accurate medical textbook. Would it relieve the suffering, however eloquently read? The analogue is Needleman's. I amplify: Is not actual treatment necessary for a cure? Reading Freud or Fromm or Horney or Stack Sullivan will not take the place of "analysis"; it may even make the patient worse. The suggestion behind the analogy seems to be that sin is disease—is, as the Buddhists say, ignorance, desire, and suffering. Most of us have heard in our modern churches few theoretical sermons on sin or salvation, few reasoned theological discourses, the equivalents perhaps of textbooks; but we have heard perhaps even yet fewer instructions on the methods of spirituality. Possibly the Sunday sermon is not the place for more than exhortation; but, if so, and even if not, there should be some regular weekday services like the old-fashioned Methodist "class-meetings" and the longer-surviving midweek prayer meetings. Already, Roman Catholics are adding gatherings for extempore Pentecostal prayer to the liturgical prayer of the church. But I do not think prayer and meditation can reach their heights without instruction. "Lord, teach us how to pray." It is hard to think that our Lord did not do more than offer a model form of words.

If the young spiritual questers are to learn how to meditate and engage in *mental* prayer, they must certainly have their teachers. Are our clergy—our parish priests and our chaplains of students—equipped and ready to teach these spiritual disciples?

Spiritual disciplines, spiritual exercises—these are what the young want, and what the old ought never to have ceased practicing; yet somehow, under the influence of yesteryear's modernism, they have dropped out. Years ago I read a book an Indian prince published, chiefly for his own people, though he wrote in a kind of English. His book was a manual of Yoga exercises, illustrated by photographs of the venerable prince in the various postures. What I have not forgotten is his express rubric that these exercises must be done facing some god-symbol—an image or a crucifix; and "if you have no god, draw an orange, sun-like circle and affix it to the wall in front of you." This mode of combining physical exercise with spiritual orientation is missing from the Western world.

But the Christian Church, especially but by no means exclusively in the monastic tradition, has preserved many ancient disciplines and exercises. There is the rule of silence: not to speak unless one could as willingly keep silence; the silent meal; the silent meeting for worship. (We live in a world full of media-noises and others—of jukeboxes and piped-in music, a world uncomfortable without "background," unlistened to but terrifying by its absence.) There is the practice of solitude, permanent or periodic—the "going apart for a while," the Retreat, the temporary withdrawal from "the trivial round, the common task."

There is the discipline of fasting, which can be assumed for the purpose not of enhanced comeliness but of "bringing the body under." The seven deadly sins include an American favorite—greed, gluttony, the perpetual snack, the insatiate mouth.

10

Fénelon salutarily reminds intellectuals, old and young, that "the mind must fast also as well as the body." A good discipline for Lent or any other season would be an abstinence from newspaper and magazine reading. The eyes have their greed as well as the mouth. And most professional readers know the greed of "covering ground," of "keeping up," and need to remember the practice of philosophers like Benjamin Whichcote, whose modest boast it was that he read *non multa sed multum*, not many but much.

In his early lectures, Emerson has much to say of spiritual hygiene as he outlines the Way for his "scholar," his spiritually questing young man; and he commonly makes some embarrassed remarks about the utility to the "scholar" of manual labor. Of its use to the monk, St. Benedict speaks in his Rule. Adventurous it need not be, still less should it be exhausting, for its value is therapeutic and disciplinary: splitting wood, weeding a garden, raking hay: I limit myself to elementary examples. Let me add, under manual labor, the habit of walking. Those who don't own a motorcar need not hitchhike for rides in the cars of others.

Traditionally, spiritual exercises belong to the ascetic stage or period of the spiritual life, the preparation for mystical experience, the direct experience of God. The disciplines aim at a settled state of recollection, union with the "unconditioned," a state of peace and joy. The use of drugs is an attempted shortcut to such supreme states of serenity and ecstacy as mystical theology postulates. There are no shortcuts to the mountains; as Hawthorne reminded us, there is no "celestial railroad." Such "new religions" as promise wisdom, recollection, an ecstacy in ten easy lessons are new versions of old heresies and frauds.

Having spoken this much of the spiritual quests of the young as, at their best, a resurgence of primal and permanent quests of man, as current examples of man's hunger and thirst for real righteousness, for the infinite love and wisdom, I want to end with some words on a persistent, but today critical, problem, that of the relation of religion to culture. Long ago, reading the nineteenth-century sages Newman and Arnold, I formulated to myself: Newman subsumes culture under religion, while Arnold reverses the subsumption. This is an intellectual maneuver I cannot emulate. Religion (high or low) is clearly the more fundamental; yet I cannot but see in culture a necessary balance or check on religion. Religion can better get on without culture than culture without religion.

11

To be sure, without religion, culture can become, if it is the culture of the gentleman, superficiality, urbanity, smooth manners, amateurism; if it is the culture of the professors, mere "booklearning," erudition, intelligence without commitment or moral responsibility, connoisseurship, skepticism. But without culture, religion can be superstition, fanaticism, bigotry, intolerance, and obscurantism. Religion stands in need simultaneously of some restraint by culture and of some relief from it. Arnold's "Hebraism and Hellenism," in his *Culture and Anarchy*, is too patronizing of both the Anglican establishment and the bibliolatric nonconformists, but it can serve as partial text. In a Shelburne essay, "Criticism," Paul Elmer More finds in Erasmus and Sainte-Beuve (and I might add Montaigne) sound checks on the influence of St. Paul and Luther. Christian humanism is the combination of religion and culture, of learning and spirituality. This proper balance—I better say—is ideal, difficult, and precarious.

There is indeed great religious thirst and appetite among today's young, even though much of it is naturally crude and elementary; but I am disturbed and disquieted by the evidences of anti-intellectualism which accompany it, the more disturbing since Americans are endemically anti-intellectual. In our universities, there is a demand only for what is judged "relevant" by the unread and inexperienced. The desire for the "existential" (at its crudest a synonym for "relevant") rules out the patient acquisition of knowledge, either as an end in itself (for the most part, at the least a harmless form of contemplation, a form of scholarly busy-work) or as material for philosophical shaping. If, two or three generations ago, the German type of research-scholarship seemed in need of subordination to a more critically oriented type, now a responsible criticism itself is suspect. It is granted that "exact sciences" cannot be learned by a free-for-all discussion; but I can indeed wonder whether, in the world of the humanities or of spirituality, one man's opinion is as good as another. It is "undemocratic" to say so, but the principle of hierarchy is at least as important as the principle of equality. All men— and all values—are not, except in specified way, equal. There is indeed a "diversity of gifts"; but there is also what the Renaissance called the principle of "degree."

It is easy to confound *a* culture with culture, *a* civilization with civilization, though we must not forget that even a civilization in decay still preserves some of its virtue. But let not the young, let not any of us, in objecting to a culture deemed obsolete, fail to build the counter-, or future-, culture with the full knowledge of the values of our own traditional culture, including our traditional religion.

(1972)

Carroll and His Alice Books

Some months ago, during prolonged trouble with my eyes, I could read only an hour a day, a severe regimen for a man of letters. To what book or books could I devote my precious permitted hour? Obviously it must be concentrated fare, sustaining and enriching, providing matter first for scrutiny and then for subsequent meditation. The books which, after I had mentally surveyed my library, almost thrust themselves into my hands as fulfilling these needs were the Alice books of Lewis Carroll, for they are a unique compound of poetry and philosophy, both prime forms which expand in the mind and sensibility. My choice of books was so right that I compose this essay in gratitude.

When my sight had sufficiently recovered, I addressed myself to my essayist's homework. One ideal reader I know, a highly intelligent woman who is neither a teacher nor a reviewer, insists on reading a famous book first without any apparatus, and only then, if at all, checking her judgment by reading what the critics, and perhaps the scholars and the biographers, have to say. But that is a procedure too pure for a bookman like me, even though I have never lost for long the sheer pleasure of reading. By habit I move back and forth between what one of my academic colleagues used to call the original work itself (the *fons et origo*, after all, of all the aids and commentaries) and the aids: biographies of Dodgson-Carroll; other writings by Dodgson and Carroll, the specialized parts of a whole Oxford bachelor don who was fond of logic, mathematics, games, puzzles, and little girls; a few critical essays on Carroll's Alice books; then back to the Alice books; them back to the aids—in and out, out and in. The final necessity for a critic is, ideally, space and time for withdrawal to achieve critical distancing.

To savor the Alice books fully one must read Martin Gardner's *Annotated Alice* (1960), the wide margins of which, like a variorum Shakespeare, provide explanation and commentary accumulated over the generations. These notes include glosses on words, some purely British, some archaic; also proposed identifications of the characters in the tales with historic personages and persons in the family life of the little Liddells; also the speculations of philosophers who have taken texts for

15

discourses on time, meaning, and identity from Carroll—especially from the philosophers' favorite, *Through the Looking-Glass.*

Critical essays on the books are strangely rare. I can recommend only two: Edmund Wilson's "C. L. Dodgson: The Poet-Logician" (1932) and William Empson's "Alice in Wonderland: The Child as Swain" (1935). Both are brilliant and suggestive—Wilson, for example, when he finds Carroll nearer to Donne and Swift than to "whimsical" writers like Barrie and Milne. Wilson more centrally addresses author and text; Empson characteristically coruscates Empsonianly all over the place, taking a wide freedom of associative interpretation.

The big biographies of Carroll by Florence Lennon (1945), an excellent book, and Derek Hudson (1954)—the latter humorless and boring—are both exhaustive, too long and too detailed for a man so slight, of daily and yearly routines so unvaried. Roger Lancelyn Green, author of another long biography, has summarized his big book in a shorter one (1960) which contains all a reader of the Alice books can possibly need. But by far the best biographical book I have found is the most recent, a 120-page sketch by John Pudney (1976), aptly called *Lewis Carroll and His World*, with copious illustrations, chiefly from contemporary magazines, with telling quotations, and with sociologically and psychologically acute comments. The pictures really illuminate Putney's text without being a substitute for it—in this respect like Tenniel's illustrations of the Alice books.

It seems natural to assume that an author is the cause and his books are the effects; that the cause, by including them, must be greater than the effects; that an author must be greater than his works. But such a theory does not tally well with what we find when we match biography with the greatest authors, which dwarf their creators. Here we may partly be contrasting the chaotic and messy lives of the giant novelists, Dostoevsky and Dickens, with the powerful and carefully ordered *Crime and Punishment* and *Bleak House*. Or we can be thinking of how brief, generally, is the period during which a creative writer is writing at his best: theorists agree on ten or fifteen years, coming earliest for lyric poets, later for dramatists and novelists. The greatest writers have their three or four periods, each with its norm and its interval of respite followed by renewal: Eliot and Yeats, Mann and Joyce, among the moderns, as well as Dante and Shakespeare and Goethe, the three supreme writers of the West.

The great books for which Carroll is remembered were written within ten years (1862–1871) when their author was in his thirties. They were written by the handsome young man with the long wavy black hair and the dreamy face whom we can see in several early photographs of him. Charles Dodgson lived to be sixty-six and, as writers will, kept on writing, and prolifically; yet, unless one makes an exception for *The Hunting of the Snark* and his letters to little girls, none of it seems worth much—even *Sylvie and Bruno,* which he intended to be his masterpiece.

Dodgson was a fussy bachelor don, bothering with endless schemes and schedules, devices, the loving inventor and contriver. The narrowness of the man contrasts sharply with the imaginative magnitude of his two read books. Some literary men lead lives which have an interest almost independent of any light they may cast on the books they wrote; sometimes, indeed, those lives are more interesting, more dramatic as myths, than the books: such are the lives of Byron and the Brontës, of Scott Fitzgerald and Hemingway. This is not the case with Dodgson. What matters to those whose interest is in his books can briefly be summarized.

Charles Dodgson was born into almost the best of Victorian worlds, for his father was a gentleman, an Oxford man, and an Anglican rector. The archdeacon held a country parish (first in Cheshire, the home of the celebrated Cat), and he reared a large family of three sons and seven daughters. His large rectory at Crofts was set in spacious grounds: here Charles had his pets—snails, toads, earthworms, little creatures such as those Alice found underground. Charles's father tutored him in mathematics and the classics during the year he spent at home, between Rugby and Oxford. At Rugby he took little interest in games, preferring long walks in the country, reading the new books, poetry and novels included (all his life he kept up with current literature, Dickens as well as Tennyson for example), and writing letters to one or another of his seven sisters. His beloved mother died when he was in his first term at Oxford, but his relations with his father were, and continued to be, not only respectful, but loving: no Oedipus complex has ever been sniffed out.

17

He was early a literary man, writing home magazines, like *The Rectory Umbrella*, for the pleasure of authorship and the entertainment of his brothers and sisters; he was a home author before he became a published one; and all his later life he kept up an amateur's kind of private literary activity, writing and publishing, at his own expense, many pamphlets on subjects from letter-writing to public reform (he also paid for the first publication of the Alice books and not only chose and supervised Tenniel but paid him for illustrating them). In a real sense he became a public author only by chance.

He spent his professional life at Christ Church, Oxford, where in 1852 he became a student (fellow) at the recommendation of Edward Pusey, the celebrated Anglo-Catholic, whose views Dodgson never shared. His first book, a *Syllabus of Plane Algebraical Geometry*, appeared in 1860; in 1861 he was ordained deacon by Bishop Wilberforce. He was lecturer in mathematics at Christ Church from 1860 till 1881, when he resigned the office; it never gave him pleasure, because he disliked teaching undergraduates. In 1882 he became curator of the senior common room at Christ Church, a fussy post which he held till 1892. The books on mathematics and logic written by Dodgson, the Oxford don, are listed in an appendix to Mrs. Lennon's book; in her chapter 15 she summarized expert opinion on the value of them: they were not much regarded in his own time or later. Yet never should we forget Dodgson's gifts to Carroll.

His external life was dull and monotonous, but his interior life was one of small but intense excitements. He had his photography, which he took up in 1856, photography divided between celebrities and little girls; and he had his letter-writing, similarly divided. "One-third of my life seems to go in receiving letters," he wrote in 1879, "and the other two-thirds in answering them."[1] His meticulous Register of Letters Received

---

[1]Morton N. Cohen, editor, with the assistance of Roger Lancelyn Green, *The Letters of Lewis Carroll*, 2 vols. (Oxford University Press, 1979) 1,246 pages. These two handsome volumes of the letters collect the immense amount which has survived. The editing is meticulous: the scholarly annotations identify nearly all the little girls to whom Carroll wrote, and what happened to them in later life, and who their descendants were. However, the best letters have already been used, and quoted, by all the biographers; and the multiplication of more and more letters does not add either to one's pleasure or to one's knowledge of Carroll's character.

and Sent, begun when he was twenty-eight, and continued for the remaining thirty-seven years of his life, recorded 98,721 sent items; and there were besides something like 5,000 letters received and sent in pursuance of his duties as curator of the senior common room.

The Oxford don had one special and strange passion which united his photography and his letter-writing, the passion for little girls of the kissable and huggable age of (approximately) from seven to fourteen. "About his child-friendships," says Pudney, "he was never secretive, indeed always quite explicit. He was totally self-centered. He knew and got what he wanted. He expected them to end with the end of childhood: as he wrote, 'About nine out of ten, I think, of my child-friendships got shipwrecked at the critical point, "where the stream and the river meet," and the child-friends, once so affectionate, became uninteresting acquaintances, whom I have no right to see again.' "

Much of Dodgson's correspondence was with the mothers of the little girls whom he wished to have friendship with, to entertain at tea or dinner, take to the theater, or photograph, preferably nude. To a male friend, one of his illustrators, he wrote: "I wish I could dispense with all costume, naked children are so perfectly pure and lovely, but 'Mrs. Grundy' would be furious." He wanted, as he became clear and un-abashed, to see the little girls singly. It is a tribute to Dodgson's character and his diplomacy that, strange as was his taste and un-Victorian as was his explicitness, he succeeded in disalarming so many mothers of prospective girlfriends. The hardest to deal with was the first, Mrs. Liddell, the wife of the dean of Christ Church and the mother of the original Alice; but he presumably learned by his fumbling practice with her.

Through the Looking-Glass was inspired by a second Alice, surnamed Raikes; *The Hunting of the Snark* by a third little girl, Gertrude Chattaway; the succession went on long after Dodgson ceased to write his masterpieces. But all the little girls were little ladies. Dodgson was an amiable but undeviating snob, as is his Alice, who took for granted a world of nurseries and home schoolrooms, of nurses and governesses and servants.

Dodgson was a stammerer, as were most of his seven sisters; but this embarrassment, which he suffered in talking to other adults, other dons, and in preaching—one of his reasons for not undertaking parish work—

disappeared in the company of little girls, with whom he became Carroll, the charming, infinitely ingenious companion and entertainer, who read their minds, knew what they thought and what they wanted.

He could speak out, become Carroll, only under the mask of the story-teller. This is an advantage which novelists have over the rest of us. They can, without shame, externalize, project, all of their plural selves, their interior conflicts, creating the saint and the villain, the fool and the wise man out of themselves. The Red Queen and the White Queen are both Carroll. Alice herself represents the sensible and the conventional part of him; the "creatures" whom Alice meets, his rebellious, questioning, speculative parts. The two Alice books are unflaggingly alive throughout; they contain none of the unreal, stagey, fictional clichés which derive not from life but from an author's unassimilated reading.

A book is not only a creation of the author's personality but a part of literary history. There are two traditional genres to which the Alice books belong: the Dream and Children's Books.

The lofty ancestors of the Alice books are Dante and *The Vision of Piers Plowman, Pilgrim's Progress,* and the Old Testament vision of Joseph and Daniel, and the book of Revelation and all apocalyptic books. The dream as literary convention is perhaps the most serious form of literature, more deeply real than the nineteenth-century realism of matter-of-fact detail, real with the reality of poetry and philosophy and religion. Freud and Jung have reinstated the psychic importance of dreams and of the subconscious from which they come. Joyce's *Finnegans Wake* has perhaps restored the dream as a literary form.

Carroll's fictive dreams are a vehicle for conveying wonders within a commonsense framework. They are not devoid of speculation on how we know which the real world is, whether that of sleep or that of waking consciousness—the topic to which Descartes devotes several pages of his *Discourse on Method.* Mainly the dream is a convention which allows Carroll to introduce talking flowers and talking animals, a world still open to small children and to adults who can suspend their tiresome anthropomorphism and listen to what flowers may have to say. And, as in our own night-dreams, the convention allows of shifts, transformations, metamorphoses: the Duchess's baby turning into a pig; the White Queen turning into an old sheep who first is a shopkeeper and then the rower of a boat; the Cheshire Cat which fades into a metaphysical grin; and not the least the constant shifts in size of Alice in relation to other things and persons—the relativity of size. In a dream mythological creatures like the Gryphon and the Unicorn and the Mock Turtle are as real as any other creature; so are the figures out of the nursery-rhymes (the small child's traditional literature), Humpty Dumpty and the Tweedle brothers. And even the food (and eating plays a large part in the Alice dreams) is animated: witness the talking leg of mutton and the sentient plum pudding at Alice's coronation feast.

Incomparably the best survey of children's books is F. J. Harvey Darton's *Children's Books in England: Five Centuries of Social Life* (1932; 1958). Darton begins with fables, romance, and courtesy books. The tradition of the fable, the talking animal story, with its moral, is long-lived. One edition of Aesop, designed for children, was illustrated by John Tenniel in 1848: it was these illustrations by the *Punch* cartoonist which prompted Carroll to engage him for the Alice books. Then came the godly books of the Puritans; then the pedlar's pack; then, at the turn from the seventeenth to the eighteenth century, the fairy tale, largely under French influence (Perrault and the Countess d'Aulnoy), and the nursery rhyme, of which the first collection was published in 1744.

Between 1700 and 1740 appeared Isaac Watts's *Divine and Moral Songs for Children* (1717), Defoe's *Robinson Crusoe* (1719), and Swift's *Gulliver's Travels* (1726): a motley group, only the first of which was addressed to children—didactic verse which Carroll parodies in his Alice books. *Gulliver* is a somber and bitter book, replete with political satire and misanthropy, but the child gets only the talking horses and the changes in size—the pygmies and the giants.

Then stories for children fell into the hands of theorists, the Rousseauists and the early Victorians: they become didactic: they teach science and morality of a prudential sort by illustrating the bad effects of disobeying the laws and the good effects of abiding by them. That didacticism might be "progressive" or it might be pious (Evangelical or High Church); but, whichever, children's books now came to be a profitable market for publishers—as they have continued to be ever since.

21

The Duchess said to Alice: "Everything's got a moral, if only you can find it"—doubtless true enough; but the morals of Victorian children's books before Alice were explicit. In the first chapter of *Alice in Wonderland* the heroine recalls having "read several nice little stories about children who had got burnt, and eaten up by wild beasts, and other unpleasant things, all because they *would* not remember the simple rules their friends had taught them: such as, that a red-hot poker will burn you if you hold it too long; and that, if you cut your finger *very* deeply with a knife, it usually bleeds; and she had never forgotten that, if you drink much from a bottle marked 'poison,' it is almost certain to disagree with you, sooner or later."

Before the Alice books, however, the reign of the didactic had already been challenged by the first English publication of Hans Andersen's fairy-tales, *Wonderful Stories for Children* (1846), by *Treasury of Pleasure Books for Young Children*, including the traditional British and French tales like "Jack the Giant-Killer" and "Cinderella" (1849), and by Edward Lear's *Book of Nonsense* (1846). 1863 is the date of Charles Kingley's *Water Babies: A Fairy Tale for a Land-Baby*. *At the Back of the North Wind* and *The Princess and the Goblin* appeared contemporaneously with *Through the Looking-Glass*; and Carroll was a friend of their author, George MacDonald, an unfrocked Presbyterian clergyman. MacDonald's books are poetical, moral, mystical; their author was the progenitor of Chesterton, Charles Williams, C. S. Lewis, and Tolkien, whose mythologies populate the neo-Christian world of our own day. "But as in Kingsley, and as not in Carroll, there was also in MacDonald an open, conscious, and sincere purpose of improving the young mind, as well as of letting its fancy roam." In writing neither to improve nor to elevate the young mind, Carroll was indeed unique.

Darton's chapter "The Sixties: Alice and After" is profitable to read in the sequence of his highly intelligent, historically oriented book; for it shows how little an historian, however intelligent, can find to say about Carroll and the Alice books. The Carroll books "fell then and still fall into the category of 'fairy-tales,' as Dodgson himself once thought of calling the wonderful book *Alice's Hour in Elfland*, though neither fairy nor elf appears. . . . There is simply magic, and even that is treated as just an extension of the natural—'curiouser and curiouser' . . . by an almost logical extension of properties inherent in this or that person or animal." And, while most fairy tales had been traditional tales of kings and queens and peasants once upon a time in a faraway kingdom (even Andersen's), the characters and situations in the Alice books were pure Carrollean invention and set in sexagesimal England.

The historian never succeeds in naming the special quality of the Alice books—their moral levity: the absence from them of evil (so present in the traditional fairy tales), sin, and sorrow. Carroll's central interests lie elsewhere: in the psychological and the metaphysical, in problems of identity (like losing one's name, or disaster in finding that one may not be Alice Liddell but Mabel, who lives in a poky little house and has almost no toys) and of meaning, in puns and riddles.

Carroll's view of life is not existentially serious, not tragic. Alice, and Carroll, live in a sheltered upper-class academic world: a world before the Fall, almost before the birth-trauma, a world of perception, imagination, and reason. And when one looks for parallels to the Alice books one is surprised to find them in Restoration comedy and *The Importance of Being Earnest* and Ronald Firbank's novels and in certain philosophers and their books. No American parallel comes to mind: our writers lack the requisite sense of social security.

Much in Dodgson reminds one of Bertrand Russell, the mathematician-logician, who all his life remained a precocious child with an overgrown head and an underdeveloped heart; and there is something too of the early I. A. Richards, the semanticist. Much of *Through the Looking-Glass* is an advance commentary on *The Meaning of Meaning*, is a practice book in exact definition and in precise use of terms, in the exposure of such logical fallacies as the undistributed middle.

In Carroll is also something of W. S. Gilbert—the *Bab Ballads* as well as the Savoy operas, with their witty dialogue interspersed with wittily rhymed patter songs. It is not surprising that Carroll tried to get Gilbert's collaborator, Sir Arthur Sullivan, to set the Alice songs to music for stage presentation. Indeed the artistic collaboration of Gilbert and Sullivan had its counterpart in Carroll's difficult but triumphant collaboration with Tenniel.

The special quality, or *note*, of the Alice books is their *Heiterkeit*: this German word, which has no exact English equivalent, lies somewhere between gaiety, cheerful serenity, and blitheness (the last a favorite word of Pater's). Without being tragic the books are serious; yet, even more, they are good-humored—perhaps like Mozart, to whom also it is difficult to find analogies, since he is serious without ponderosity; perhaps like Goethe, without the romantic note, entirely without *Weltschmerz*; like Auden in his old age.

Alice in Wonderland begins by describing a book which Alice's sister is reading, one with no pictures or conversations in it. And "what is the use of a book," thought Alice, "without pictures or conversations?" This is text for Carroll's own books, which mostly comprise a series of conversations or dialogues (some of them between Alice and herself) with interspersed pictures: first those drawn by the writer himself, who had an amateur's gift, and then by Tenniel, who now meticulously if grumblingly followed the prescriptions of Carroll. The detail in the Tenniel pictures calls one's close attention to the detail of the text: the two must be read together.

Lyric (or song) is the other ingredient in these books besides dialogue and picture. Carroll was a wretched poet when he tried to be serious: he became mawkish or sentimental. But Carroll was a masterly poet when he parodied—either a particular poem like Wordsworth's "Resolutions and Independence" or a type of poem like the ballad. The celebrated "Jabberwocky" is a parody of Anglo-Saxon poetry, as Carroll originally printed its first stanza as being—Old English poetry as it would appear to the modern reader. It was probably also a fun-making at the expense of antiquarian scholars who made so much of the archaic poetry which was not to the taste of Carroll: he was very much a modern and a Tennyson-worshipper.

Generations of scholars have worked at the identification of the poems Carroll parodied: the results of these inquiries are accumulated on the margins of Gardner's *Annotated Alice*. "You are old, Father William" is a comic reversal of Southey's "The Old Man's Comforts," and "Soup of the evening, beautiful Soup" parodies a music-hall song, "Star of the Evening," which Carroll had heard the Liddell girls sing. Sometimes Carroll was poking fun at a didactic poem like Isaac Watts's "The Sluggard"; but like all good parodists he was capable too of parodying poems and poets he admired (as, in our own time, Henry Reed's "Chard

Whitlock" can be a brilliant parody of "Burnt Norton" without implying any denigration to T. S. Eliot). Parody is a highly ambivalent art, capable of praising out of one side of its mouth—for it is a critical act to select a poem as important enough to ridicule—and fun-making out of the other. No single straightforward unequivocal judgment is intended.

The two Alice books are often treated as one; and it is sometimes hard to recall in which book a chapter occurs. But perceptive readers notice a difference in method and tone between the two books, which were written seven years apart. *Wonderland* is nearer to the fairy tale (indeed in the fourth chapter Alice says she finds herself "in the middle of one"); and it is more spontaneous: the first three chapters, which narrate the fall down the rabbit-hole, the first changes of size, and the pool of Alice's tears, in which all sorts of little birds and animals swim around with Alice, is all one flight of delightful fantasy; another such sequence embraces the ugly Duchess, her cook, her baby, and her cat.

Only eventually, after the Mad Tea-Party, do we settle down to a pattern, a scheme, based upon two motifs, a croquet game and a pack of playing cards. (Had he written this book later, Carroll might have contrived the architecture of the whole as a card game.) As it is, the whole book forms a sequence of blocks, like the two chapters on the Mock Turtle and the Gryphon, two mythological creatures who (as Gardner says) suggest two alumni sentimentally recreating the studies and the sports of their schooldays. But just as the book begins to seem a sequence of unrelated episodes and characters, related only as a picaresque tale is by the continuing figure of the protagonist, Carroll brings back, at the Queen's Croquet Ground, the Cheshire Cat, the White Rabbit, and the Duchess; so his story rounds itself into a story, ending with the nursery ballad of the Queen's tarts and the trial to discover the culprit who stole them.

The first book does not end as well as it began. The story in its early chapters hovers around Alice's cat, Dinah, of whose skill at catching mice and birds Alice is ever, to the dismay of the little creatures in the pool with her, being reminded. It should end with Alice's awaking ("You're nothing but a pack of cards!") and going in late to her tea. But instead it ends with a sentimental two pages in which Alice's sister, "dreaming after a fashion," relives Alice's dream and pictures how Alice, grown and herself a mother, yet keeping "the simple and loving heart of her childhood," will gather around her her children and tell them the story of her dream. This is too literary and sentimental and Victorian—qualities the book itself so strangely and wonderfully escapes, perhaps because, as Carroll said afterward, he started with the descent into the rabbit-hole without thinking how the story (originally told orally) would go on from there. That oral quality, of a story told aloud, with the author improvising as he goes along, weaving into the narrative events and persons recognized by the children who listen, remains never far underground in Carroll's first book, surviving its translation from the oral story and its first writing down immediately afterward as the *Adventures under Ground*, illustrated by its author's drawings, into the book we know.

Through the Looking-Glass, written seven years later—written without ever being told—is one of the rare sequels which match their predecessors in quality. *The Looking-Glass* is unavoidably more self-conscious. A man who has published a successful book can scarcely undertake another without wondering whether he can equal his first running. And the second book is more systematically ordered. The chess-game, one which Carroll demonstrated could actually be played, gave skeleton to the book as no card- or croquet-game (afterthoughts to the narrator) did to the earlier book. And a secondary structure of motifs involves the three nursery rhymes, "The Lion and the Unicorn," "Tweedledum and Tweedledee," and "Humpty Dumpty" (advice picked up from the use of one, "The Queen of Hearts," in the preceding book).

If the first book is the book of a poet and a mythmaker, the second is that of a philosopher. The *Looking-Glass* concentrates on problems of language (semantics and semiotics), psychology, logic, and metaphysics; on the problem of faith (belief, credence), believing (like the neo-Catholics, six impossible things before breakfast), and doubt: the Unicorn says to Alice, "If you'll believe in me, I'll believe in you"; of definition: the Unicorn, again, calls Alice a *monster* (what she, of course, believes he is); of identity: Alice forgets her name when, in the wood, she is talking to a faun. Finally there is the ultimate question concerning the nature of Reality. The Tweedle brothers explain to Alice that she is part of the Red King's dream, a claim she denies. But is he a part, instead, of

26

hers? Who is the dreamer and who the dream? Is life an illusion, dreamed by God or the Absolute? Has God dreamed us, or have we dreamed God? In this traditional commonplace, shared by literature and Oriental religions, Carroll strikes his deepest metaphysical note, not insisted on but reverberating through his book.

The central character is Alice herself, a correctly reared, upper-class little girl of seven and a half who will one day grow into being a well-balanced, sensitive, and sensible woman, responsive and still more responsible, very British, the mainstay of the British empire; she has something of Victoria herself about her.

In bad dreams most of us know what it is to feel menaced; to feel always in the wrong, unable to rectify the situation and reinstate ourselves in our good opinion of ourselves; to lose our name or that of the distinction for which we are bound—our ticket, or the money with which to pay our train-fare: these are dreams of lostness and persecution. Resourceful and socially secure Alice never reaches that plight, or is never in it more than briefly. The "creatures" order her around and rudely question her, but she is always at least mildly polite, even with what in her waking world are clearly her inferiors. Though metaphysical, psychological, and semantic questions puzzle her, her biological sense of well-being and her "will to live" always quickly assert themselves. Both of Alice's dreams end by her doing something decisive. She shakes the Red Queen, who turns out to be her own cat, Dinah. Shaking is waking.

Red, in both books, is the color of vigor, violence, and passion; white, that of ineffectuality. The weak in Carroll are white, whether rabbit or queen or knight; red is the color of strength, and women are the strong sex. The Duchess, that later addition to the original *Alice*: is she red or white? A question not clearly answered. In her kitchen she is surely psychologically red; later, on the croquet grounds, she is less powerful than the Queen of Hearts, her subordinate; but, as she talks with Alice on the croquet grounds, digging her head into Alice's shoulder and moralizing, she resumes something of redness. On the evidence of the Alice books, Carroll disliked and feared older women, symbolized for him doubtless by Mrs. Dean Liddell, who disapproved of him and burned his letters to her daughter, and by Miss Pritchett, Alice's governess, who is perhaps the Red Queen.

27

Except for Alice and the Queens, Carroll's is a man's world, one of men ineffectual in action but theorizing and argumentative, like the dons and fellows at Oxford ("How the creatures like to argue"). The White Rabbit, with his kid gloves and his fan, a kind of obsequious fop, is as ineffectual as the White Knight in the other book.

The White Knight is Carroll's portrait of himself, a man endlessly ingenious but without any practical skill or power. The portrait shows Carroll capable of self-mockery: even the "aged aged man / A-sitting on a gate" is Carroll as well as the old man's interlocutor; the Knight is ingenuous, ingenious, undaunted—comic and pathetic, "a faint smile lighting up his gentle, foolish face." Our author singles out the White Knight (his stand-in) as what, "years afterwards," Alice could most clearly remember out of her dream. According to Empson "it is the childishness of the Knight that lets him combine the virtues of the poet and the [Victorian] scientist, and one must expect a creature so finely suited to life to be absurd because life itself is absurd." Among Carroll's self-portraits, I think, is even the figure of the Gnat, the little creature who keeps whispering bad puns, an entertainer conscious of being pathetic, an insect but inoffensive—a psychically *white* character.

If the White Knight is the unworldly intelligence of the second Alice book, the Cheshire Cat is the presiding intelligence of the first—the Comic Spirit of Carroll, the "ideal of intellectual detachment," as Empson calls it: the grin without a body.

In her first conversation with the Cat, Alice asks directions:

"Would you tell me, please, which way I ought to go from here?"
"That depends a good deal on where you want to get to," said the Cat.
"I don't much care where—" said Alice.
"Then it doesn't matter which way you go," said the Cat.
"—so long as I get *somewhere*," Alice added as an explanation.
"Oh, you're sure to do that," said the Cat, "if you only walk long enough."

This, the first conversational specimen I quote from Carroll, illustrates the close attention to exact language, the language of a logician and a semanticist, which characterizes most of the dialogues between Alice and the "creatures." Well-bred Alice, with her schoolroom knowledge of history and geography, and, above all, of the Rules of Good Society, is rarely a match for these trained, if sometimes also whimsical, wits. Not knowing the rules of logic, and not trained in precision of language, she is often confused by what they say and often vexed; but she is sustained by her manners and her woman's sanity.

The same conversation goes on. Alice asks: "What sort of people live about here?"—meaning Are they *nice* people, such as I am accustomed to at home?—only to be told they're mad. "We're all mad here. I'm mad. You're mad." This contention the Cat proceeds to "prove" by specious argument; but the mind of the reader lingers over the Cat's visionary axiom "We're all mad," one of Carroll's philosophical *Weltanschauungen*, like the view, in the second Alice book, that we all may be shadow shapes in someone's dream. There is a touch of R. D. Laing in raising the question Who are sane, and who insane, and what, anyway, is sanity? Such questions about the nature of ultimate reality are briefly raised and then dropped; but they contribute to the depth and resonance of the books, the texture of which is made up of brittler, fresher, and more sparkling "upperwork" of logic and semantics.

This texture of the books, both of them, is made up of jokes involving faulty syllogisms or puns and other linguistic tricks. For example, the Pigeon argues, all serpents eat eggs: therefore a little girl is a serpent. Or, more elaborate, the falsely reversed proposition that "I say what I mean" is the same, according to Alice, as "I mean what I say." Hatter, Hare, and Dormouse all pounce upon her: "You might just as well say that 'I see what I eat' is the same thing as 'I eat what I see'!"

There are specimens of a precision half-logical, half-verbal. For example, at the Mad Hatter's Tea-Party, Alice is bidden, "Take some more tea"; and when she replies, "I've had nothing yet, so I can't take more," she is told, "You mean you can't take *less*."

The wordplays are endlessly varied. Quintilian, Puttenham, and Sister Miriam Joseph could technically name them; I shall not try. Several times characters play the British parlor game of stringing together words starting with the same letter, as when the Dormouse remarks of the three little sisters who lived in a well ("well in") that they "drew all manner of things—everything that begins with an M . . . such as mouse-traps and the moon, and memory, and madness"; or, more splendidly, in the second book, Alice recites to the White King, of the Anglo-Saxon Messenger Haigha, "I love my love with an H, . . . because he is Happy. I hate him with an H, because he is Hideous. I fed him with . . . Hamsandwiches

29

and Hay . . . and he lives—" which sentence the King fills out with "on the Hill." And this dialogue between King and Queen-to-be Alice occurs on the same page with Alice's remark "I see nobody on the road," upon which the King comments: "I only wish *I* had such eyes . . . to be able to see Nobody!" The shift produced by capitalizing, and so personifying, the neutral "nobody" which amounts merely to a negation reminds one of a passage in the first book in which Alice's wasting time and beating time are brought up by the Hatter against the reanimated figure of Father Time, who would do almost anything for one who kept on good terms with him. A bravura piece of punning is the Mock Turtle's story of his education under an old Turtle, called the Tortoise "because he taught us," the piece which includes the courses of study, with "the different branches of Arithmetic—Ambition, Distraction, Uglification, and Derision"—an account which explains "uglify" as the antonym of "beautify."

The sixth chapter of *Through the Looking-Glass* centers on language; here Humpty Dumpty, at Alice's request, gives a word-by-word exegesis of "Jabberwocky," the poem Alice has read in the first chapter. ("You seem very clever at explaining words, Sir.") Humpty Dumpty proposes his theory on the portmanteau word—"two meanings packed up into one word"—after having analyzed "slithy" as "lithe and slimy." He proposes also the ancient theory that names mean something: "*My* name means the shape I am"; but what does "Alice" mean? But he also propounds that words mean what he wants them to mean, unrestricted by convention.

> "When *I* use a word," Humpty Dumpty said, in rather a scornful tone, "it means just what I choose it to mean—neither more nor less."
> "The question is," said Alice, "whether you *can* make words mean so many different things."
> "The question is," said Humpty Dumpty, "which is to be master— that's all."

This much "puzzled" Alice, who indeed is often puzzled by the assertions and arguments with which the creatures engage her; but of course Humpty, if we may think of him as speaking for the poet, is partly right, for such a writer, not of plain prose which must be readily intelligible to the plain reader, can in part bend language to his purpose.

To this chapter there adheres a further interest: in Good Manners, at the Rules of which Alice is never at a loss, and in the rules of Polite

Conversation, which Humpty Dumpty seems either not to know or knowingly to flout. To argue when one is not engaged in formal debate is just plain bad manners: Alice is ever "not wishing to begin an argument"—nor indeed to engage in argument at all. Nor does she like Humpty's talk about "my turn to choose a subject" for conversation. ("He talks about it just as if it was a game!")

This is also a good chapter in which to observe Carroll's skill in handling dialogue, especially the difficulty of handling the simple problem of who said what. Sometimes just "said" follows the quoted sentences of talk, but mostly it is followed by some adverb or phrase of attitude or manners—*e.g.*, " 'I never ask advice about growing,' Alice said indignantly." She does sometimes grow indignant, and once she utters the British monosyllable *oh*, "too much puzzled to make any other remark"; but mostly she is tactful, polite, occasionally calls her host "sir," and says " 'Thank you' rather sadly," when good manners oblige her to listen to Humpty's repeating of his "piece."

Like all successful authors, Carroll was often asked, by letter or by word of mouth, what he meant by his books. His replies all amount to the same reply. About the Alice books he said: "I can guarantee that the books have no religious teaching whatever in them—in fact they do not teach anything at all." To questions about *The Hunting of the Snark* his answer was: "I'm afraid I didn't mean anything but nonsense! Still, you know, words mean more than we meant to express when we use them; so a whole book ought to mean a great deal more than the writer meant."

E. D. Hirsch has written a book at once brilliant and closely reasoned called *Validity in Interpretation* (1967), which I often read, or read in. This sober book abounds in so many terms and distinctions that it is difficult to keep them straight. His central distinction lies between *interpretation* and *criticism*: interpretation is concerned with a work's textual meaning, which is the author's intended meaning, interpreted historically as what, in his lifetime, he could have meant; and criticism involves the judgment of a work's *significance*—of its larger bearings and application and its value. This is the distinction between the work of the scholar and the work of the critic, work sometimes performed by the same man, but commonly divided, with the responsible critic undertaking to assimilate the scholar's finding before he begins his own. Historicism is not enough: it leaves the illustrious authors embalmed, yet still in their coffins. Far-flung speculations which heed neither the illustrious authors nor their fictive creations but aggrandize the "creative" critic and flout adherence to their texts are an abomination. So delicate is the act of resuscitation, of resurrection. Yet the immortal, the incarnate parts of the dead, their perceptions and cerebrations, clothed in the flesh of their very words, must be kept alive—else there is no continuity, no inheritable culture. The final word must be: meaning is, and meaning accrues, is not time-bound.

Almost nothing in the Alice books dates, because all is so readily translatable, so lends itself to *application*. After Shakespeare no author is so frequently quoted in the English-speaking world as Carroll, especially by statesmen and philosophers. Today probably the aptest sentence is the Red Queen's "It takes all the running *you* can do to keep in the same place." But the books not only are, like *Hamlet,* "full of quotations"; they also abound in situations widely *applicable*. There is the Caucus-Race in which all have won, and all receive prizes (each animal, including man, excels at something). And the fight between Tweedledee and Dum over a rattle suggests one aspect of wars. This large applicability, or "significance," of the Alice situations has certainly much to do with the natural symbolism of Carroll's images; running, fighting, the river, the wood (the "state of nature"). Carroll's books, although they transcend the Victorian age, were immediately intelligible; they are timeless by including their own time, not by skipping over it.

They have also proved universal. Warren Weaver's *Alice in Many Tongues* (1964) engagingly deals with the translations of *Alice in Wonderland* (its sequel has been neglected). By now it has been translated into nearly fifty languages, among them Hebrew, Arabic, modern Greek, Chinese, and Japanese. There are over three hundred translations in all, the majority done in our century; the Chinese and many Japanese versions (at least sixteen of them) all date since 1920.

Alice seems so British a classic—indeed first of all Victorian upper-middle-class British—that this universal dimension is even more surprising than its timelessness. It would seem also to be so tied to its style as to be, like poetry, untranslatable. Thus the most engaging part of

Weaver's book is concerned with how the translators handled its special difficulties: the parodies, the puns, the nonsense words, the jokes which involve logic, and the "unclassifiable Carroll twists of meaning with underlying humor." The principle is that the mixture must remain the same.

The translator must remember that *Alice* appeals—and has ever since it appeared appealed—to "children of all ages," who can be divided into literal children and imaginative or philosophical adults. Children chiefly enjoy the narrative; adults, the linguistic and logical puzzles. Like *Pilgrim's Progress* (which Hawthorne cherished as a boy) or *Gulliver*, the Alice books offer characters and wonders in a dream/fairy-tale narrative which can entertain children of almost any culture, constantly overlaid by, and blended with, the elements adults find so irresistible. Yet they must finally be read or listened to in English, for Carroll is a master of style and tone, and the narration and the witty dialogue are not finally disjoined, but merged.

I have remarked the paucity of essays on the Alice books. Having attempted one myself, I am not surprised at that paucity. Occasionally I have written a critical essay which, to my own perception, so plucked out the secret of the books addressed that I felt no further need to continue reading them. Now, however, my critic's pride is humbled. I may to my satisfaction dispose of Dodgson, but I cannot lay by the books Carroll produced; I can but go on reading them.

(1980)

Herrick Revisited

I first read some of Herrick's anthologized poems in the *Century Readings in English Literature*, a pioneer "survey" book. The year was 1917; the place was Wesleyan University. We sophomores read "Corinna" and "Gather Ye Rosebuds While Ye May." The latter poem I took to my heart and memory along with certain stanzas from Fitzgerald's *Omar*, also in our anthology. Both poems gave me a delicious shudder at the thought of the fragility of life and the beauty of beauty: "And that same flower that smiles today Tomorrow will be dying." Later, I could link with them the "Conclusion" to Pater's *Renaissance*: "While all melts under our feet, we may well grasp at any exquisite passion. . . . Not to discriminate every moment . . . is on this short day of frost and sun, to sleep before evening. . . ."

When first I read Herrick's anthology piece, I did not notice that the poet wrote "rosebuds" and not "roses," which would also have fitted his meter, though the effect would not have been so subtle, for, though both are disyllabic, the former has a secondary stress as well as a primary. Only the other day did I take in that word which, with precision, the poet chose. In untutored youth, the sentiment and the rhythm suffice: the exactness of the language goes unnoticed. And in later life a remembered favorite escapes exact attention because we think we know it so well.

A year after first looking into Herrick, I read Horace with Karl Harrington, the Latin professor under whom I majored. I much preferred Catullus, the more "spontaneous" and "lyric" and palpably emotional and more "original" of the two: he must have been, after Virgil, read in high school, and Herrick, the next poet I felt as a poet. But I did savor the "wisdom" of Horace, his *aurea mediocritas*, his gnomic tags, his Herrickean *carpe diem*. And indeed Professor Harrington, who gave me an English title for each Horatian poem, supplied "Gather Ye Rosebuds" as the epigraph for the Third Ode of Book Two.

As a young Instructor I in turn taught selections from Herrick to sophomores. Fresh from the powerful indoctrination of Irving Babbitt at Harvard, I found nothing much to say about the poems,—merely exposited the theme of *carpe diem* and almost certainly uttered some warning against its unwisdom. But towards the end of my thirties, I met with, and taught, the first edition of Cleanth Brooks and Robert Penn Warren's *Understanding Poetry* (1939), and I recall being struck by the comments and questions of Herrick's "Litany to the Holy Spirit," especially those on stanzas four, five, and seven, so wryly, grotesquely, "cynically" interspersed amid more conventional stanzas—semantic dissonances. Herrick was certainly more "complex" and "ironic" than I had thought.

After these preliminary studies in the apprehension of poetry, still a relatively innocent reader of Herrick, I had a magisterial lesson in reading from Cleanth Brooks, whose exegesis of "Corinna's Going a-Maying," published in 1947, perhaps remains the single indispensable essay on Herrick, as the poem is probably Herrick's greatest single poem. After having studied that essay, matching its exegesis line by line with the poem, one can never again think of Herrick as a facile writer: one sees him more and more as a precise artist who weighs every word and who never spares the *labor limae*—an endless revisionist. One sees also, with Brooks, that "Herrick's process of making the poem was probably a process of exploration too," *i.e.*, that the meaning of the poem was discovered by the poet partly in the act of writing it; that it did not preexist and cannot be reduced to paraphrase. Lastly, Brooks properly relates Herrick to *The Golden Bough*, i.e., to Comparative Religion. So Herrick is not only a poet of impeccable verbal texture: he has also a worldview.

In humanistic studies as in scientific, it is common that the same or analogous discoveries are concurrently being made. Though I did not read him till much later, Sidney Musgrove, in New Zealand, was independently working out another serious and status-raising view of the poet in his *The Universe of Robert Herrick*, first published in 1950. The word "universe" (or worldview) is significant; and this little book offers another close reading of "Corinna," less keen than Brook's, but better than anything earlier, and gives a really brilliant reading of Herrick's "Proem." Musgrove makes Herrick out to be far more orthodoxly Christian than would Brooks, or I, and in general makes Herrick far more of his own time, far more standardly Elizabethan, than would I; but his essay is a valuable piece of criticism, especially its thesis-stating, provocative, first few pages.

Popular and anthologized as Herrick was throughout the nineteenth century, it has only been since 1940 that some kind of consolidated serious view of this poet has emerged. This has probably been the joint consequence of the New Criticism, with its "close reading," and of folklore and the New Anthropology and Comparative Religion.

Eliot's essay, "What is Minor Poetry?" (1944) juxtaposes the names of George Herbert and Herrick, a juxtaposition which may have suggested Marchette Chute's intelligent and careful joint biography (with interspersed criticism, often excellent), *Two Gentle Men* (1959).[1] Eliot obviously knew Herbert's poetry much more closely than Herrick's; but he speaks with more admiration of Herrick than one might expect, though not, I think, with his usual perceptiveness. From Herrick's poems, he says approvingly, we "get the feeling of a unifying personality" and "having read all of his poems, we enjoy still better the ones we like best."

Eliot blunders, however, when he says that the "personality expressed" in the *Hesperides* is charming by virtue of its "honest ordinariness." To my perception, it would be hard to find an adjective and a noun less accurate. Herrick was far too much of an artist to be "ordinary" (no artist can be that), and far too subtle and precise of language and oblique of view to be "honest" in any sense Eliot can intend.

But, indeed, even after Miss Chute's careful book, augmented by chapters of Civil War history, and Miss Easton's *Youth Immortal* (1934), padded with full-length portraits of Herrick's family, friends, and acquaintances, and after Rose Macaulay's over-scholarly and insufficiently living historical novel, *The Shadow Passes* (1932), I still lack, without much extrapolation, any sure intuition of Herrick's "unifying

---

[1]To the essays by Brooks, Musgrove, and Eliot should be added Douglas Bush's fine pages on Herrick in his *English Literature in the Earlier Seventeenth Century* (1945) and the really masterly essay by Thomas Whittaker, "Herrick and the Fruits of the Garden," *ELH* (22) 1955. Two earlier books on Herric are still useful,—those by Floris Delattre (a French dissertation) and by F. W. Moorman, both of 1912. The most recent monograph, Roger B. Rollin's *Herrick* (New York: Twayne, 1966), "new critical" in method, offers many close readings; is generally sound. The best text is *The Complete Poetry of Herrick* (New York: Anchor Books, 1963), admirably edited, with full and valuable notes, by J. Max Patrick. This is the edition I have used.

personality." The one thing I do not suppose Herrick to have been is simple; and I think it quite unlikely that he fully understood himself except so far as he found himself expressed on paper by writing his poems in search of that earthly even if only literary immortality which, after illustrious precedent, he was always promising himself.

II.

Three topics engage me in 1975. They so overlap that I have difficulty in separating them; but I will attempt so to do. The first is the unity of Herrick; the second is the nature of his religion; and the third is his rank as a poet.

The "unifying personality" of a poet is certainly one test of his stature. The poet of an anthologized poem or few poems does not count as a poet. There must be some scope and bulk; and yet there must be unity as well. That unity must be found in the poems; it may or may not be found correspondingly in the life.

In his poems, Herrick appears, even more than most poets, to be autobiographical; yet when we compare the scant information we possess about his life with his poetry, we see that the poet abounds in *personae*: for example, he sometimes represents himself as married or about to marry, though in point of fact he never did. And in his "Ternary of Littles," he speaks of his little church and little vicarage, though small they were really not; the whole poem, indeed, is an affectionate and pseudo-humble stylistic exercise.

It is impossible to bear down on what appears to be autobiographical, so saturated is he with his poetic antecedents. I will take one example. Especially in relation to his "mistresses," he frequently writes of his old age. Yet we have only to read the Odes of Anacreon, in which the conjunction of old age and young women is a persistent *topos*, to doubt whether Herrick's poems in similar vein were written when he was really old; indeed, we know that they were not: his book was published when he was fifty-seven. They were written when he *felt* old, which could come before, at thirty-nine when he became Vicar of Dean Prior; or they were written when he tried to anticipate what it would be like to feel old.

Are his many "fresh and fragrant"—or "dainty"—mistresses real or devised? No definitive answer can be given to this question. Does any artist, whether novelist or poet, either draw literally the people he has known or not draw upon observation? Herrick writes not about women but aspects of women,—women as flowers, or women as clothes, or women as ritual: anything, we might say, except women as wives or procreating mothers. The term "mistress" is, for him, as for his century, a purely neutral term for any woman, or any young woman, to any degree or in any relation admired, the object of devotion or affection (*cf.* Cowley's *The Mistress* or Crashaw's "To His Supposed Mistress"). Some of Herrick's "mistresses" were given their literal English names; others, Roman names out of the Roman poets. I am inclined to agree with Grosse that Julia was a real woman,—a Londoner, I would suppose, out of Herrick's pre-Devon years and out of his pre-clerical years; but the others,—Corinna, Anthea, and so on, may be either, as Miss Easton thinks, variant names for "Julia," or separate women, or mere inventions: I see no way of knowing.

In "His Age," dedicated to Wickes, his Cambridge friend, ordained with him, and now, like him, a Devon parson, Herrick imagines himself not only old but equipped with "an old leane" wife, Baucis, and a young son Iulus, his illegitimate son—by "Julia," it would seem, for he admits to his old wife, "these were my sins of youth." It is a "frantick crazy man" who speaks and who, listening to his son sing one of the songs he made, must

> Flutter and crow, as in a fit
> Of flesh concupiscence, and cry
> *No lust there's like to Poetry.*

This last line, italicized by the poet, seems a kind of epitaph, and epitome of Herrick's hierarchy of passions, as well as a comment on this fiction.

If there was a Julia, she presumably belongs to the years before his ordination, at the age of thirty-two, when he wrote his "Farewell to Poetry"—at least to secular poetry, including certainly poetry about women. This "Farewell," the authenticity of which is indubitable, was never published in his book; for he subsequently changed his intention.

Though he later decided to add some pious pieces, he was able to persuade himself that his earlier work could stand the tolerant inspection of God if, when he published, he made formal apology for his "unbaptized Rhimes" written in his "wild unhallowed" years.

A reader of our time feels a discrepancy between Herrick's office as cleric and the personality and attitudes to be found in the *Hesperides*. How could Herrick have reconciled the one with the other?

Perhaps the best answer is that seventeenth-century minimum standards for clergymen did not require any special profession of piety any more than they required special theological preparation. Indeed, specific training for men who were going to become Anglican priests was not thought necessary before the second half of the nineteenth century, when the divorce between religion and general culture came increasingly to be felt.

In Herrick's time and until very long after, any graduate of either university, not of scandalous life, who presented himself, was briefly examined by the Bishop or the Bishop's chaplain, and any such graduate who assented to the Creeds and the Thirty-Nine Articles, and who had secured a patron to present him to a "living," could be ordained a priest. [Special piety was not ordinarily required—might indeed be considered Puritanical.] Desiderated was a "gentleman and a scholar," a University man, fit to be chaplain to a nobleman (as Herrick was to the Duke of Buckingham on his military journey to the Isle of Rhé), or to be the responsible head, as rector or vicar, of a parish—the *parson* or person of the community. The University Colleges all had their chapels, with daily Morning and Evening Prayer, in Latin, and their chaplains and *catechists*, theological tutors: it was enough, this Anglican *ethos* which surrounded the undergraduate, to prepare a man for ordinary parish duties.

The Anglican priest, until the nineteenth century, and often since, is partly a representative of the Establishment, the Established Church, a State Church, which in Herrick's time was Royalist and hierarchic, closely allied with the cause of the King and the nobles and the country gentlemen—thoroughly aristocratic in point of view. This general allegiance was one Herrick, a devoted Royalist, a believer in the divine right of the Stuarts, accepted *ex anima*.

To turn from Herrick's profession to the self which wrote the poems: What "unifying personality" can we infer from the poems, treating them as autonomous? This is the portrait I see.

First of all, that personality is one of a poet, and being a poet he is not an ordinary man, but he is as obsessed with being a poet, with belief in himself and his literary immortality, as any poet one can think of. He is a Horace, an Ovid; he is also a Landor and a Swinburne.

He is also a consummate egoist. He is a Montaigne, a Robert Burton, and a Walt Whitman—a man of one Book, which went on augmenting its size and scope, a Book held together by the persistence of a born and inveterate and ever-revising writer—a combination of autobiographer and artist for whom to write was to live. He must have ceased to live, in effect, when, at the age of fifty-seven, he had the pleasure of seeing his Book in print.

There is a strange, paradoxical contrast between the gross face of Herrick's portrait and his predilection for the little and the delicate— strange but not entirely incredible. His face is sensual—or at least sensuous. He is an epicure and an aesthete. He is a lover of flowers and girls, but evidently content to look at both or engage in *badinage*: he doesn't desire to possess; for to possess is to be possessed. He is fond of a home, as some, if not many, bachelors are, but not fond of domesticity —not fond of monogamy, and not fond of children: he doesn't want to be tied down; he wants something of "many fresh and fragrant mistresses," not all of one. In many, there is freedom from bondage; and Herrick loves his liberty.

He is a man of moods—even though the gamut of his moods is far from infinite. He can go from (in the popular sense of the words) the Epicurean to the Stoic: he can enjoy life when it goes ecstatically, or even well; and he can bear it with good sense and control when it doesn't. He can be content with little, and yet respond fully and gaily and joyfully to the unpredictable height of intense pleasure.

With Herrick, the poet, the style is almost everything. He is enamoured of surfaces (textures, jewels, fabrics). And he is a close writer. There are all sorts of sly close fingerings in his verses: in the "Proem," he writes, "I sing of Hell and Heaven—and hope to have it after all." Later, in *Noble Numbers*, he asserts Heaven will be attained by "the good and I." He loves detail (even at times, lists). He loves diminutives—stylistic expression of his fondness for "little things."

Herrick is a snob. His friends, of whom he is proud, are all country gentlemen or lawyers, or, like himself, priests. He has no friends among the village folk—indeed is repelled by them, as his epigrams witness: they are illiterate, petty-minded, filthy (all his daintiness is offended by their stench). But peasants, farm labourers are proper enough in the station in which it has pleased God to place them. What the lower classes are good for is to till the soil and to look up to their superiors. Their rewards are their duties; but they have their pleasure also in the rural agrarian festivals, the sponsoring of which the gentry undertake.

City-born, Herrick thinks of himself as Londoner, a Roman citizen who, for much of his life, has lived on his Sabine farm. He is not a Stephen Duck, a Burns, or a Whittier writing about country life and labor which he has himself shared. He is not a peasant or proletarian nor a regional or dialect poet; an observer, he is a writer of pastorals and bucolics.

Herrick's worlds were those of city and court, of the university and its classical culture, of Ben Jonson's circle. What held all these worlds together? The Monarchy and the Established Church. No wonder he was hostile to Parliament, the Presbyterians and the Independents. They had killed the King, the secular representation of God, and destroyed the Church; they had undermined the whole hierarchic world; and probably would have destroyed the regular successions of the seasons had they been able. The poet, to be sure, was fond of minor and artful disorder, the "sweet disorder of dress" and the like, but these were but poetic deviations, descants which implied a *cantus firmus*.

Perhaps the dominant notes or tones of Herrick's poetry are relaxation and contentment. He is not relaxed as a craftsman but relaxed in his attitude towards life—content with the *status quo*; no revolutionary, he is indeed ultimately hostile only to revolutionists. Even the objects of his acerb epigrams deserve to exist in order that they may be satirized.

He was a contented man. In his *Holy Living*, Jeremy Taylor has a chapter on Contentment, a chapter filled with quotations from the Stoic philosophers as well as Scripture. Herrick's contentment, not so stringent, more Horatian and Epicurean, is basic to him.

Herrick accepts the universe, including himself. He has little or no sense of personal sin or of cosmic evil. The deeper Christian notes of sin, so morbidly present in Kierkegaard, so present in George Herbert, are absent from him. He knows neither *acedia* nor despair. His irritation or vexation is addressed at other people, not himself.

Herrick did not desire this man's art and that man's scope. He accepts not only his station but his temperament. He delights in his own poetry. Others, he keeps saying, may criticize it, but he thinks it good. He will not select among his poems—only add more. Everything which interests him should interest his reader; everything he has written seems to him precious.

This is my portrait of Herrick drawn from the poetry; and it is, I think, the portrait of a reasonably unified personality.

III.

Herrick had, held, a series of religions—that of art—of poetry; that of his ancestral Christianity; that of classical Graeco-Roman religion, philosophy, and culture; and that of British folklore, the local version of the religion of Nature.

How far Herrick was aware of gaps and discrepancies between these religions or loyalties is not clear. He was in no way a thinker—had no *mind* in any strict sense; was a man of perception and intuition and awareness, an artist—but not an intellectual artist like Donne or Eliot or Thomas Mann.

How Herrick's reconciliation of attitudes and loyalties could have been understood in his own time, I am at a loss to know, for I can find no contemporary Englishman whose position was at all parallel. Though professionally an Anglican priest or "parson," he does not fit into any of the categories or parties of the seventeenth-century Anglican theology. Obviously not a Puritan, he was almost as obviously not a Laudian Anglo-Catholic. One recent scholar has called him an Anglican Latitudinarian; yet he has nothing in common with the Cambridge Platonists or with Lord Herbert, the proto-Deist, or with Chillingworth, save his dissent from the more pronounced parties of his time. The nearest parallel one can produce is Jeremy Taylor, his only approximate contemporary (as Douglas Bush has remarked before me) who shows equal saturation in Roman culture, who quotes almost as much from the classics as from the Bible. But one can hardly think of Herrick as reading, and certainly not of writing, *Holy Living* and *Holy Dying*.

To make total sense out of Herrick's religion, one has to reach the nineteenth century at least, and then—at whatever peril of being unscholarly, that is, unhistorical—to read back into Herrick a syncretistic point of view, that of the comparative religionist who sees, or stresses, rather the similarities between the historic world religions that their diversities—who sees Santa Maria as indeed *Sopra Minerva* and Christ the Shepherd as the "great God Pan" kindly come to live among us, who is sensitively aware of the heritage of the Christian Church as "debtor both to the Jew and to the Greek"; that of the student of history who sees, and feels, the continuity of culture.

The later nineteenth century was capable of adumbrating such a syncretistic view; and, when I began rereading Herrick, I instinctively turned to Pater, to *The Renaissance*, especially the essay on Pico della Mirandola, and yet more particularly to *Marius the Epicurean*, especially the early chapters, "The Religion of Numa" and "White-Nights":—the whole book, however—which (it will be remembered) ends with the death of Marius, in the "Church Porch," on the threshold of conversion to the new city religion of Christianity—is relevant to the understanding of Herrick.

On the second page of *Marius*, Pater quotes, from Tibullus, one of Herrick's favorite poets,

> At mihi contingat patrios celebrare Penates
> Reddereque antiquo menstrua tura Lari.

"And may it be mine many times to stand before the shrine of my sires' Penates and to offer incense, as the months come round, to the old Lar of my house." The Lares and Penates, the household and family gods, those of the hearth and one's ancestors: how dear these lesser or "Little" gods are to Herrick, the lover of the small, the familiar, the ungrandiose.

In *Marius*, I am struck with the unabashed fashion in which Pater juxtaposes his reading of Augustan Romans with parallel allusions to later

44

figures in Western culture—to Wordsworth, to "a quaint German mystic," to St. Augustine; how he speaks of the "college" of Aesculapius as coming "nearest, perhaps, of all the institutions of the pagan world, to the Christian priesthood." More persuasively, and so beyond the reach of quotation, Pater tries to make classical culture live again by making it continuous with the present. The parallel between Pater and Herrick is helpful in many ways: not only for the mode in which both felt the livingness and concurrence of the past but for the delicate insistence both placed on the civilizing function of art and ceremonial, on myth and ritual.

How did Herrick reconcile his attraction to the "religion of Numa," the primitive Roman religion revived by Augustus and the Augustans, with his absorbed fascination in the British folk-festivals and rites which survived outside of London, and these in turn with Christianity in its reformed Anglican mode?

Presumably he took his Anglicanism rather easily, as the local form of religion in his own country and time. He was instinctively a man for the established order of things, in state and church—a lover of the good old ways and the good old times, a lover of stability, hierarchy, in a word, order. Breaks in continuity, lapses in culture, deviations from tradition, expressions of private opinion, enthusiasms (outside of the poet's time-hallowed and universal *furor*): these were all distasteful, or worse, to this "gentle man."

The old "Popish" religion was assuredly less offensive to him than Puritanism: had it been still the "established" religion, he could certainly still have been the vicar of Bray—or of Dean Prior. When, in "The Fairie Temple," he speaks of the "little people" as having a "mixed religion," "part pagan, part Papisticall," he might almost be said to be describing his own; though I note that the fairies have also their Anglican aids to doctrine and discipline, their book of Canons, their book of Thirty-Nine Articles, their book of Homilies.

Herrick has a considerable vocabulary of Roman Catholic words which he uses perfectly neutrally—words like *dirge* (sung in the Latin office for the dead) and *trental* (popularly called today the "month's mind mass," said thirty days after a death,) and *beadsman*; he has Julia say her "*Ave* Mary." In "Mattens, or Morning Prayer," he instructs one to rise early, "Crossing thyself," and urges that one "humbly kneel" (*i.e.,*

45

genuflect) to the Altar. It is difficult, if not indeed impossible, to suppose that Herrick himself engaged in these pious practices or insisted that his parishioners at Dean Prior do so, but these—along with incense—are at least acceptable figures of ritual speech. So in "Pray and Prosper," in which we are bidden "First offer incense," and then our meadows shall "smile and smell the better" by our "beads": this amounts probably to saying, "Let my prayers be set forth in thy sight *as* the incense." For the incense, presumably never used at St. George's Church of Dean Prior, Herrick could cite Hebrew Scripture as well as Tibullus, Ovid, and Horace.

A better-known example of Papistical imagery is his "Prayer to Ben Jonson," in which he proposes to canonize his poet-father—to set aside for him an altar and candles and to inscribe Ben's name in his Psalter (*i.e.*, to dedicate a day to this black-letter minor saint, Saint Ben). In the concentrated first stanza, Herrick says that before ever he writes a poem, he invokes Saint Ben, "For old Religion's sake." What does "old Religion" mean? In his note on the poem, Mr. Patrick cites from Ovid's *Fasti* the phrase *antiqua religione*, and suggests classical Roman glosses of *Pietas*. But the "conceit" of the poem is surely that of Catholic canonization; indeed this very phrase is used by Anglican Bishop Corbett in his poem, "Goodbye, Rewards and Fairies"; the "little people," he says "were of the Old Religion."

The same phrase, "Old Religion," is also used in "The Sacrifice": here, the question is whether by it is meant the religion of the Old Testament or that of the Greeks and Romans; and the final gloss to be made on the phrase should be, I think, that for Herrick all religion is "old": the phrase is almost tautological for one so devoted to tradition. Religion is what binds us to the past; and our shared past is what, far more than contracts or abstract principles, binds us together.

This devotion to continuity made Herrick a classicist; and one can make no better preparation for reading the *Hesperides* than to saturate oneself in the ancient writers who were the poet's stay. He certainly knew Anacreon in some version, probably in Latin, and, it would seem, the *Greek Anthology*, on which his own small hymns to the gods are modelled, and he had presumably looked into Homer; but Catullus and Horace, Virgil and Tibullus and Marial are the authors he knew best: he must first have read them in his grammar school years, wherever passed,

46

and again at Cambridge; and they must have accompanied him into Devon. The *Eclogues* and *Georgics* of Virgil; the *Fasti* of Ovid; the Odes of Horace: out of these sacred books one can collect Herrick's worldview.

It was not primarily to the grand Graeco-Roman pantheon that Herrick was attracted. The great gods are mostly absent from Herrick's classical theology—notably the *Magna Mater*, but also, really, the *Magnus Pater*, Zeus. He wrote a group of short hymns addressed to the gods which are neither quite serious nor yet mere exercises, as I read them. Here, in its entirety, is the "short hymn" to Neptune, one of the second rank of gods:

> Mighty Neptune, may it please
> Thee, the Rector of the Seas,
> That my Barque may safely runne
> Through thy watrie-region;
> And a Tunnie-fish shall be
> Offer'd up, with thanks to thee.

Each prayer is followed, after the fashion of both the *Anthology* and the popular practice in Roman Catholic countries, by promise of a votive offering. The "hymn" to Neptune is preceded, however, by another to Lar, the household god of the homeloving bachelor priest. It is this domestic god, along with the *genius* of house or country, and the *penates*, the effigies or representatives of the family's ancestors down to the parents, who Herrick chiefly invokes.

Classical religion naturally most occurs to him when matters of family are concerned, matters of marriage and death—the times when even the customarily unreligious turn to Church and priesthood for sanction.

His nuptial Songs or Epithalamia follow in general the pattern of those in Catullus, though he knew Jonson's *Hymenaei* and may have known Spenser's pieces in the *genre*. Of the *Epithalamia* to Sir Robert Southwell and his Lady, Mr. Patrick remarks, "The marriage customs described are not accurately classical": Herrick "seems to have sought the universality of imprecision." To blend the classical with the English is to show the continuity of culture.

Death was a thought never far from him: it was the ever-present winter backdrop of his *carpe diem*; the fragility of life enhanced its preciousness: "Let us eat, drink, and be merry; for tomorrow we die." This is scarcely a Christian attitude: according to St. Paul, this is what the pagans say. In his *Noble Numbers* Herrick remembers Heaven and Hell; and occasionally in his secular poems—for example, "The Transfiguration," he refers to his "immortal clothing" and his "eternal mansion." But mostly he forgets them: I venture to think that he finds mention of them a little indelicate. The only refined, that is, humanistic, immortality is that of poetry. In an almost mystical poem to "His Winding Sheet," the shroud is addressed as "the Wine Whit / Of all I've writ." [What he must mean, in these opening lines, is that the thought of Death has been his inspiration.]

Herrick liked to write elegies and epitaphs, including some for the not yet dead—for his housekeeper, Prue, and especially for himself, Robin Herrick, who, dead, should have a grave visited and ceremonially strewn by all his mistresses.

Probably the finest of his elegies, as it is one of his finest poems, is "To the reverend shade of his religious Father." The elegy is a masterpiece of dignified translation from England and its Church to pagan Rome and its burial ceremonies—a piece of unfaked classicism. Mr. Patrick suggests that the poet, by 1627 a priest, read the proper Anglican burial service in the churchyard, but, "as is usual in *Hesperides*, . . . refers to the Graeco-Roman equivalent."

> That for seven *Lusters* I did never come
> To do the *Rites* to Thy Religious Tombe;
> That neither haire was cut, or true Tears shed
> By me, o'er the (*as justments to the dead*)
> Forgive, forgive me . . .

Now he brings to the grave the "Effused Offering," together with the "smallage" (celery or parsley), "Nightshade, Cypress, Yew" requisite; and he promises to make his father immortal in verse.

Papistical, classical (of the two Romes) as his imagery runs, there is yet a third world of central discourse in Herrick's poems—that of native English charms and rural festivals. Examples abound. I would cite particularly "A New Yeare's Gift sent to Sir Simeon Seward." But after "Corinna's Going a-Maying," perhaps Herrick's richest poem about country ceremonies, is "The Hock-Cart, or Harvest Home," which celebrates the rites of autumn as the other had the rites of spring.

> "Come Sons of summer, by whose toile,
> We are the Lords of Wine and Oile."

"We" are the aristocrats and country gentlemen, such as the Earl of Westmorland, to whom this poem is inscribed—they and their friends and guests, such as the poet. Like "Corinna," this poem is about the country festivals of peasants but seen from the point of view of the gentry, who are pleased to witness and to reward. "Wine and Oile" are not the products of English agriculture; they immediately connect the English harvest with Mediterranean culture; elsewhere Herrick repeats this conjunction.

After the procession of the cart, with its adornments of sheaves of wheat and its "malkin" and its oaken leaves, drawn by horses clad in white linen, there follows a bountiful feast for the farm workers—all kinds of meat with sweet dishes to follow. The accompanying beverage is not wine—which is for gentlemen and poets—but beer.

"Drink frolick boyes, till all be blythe"; drink a toast to the lord of the manor; then to your plow, sickle, and scythe, then to the country maids; then remember the farm animals. And the poem ends with a look forward to the Plough and Harrow and the coming of Spring.

The final ingredient in Herrick's poetic religion is poetry itself. Of the art he takes a high view, as well as of himself for being its practitioner. Far from all of his poems are of the ecstatic, the Dionysiac mode; yet when he writes about poetry almost always he thinks of it as an ecstatic art, associated with high spirits and inebriation. Sack and Poetry go together. Poetry is not for the sober morning but for night, when, the labors of the day performed, one is free to wax high. Poetry is the celebration of life; the experience of it, whether that of the poet or of his reader, is a peak experience. "When he would have his verses read" is

> When up the *Thyrse* is rais'd, and when the sound
> Of sacred *Orgies* flyes, A round, A round.

49

Herrick is the priest and celebrator of life. His worldview is that of a neo-pagan who is also, professionally, a Christian priest—one who feels that in a loose way, a relaxed way, all his loyalties hold together but feels no need consciously and critically to coordinate them.

That the *Noble Numbers* do not well cohere with the *Hesperides*, the bulk of Herrick's single volume, has almost invariably been felt by critical readers. The poet adds, whatever his motives, an Anglican chapel to his pagan church. A bolder solution would have been better: to incorporate the Anglican poems, as he did his poems of gnomic wisdom, into his basic book.

In general, the separation of the two parts of his Book seems mechanically formal, and finally to violate Herrick's whole, though never wholly conscious, view that all life is holy—a view which comes to the surface in "The Argument," when he speaks of his love poems as songs of "cleanly Wantonesse," or when he "gravely" encourages the Divine Being to read his secular poems, assuring Him that

> Thou, my God, mays't on this impure look
> Yet take no tincture from my sinfull book,

a couplet within which *impure* and *sinful* seem almost perfunctory or relative.

Surely Herrick could not, as he did, publish and proofread his own book, most of it allegedly secular, unless he supposed all his work to be, if not technically religious, still innocent, such as a Christian (and Anglican priest) might publish without intending any offense to the morals of the Christian reader. This was a large and bland assumption on his part, but I have to conceive that he, who was mostly uncritical of himself, pleased with himself and his own work, was not consciously insincere in making it.[2]

Behind the technical or ritual separation of Christianity and non-Christianity, Herrick must have felt their unity in the form of some higher

---

[2]M. K. Starkman, in an essay contributed to J. A. Mazzeo, editor, *Reason and Imagination* (New York: 1962), has written the most plausible defense of *Noble Numbers* we have; yet I think it finally unconvincing since she never attempts to relate this part of Herrick's work to the *Hesperides*, the larger and distinctly superior part of it.

but larger religion, some *pietas* which includes the rites of classical Rome, always available to him to his poetic use as a partial equivalent of Christian rites, and the folk-festivals of the English countryside, all bound up with the rites of the natural cycle, from spring to autumn harvest—all the customs which give ceremonial form to man's acceptance of the universe.

IV.

What is Herrick's rank? Is he a "major" poet? The very question seems academic; and it is certainly not to be asked by persons incapable of judging whether or not poetry is "genuine," is poetry. But the very inquiry, historically, critically, philosophically pursued, is a useful occupation, even though it less establishes the rank of poets (never to be done once and for all time) than clarifies our own criteria—whether or not, and how far, they are purely aesthetic, and how far extra-aesthetic considerations have their weight.

The history of Herrick's reputation can be stated briefly. For whatever reasons, his poetry was little known in his own time, to which he did not, literally, quite belong. He was not really a "metaphysical" poet; was perhaps too late what he has sometimes been called, a "late Elizabethan." He thought himself a "son of Ben," but he lacked Jonson's breadth and sturdiness, his masculinity; indeed prettiness and preciosity sometimes suggest the epicene. Perhaps the nature of his religion was puzzling and disquieting to the few who read his book.

The neoclassical period passed him by. It was not till the Romantic period that he began to be appreciated—first publicly by Nathan Drake in his 1800 *Literary Hours*—yet his real acclaim comes yet later, at the end of the nineteenth century, with the first important edition, that of A. W. Pollard in 1891, and with the critical praise of Swinburne and Gosse. The first important monograph on him is that of F. W. Moorman, 1915. It is the aesthetic "nineties" when Herrick achieved his first full recognition. The sensibility which savored Fitzgerald's *Omar* found much of Herrick also to its taste; so did the sensibility which responded to Pater. Reaction against Victorian didacticism and "high seriousness" found in Herrick's Epicureanism a light and elegant antidote. And one "reading" of Herrick that is—distinctly a "period reading," but a possible one for a critic.

Our century, nor far advanced, has elevated Herrick's position. H. J. Massingham, a sensible and sensitive critic of his generation, excludes Herrick as well as Milton from his 1919 *Treasury of Seventeenth Century English Verse* on the ground of their "towering stature." Mr. Musgrove, in 1950, judges that Herrick is to be ranked with Donne and Marvell, neither of whom Massingham would have put into a class with Milton. To my literary generation, Musgrove's rating seems high, but not to be dismissed.

All literary judgments are comparative. To get beyond analysis of a book or author to evaluation involves comparison—this poem, this poet, is better or worse, greater or less great than another, especially, of course, within the same *kind* (however flexible or rigid one's conception of *kind*). And ultimately, all comparisons should invoke, not, as do the two just cited, poets writing in the same language and during the same literary-historical period, but the full resources of "comparative literature," of world literature. Let me confine myself to European poetry and inquire, without answering, how does Herrick rank in comparison with Anacreon, Catullus, Horace (whose work he knew), with Villon, Ronsard, Baudelaire, Heine, Rilke—with such later poets writing in English as Landor, Shelley, Keats, Yeats, Dylan Thomas—or, to come to nearer controversial range, to Eliot, Pound, e. e. cummings, John Ransom, Dr. Williams, Wallace Stevens, Richard Wilbur, Charles Olson?

In what follows, I attempt my own estimate of Herrick, beginning with purely, or nearly purely, aesthetic criteria.

From considerations of rank, it is still almost impossible to rule out entirely the quantitative criterion—the bulk, the persistence. The great writer is commonly copious. Herrick, like Milton, Wordsworth, and Whitman, is copious; but, unlike Virgil, Spenser, and Milton, he has no long work, no *major* poem; his genius is for the minor—and the many.

What, aesthetically, I miss in Herrick's work, his *opus*, is a calculated structure. After the first eight poems, all prefaces to his poetry, defenses of it against all assailers, he observes no scheme of placement. One ordering might have been chronological—the order of composition. Delattre, in 1913, attempted such an arrangement for Herrick, indeed thought that, in general, Herrick *had* arranged them chronologically. The French scholar assigns most of the longer pieces, including the fairy divertissements and the florid and fluid and eloquent "Farewells" to Sack and to Poetry, to the period before the vicarage in Devon; to the mature period of the poet's incumbency of Dean Prior (1629–1640), he assigns the poems of rural naturalism which take the place of literary-classical pastoralism, and the folklore poems, *un peu naïf et rude*, which succeeded to Elizabethan fairylore. And them Delattre finds a third period, during the Civil War, in which Herrick, a quondam disciple of Horace and Jonson, turns himself, now more grave and sombre, into a sacred poet. About this period, I remain agnostic; for the characterization of the two earlier periods more credence can be given. But finally Delattre almost gives his whole case away by the remark—one often repeated by later defenders of Herrick—that "the very numerous exceptions to this chronological order are due to the poet's desire to introduce into his work all the variety and all the desired contrasts of life."

The exceptions to chronological order—or indeed any other kind of order, are so numerous that readers of the *Hesperides* who read it through, instead of dipping into it, can scarcely avoid some irritation at its seeming pleasure in a Shandyan helter-skelter for which our poet certainly found no warrant in the *Works* of his putative master, Jonson. In this, there is some suggestion of Erasmus' *Praise of Folly*, of Rabelais, of Burton's *Anatomy*, a book, one of the few "modern" books, Herrick is known to have read—and used. A "tradition" can be made out for such calculated but not for long amusing disorder, disarrangement. But, at the risk of seeming neoclassically rigid, I fervently wish that Herrick had used some system—literally generic (epithalamia, epigrams) or topical (poems in praise of country life, poems on women, poems of flowers as women, poems on women as flowers). He would not thereby have diminished his range.

One ordering he did make I regret. I could wish that Herrick had not separated his Christian poems but, boldly, had incorporated them into his *Hesperides*. Inferior to the best of the secular poems, that inferiority would not have been so apparent; and what I take to have been his "real" point of view would have prevailed. I can only conjecture what may have prompted this separation: for Herrick, who prides himself on his putting acetic epigram and luscious lyric side by side, this separation is abnormal.

His book suffers, too, from its unselectiveness, the lack of the critic within the poet (here I instinctively echo Pope and Eliot). Like Whitman, Herrick, *homo unius libri,* went on adding to his book, indifferent to whether or not he has written virtually the same poem before. All which he writes, or has brought to a state of craftsmanship, is precious to him— he will not discriminate among his children! Whatever a carping critic may object to, all are worthy of entrances into the Ark. Thomas Whittaker, perhaps Herrick's best critic, has proposed a critical canon reducing the poems to fifty. William Jay Smith, who has edited an exemplary "Laurel Series" edition, has nearly effected that critical reduction.

The final effect of Herrick's unselection is to make his work seem a kind of Notebook, like the work of Dr. Williams, a name engaging to associate with his—a name invoked by one of my middle-aged literary friends. And yet: the art of poetry is not, finally, a series of jottings, of perceptive memorabilia: it is a work of selection and arrangement, a triumph of art over refractory lives, and life. Only so has one, in the Horatian phrase, built a monument more enduring than bronze.

One's final judgment of Herrick's stature involves extra-aesthetic criteria, specifically what I have earlier called his syncretistic religion, the presence of which in his poetry I take to be one of the reasons why it came into fullest appreciation only at the end of the nineteenth century. This "ecumenical" religion is certainly at the base of our century's yet higher evaluation of Herrick—this perception of his "piety."

His imaginatively envisaged "system" is never quite delivered—that is, articulated. For that, a cerebrality beyond him was requisite. I can't even say that he is straining towards it: he is, with regard to such concerns, too relaxed. He adumbrates, but never quite reaches, an encompassing myth or mythic philosophy. In his work the Christian and the pagan world are "imperfectly coordinated": Herrick is "reaching for a reality that transcends them both, part pagan, part Christian; but he did not discover and could not devise a central myth which would completely reconcile them."

The phrases quoted I take from Whittaker's essay, with which I am in substantial concurrence. I value Whittaker for applying severe tests to Herrick, for treating him as more than a charming craftsman or even— one of the standard phrases for Herrick—a "consummate artist"—for thinking that he suggests a poet yet greater than he actually is.

In Herrick's total work, there is too much that is fragmentary perception, and overabundance of delicacy, even "cuteness"—too much also that is merely personal, too much about "Robin" Herrick, the coy artist. We honor Herrick by regretting the amount of self-indulgence he good-humoredly allows himself.

We honor him when we measure him by higher standards than he set himself. It gives pleasurable instruction to invoke parallels and proto- types. Retrospectively, he recalls Spenser, a sensuous artist with an in- herited moral mythology; anticipatorily, he suggests Shelley or Keats (the latter's weaknesses Whittaker remarks in Herrick); he prophesies Wallace Stevens (first, the *Harmonium* and then the long poems on the fictive power of the imagination) and finally W. B. Yeats, who, in *A Vision*, forged himself a mythical system to serve as framework for his poems.

It is in this high—if not highest—company that I leave Herrick. His literary place, well up on one of the slopes of Parnassus, seems—so far as such predictions may be made—assured.

(1976)

Frost Revisited

If it is important with all poets, it is certainly much more so with Frost, to distinguish three persons:—the biographical man; the theorist and commentator on poetry (the letter writer, lecturer, talker); and, finally, the poet, that is, his poetry.

The man Frost was ambitious of fame as a poet, even for fame; ambitious to be a "man of power." Till he was 39, he was a failure in the eyes of everyone except his wife. Then, in 1913, with the publication during a two years' stay in England of *A Boy's Will* and a year later the book which made him really famous, *North of Boston*, he was a literary success. First he made the grade of ranking with Robinson, his fellow New Englander, and with Lindsay, Masters, and Sandburg, the other members of the 1912 New Poetry generation "promoted" by Amy Lowell in her *Tendencies of Modern American Poetry*. This rank did not content him. In his Norton lectures at Harvard in 1936, when and where he followed T. S. Eliot, who had there delivered four years earlier his *The Use of Poetry and the Use of Criticism*, he made it clear to his listeners, of whom I was one, that the real rivals, whom he sought to dispose of by paltry jokes and other denigrations, were Yeats, Pound, and Eliot. In his later life, Stevens could probably be added to the list, and possibly Williams.

What distinguished Frost's ambition from that of his literarily acclaimed rivals, especially Eliot, was his early aim for a double audience —the select company of intellectuals who had appropriated them, but also the wide middleclass and middlebrow company of persons, including many professors of English, who found the acclaimed contemporary poetry too allusive and otherwise obscure. He wanted for himself the combined audiences divided in the nineteenth century between Browning and Tennyson, or, at home, between Longfellow and Emerson. In his letters he made it clear that he wanted cash as well as credit.

During his uncommonly long life he never managed to win both audiences. He received Pulitzer prizes and nearly twenty honorary degrees from universities; and he was made virtually poet-laureate of his country in being the first poet to perform, by invitation, at a President's inaugural ceremony. Frost was a skillful public performer, of his poetry and of himself—too skillful. Though he despised Sandburg, he was equally a self-dramatizer. Whitehaired and tousleheaded, carelessly dressed, he seemed, what he was not, the ordinary American, more specially the rural American. He put on an act as the bucolic sage, not only on the platform but in the hours of drink and talk which followed the performance.

But he paid severely for his popularity, and for his popular-academic acclaim. While he was Norton lecturer, he was aware that real literary people like F. O. Matthiessen discounted his stock, contrasting him with Eliot, to his distinct disadvantage. And his *Further Range*, which appeared in the year of his lectures, 1936, was unfavorably reviewed by such leftist intellectuals as Newton Arvin and Matthiessen in the *Partisan Review* and the *New Republic*: he was looked upon as a reactionary in politics, as well as, in poetry, superseded by Eliot and Joyce.

Frost died in 1963. In the following years there appeared his *Selected Letters*, overlong but of real interest and use, edited by Lawrance Thompson, a Princeton professor, whom Frost had appointed his official biographer. The biography itself was published in three volumes, 1966, 1970, and 1976, the last completed after the death of the biographer, for twenty-five years at work on his Frostean labors; his volumes, wearisomely long and often irrelevantly detailed, are further amplified by lengthy notes, appendices, and indices (the last-named worth looking into for the tabulation of Frost's character traits and opinions). Thompson came increasingly to hate the man to whom he had toadied; and, a meticulous scholar but no critic, he felt the old antagonism of the academic towards a poet encountered in the flesh. The effect of his work on the general reading public was, as successive reviews in *Time* and *Newsweek* would show, to damage Frost's reputation. That Thompson was aware of this probable effect is made clear by the best as well as most generous thing he ever wrote, his introduction to the *Letters*: "Those who know the poet largely from his poetry and his public appearances . . . may not be prepared to see how often his private correspondence reveals periods of gloom, jealousies, obsessive resentments, sullen displays of temper, nervous rages and vindictive retaliations." The gap between man and artist, between family man, husband and father with "promises to keep," and the poet, for whom poetry had ever the higher claim: to bridge this gap is difficult for poets in general, but doubly and triply so for a

58

poet who seeks to be a popular, even if such is still possible a family, poet as well as a great one.

How can one so jealous, vindictive, and selfish have been a great poet? A hard question to answer for a lover of poetry who is at the same time a moralist. But, since the Romantic movement, with its alienation of the artist from the bourgeois, an alienation concurrent with the rise of finance-capitalism and industrialism, the question has become oppressive. The days are gone in which the artist was a craftsman whose general standards were those of the civilization to which he belonged, the days of Dryden and Pope, of Molière and Racine. Now almost every artist of stature, as well as vastly more men who are only near-artists or not artists at all, are neurotics; and, though the word seems never applied to him, a neurotic Frost surely was, a man so beset by fears and anxieties, so abrasive yet so stricken of conscience. If one finally settles to admire modern art, one must accept the conditions under which it is produced; accept the fact that it is chiefly produced by vain, self-conscious, and self-centered men and women who are hard to live with, who make life comfortable neither for themselves or others. Frost's poetry was the best of Frost, but it was a clarity he achieved out of his turbulence.

Reading Poirier's recent book, I am at least half surprised to consider how little significant criticism of Frost has appeared since the reviews of *A Further Range*.[1] Even scholarship, that thriving industry which has been so lavish of meticulous work on Keats, Joyce, and Eliot (as on Melville, Thoreau, Hawthorne, James and Faulkner) has passed him by, the explanation being, I think, that literary scholarship chiefly follows, at some interval, the critical estimates made of their fellows by other creators; and here estimates have been sparse and cautious.

Yvor Winters, author of the best book we have on Robinson, his spiritual congener, declared Frost (as he did in fact Emerson) a "spiritual drifter." In *Modern Poets and the Tradition* (1939), Cleanth Brooks, putting Auden and Frost into the same chapter, had a few good words to say "achievement in maintaining integrity of tone"; and the highly influential *Understanding Poetry* (1938), in which Brooks collaborated with Robert Penn Warren, well represented Frost. Auden, the adoptive American (and

---

[1]Richard Poirier, *Robert Frost: The Work of Knowing* (New York: Oxford University Press, 1977).

New Yorker) spoke well, though not to my perception quite hitting the mark, in an essay on Frost collected, together with a much better one on American Poetry from its beginnings, in *The Dyer's Hand* (1962). But by far the best appreciations of Frost are the two essays by the Southern poet, Randall Jarrell, in his *Poetry and the Age* (1953), essays remarkably independent in their perception and, like his equally brilliant essay on Whitman, excelling in the quotation of disregarded passages or whole poems. And, lastly, in an address given at Frost's eighty-fifth birthday, Lionel Trilling, to the astonishment of his listeners, called him a "terrifying poet," implying that he had continued the noble and heroic line of dissent, was radical in the classic American tradition.

Poirier's *Robert Frost: The Work of Knowing*, a critical study, is such a book on Frost as I had not anticipated, for which, with what reservations I shall hereafter state, I have welcome, and from which I have learned much. A more or less lifelong adherent of the New England poet's rivals, Yeats, the early Stevens, Hart Crane, and above the others, Eliot, and also one with a more than passing acquaintance with Frost, whom I so disliked that the image of the man came between me and his poetry, I can call myself one type of reader to whom Poirier addresses himself. He makes a plausible cause for reconsidering the rank of Frost's poetry, to giving it equal status to that of the rival claimants.

Poirier's book must be read slowly. Unlike its immediate predecessor, *The Performing Self*, a work I found suggestive, exciting, but irritatingly arrogant and often obscure, this is not a book in which the reader, especially if he be a fellow critic, can disregard the quotations and enjoy himself with following the generalized argument, titillated by the cerebral brilliance of the criticism. *Robert Frost* cannot so be read: the critical speed-reader will have little profit from it. Poirier quotes some forty or fifty of Frost's poems in their entirety (and one must read the poems) and gives a close, attentive, if sometimes overstrained, reading of each, and then groups these poems together in six chapters topically centered— keeping in good balance the poems, with perceptive interpretations, and relevant generalizations.

Poirier gives a close reading to a poet who heretofore has been loosely read for his epigrams or his sententious endings, as though the poems existed for their summary doctrine not their wholeness or, as we used to say, their "structure and their texture." He passes lightly over didactic pieces like "New Hampshire," "Build Soil," and the two Masques to give attention to the lyrics and the dramatic pieces in *North of Boston*. The poems he analyzes are for the most part not the over-familiar ones such as "The Road Not Taken" but such as "Rose Pogonias" and "Trial by Existence," both of which appear in the first volume, *A Boy's Will*. He calls attention to Frost's sonnets (it is not generally known that Frost wrote sonnets, but he did, from youth to age. The late volume *A Steeple Bush*, 1947, contains a whole cluster of sonnets, variously regular).

With Frost's rivals ever in mind, Poirier has some important points to make. First, that Frost was not one of what Southey called the "Uneducated Poets," but well read in poetry and the classics and in philosophy; secondly, that as a poet he was an artist, a master-craftsman; thirdly, that he too was a modern poet. I shall deal with each of these in turn.

The second chapter, "Beginnings," the most informative and instructive, is concerned with both his education in poetry and his poetic artistry. Of *A Boy's Will* Poirier demonstrates that Frost planned its structure with care, intending it as a backward look at adolescence and youth; that he excluded from this book the narrative and dramatic pieces which he reserved for his next, together with such lyrics as, not fitting his scheme, were reserved for his third volume; that he accompanied the poems with glosses (omitted from the 1939 *Collected Poems* on) which paralleled in style and function the titles Yeats affixed to his poems in *The Wind among the Reeds*. And Frost was well versed in poetry anterior to and contemporary with his own. In high school and at Harvard, he excelled at Latin and Greek. He shared his mother's taste for Emerson's poetry. He studied Palgrave's *Golden Treasury*, which, as Poirier remarks, contains many seventeenth-century poems, though I do not find convincing Poirier's claim that these much influenced Frost. In England, he knew personally as well as read Yeats, Pound, and the Georgians. While Pound and Eliot displayed their literary erudition by their allusions, Frost underplayed his.

In his preface, Poirier writes, "there has yet to be thoroughgoing assimilation of what Emerson and William James, Frost's two most potent American forebears, have to offer." Throughout his book, the critic comes back to what these two unacademic philosophers who wrote, like Frost, in his critical prose as well as in his poetry, in nontechnical language, meant to the poet. Like Frost himself, these two, born tender-minded, had made themselves, in James's word, "toughminded." The later Emerson of *Conduct of Life*, which Nietzsche admired, was already present in essays like "Experience," which Poirier often invokes, as well as in "Monadnock" and "Uriel," poems Frost especially admired; it was by Frost's own choice that his Poetry Fellowship at Harvard was called the Emerson Fellowship. His debt to William James is less well known; but Poirier convincingly shows the influence of *Pragmatism* and *Talks to Teachers of Psychology*, both books which Frost taught at the Plymouth Normal School in New Hampshire. A third philosopher who excited Frost was Bergson, whose *Creative Evolution* offered the poet an alternative to Darwin.

Poirier certainly makes his first two points; about his third I have my dubieties. He is out to show, or to insinuate, that Frost is as modern as are Pound, Eliot, and Joyce, despite the fact that, unlike those of the "certified modernists," his chaos and confusion have no "historical localizations," that he is more aware of man in relation to nature than man in relation to history. Oliver Goldsmith wrote: "How small, of all that human hearts endure, / That part which laws or kings can cause or cure!" Frost was a humanist, almost a Christian humanist, who considered the human lot neither a happy one nor a hopeless one, but assuredly not one of miseries which only Communism or the New Deal could substantially abate. Man, for him, is always facing chaos; poetry is, like civilization itself, a man's temporary victory over his own sloth and despair, a "momentary stay against confusion"—a phrase of Frost's. Is Frost not "modern" because he writes about the country and not the city? The solitude he sought, when he sought it, the flights he was ever proposing to take, were as much from the thinly populated country as from the overpopulated city (*cf.* Emerson's *Society and Solitude*). Frost tried deliberately not to be a modernist, not to "keep up" except by trying, like Chesterton, to combat and correct modern heresies. He aimed at a modernity which would not date, hence at the universals of experience, better observed in rural life than in that of the city.

Important to Frost's modernity was his simplification of language, his adoption of speech-rhythms—his attempt, at which he shared common ground with his generation, to dispense with all traditional poetic diction, to approximate, so far as it is compatible with "writing regular" (Frost's own phrase)—that is, in meter and rhyme, with their counterpoints to prose rhythm, the rhythm of prose, of conversation. Auden writes of him, "the music is always that of the speaking voice . . . ; and I cannot think of any other modern poet, except Cavafy, who uses language more simply. He rarely employs metaphor, and there is not a word, not a historical or literary reference in the whole of his work which would be strange to an unbookish boy of fifteen." This last clause exaggerates; but that it can be made shows the success of Frost's effort. Frost himself was fond, in letters, prefaces, and talks, of phrases "sentence sounds—the sound of sense," and "talk-song," especially of the first-named. What did he mean by "sound of the sentence"? Poirier attaches high importance to it, but cannot convey much more than Auden says and others have said, acclaiming the achievement for which Frost was immediately acclaimed by his contemporaries, that of making conversational poetry, whether in lyric or narrative, in which the natural word-order is followed and which uses the natural language of men.

The trouble with Poirier's claim that Frost is modern is that no definition of the term is given. Often used to mean the method of Pound, Joyce, and Eliot, that of ironically juxtaposing the past and the present, the civilized past and the barbaric present, this is but one of its possible meanings; and obviously in that sense Frost was not, deliberately chose not to be, modern, or, better, a modernist. Nor was he modern in the wider sense intended by Irving Howe's anthology *Literary Modernism* (1967), which contains Trilling's confessional essay, "On Teaching Modern Literature." But modern he is in the sense Irving Babbitt used the term, when he speaks of "the positive and critical spirit, the spirit which refuses to take things on authority." Using a term which, whatever it means, is always in fashion, Poirier wants to claim for Frost what is currently denied him, continued "relevance." This term, fashionable at least for a time among the young, and still useful, is praise for any work of literature which, whatever its date, is universal enough still to speak to us today—which is what we used to mean by calling a work a "classic."

Poirier's third chapter, "Outward Bound (Home and Extravagance; Women at Home; Soundings for Home)," is at once his clearest and his most brilliant. Its materials are chiefly drawn from *North of Boston*, the narrative and dramatic pieces in blank verse which the reader mistakenly thinks he already knows. The themes of this chapter are the tensions, and the equipoises, in Frost's poetry (as well as in Frost the man) between fixity and flight, between wildness and domesticity, and the tension and equipoise, between women and men. "Sexuality in Frost has been noted, when at all, with a kind of surprise," says Poirier, who groups Frost with Milton, of whose scenes in Paradise he is presumably thinking, as uniquely a poet of married love, and explicitly ungroups him from Eliot —and presumably Stevens. But Poirier doesn't limit Frost's sexuality to husband and wife poems like "Home Burial," "The Death of the Hired Man," or "West-running Brook"; he finds it pervasive. If he particularly stresses its presence in the early sonnets, "Putting in the Seed," he finds it everywhere, finds it with a fantasy of extension beyond my following, in the poetic process, especially in metaphor.

Chapter VI, "The Work of Knowing," Poirier's titular and climactic chapter, is the least clear. What he means by his title I do not know except so far as his own antimetabole glosses it as "his poems of work and the work of his poems." And I certainly don't agree that Frost's "poetry of work" is quite directly about the correlative work of writing a poem and of reading it, an equation of which Poirier is fond. Any genuine work, whether it is building a load of hay or carpentering a table or constructing a theology or writing a poem—or, I concede, reading a poem and not just reacting to it—is hard; but they are not the same. Particularly I protest against equating the poet's discovery, in the act of writing a poem, of what he means, a movement from the unconscious to knowledge, with the process of attentive reading, which is a movement in reverse direction—from surface to center. This writing-reading equation is Poirier's, not Frost's.

To be sure, the equivalent importance of other men's work is occasionally suggested in Frost's poems, but it appears much more often and overtly in his talks and essays—in "The Constant Symbol," for example, in which he compares, for commitments, strong spending in "art, politics, school, church, business, love, and marriage," with the poet's commitment to his poem: in which he compares the poet to the President of the United States or the clergyman who has to fulfil his early pledge (elsewhere he compares the poet with the athlete). These are the poet's honorific defenses of himself and his profession as doing a man's work in the contemporary American world which has not room for the dilettante or the idly leisured. The poet, Frost implies, works as hard as anyone else; that he works harder is his own secret.

64

Probably by the "work of knowing" Poirier means that Frost's poems, like the acclaimed rival poems of Stevens, are really about the writing of poetry, a notion at which the critic hints from the first chapter on. This is a fashionable doctrine, one espoused and exemplified by many lesser poets as well as by Stevens; but I think it does Frost an injustice to claim it for him. When Frost accused Stevens of writing about bric-a-brac (works of art), Stevens countered with the accusation that Frost wrote about "things" (matter, the real world, not the imagined). Frost's poems "imitate" human life, persons, and their interrelation with other persons, and they "criticize," interpret, real life.

On the subject of metaphor Poirier is virtually silent; but, despite the disparity between Frost's infrequent use of this specific rhetorical figure, a fact noted by both Cleanth Brooks and Auden, Frost, in his "Education by Poetry," makes metaphor and poetry almost synonymous. The critical observers are speaking of a localized device like simile; but Frost uses it more broadly and philosophically to mean talking of one thing in terms of another, of matter as though it were mind, of spirit as though it were matter, of the man as animal or animal as man ("The Drumlin Woodchuck"). Years ago, in "Image, Metaphor, Symbol, Myth," in *Theory of Literature*, I wrote of Frost as using public, natural, symbolic, or archetypal images, citing "The Road not Taken," "Mending Wall," "The Mountain," and "Stopping by Woods on a Snowy Evening." Walks, journeys, outward movements of excursion or flight, are balanced against homes; graveyards and deserted villages against the counterpointing images of life, birch trees, and birds; the snowstorm against the signs of spring. Metaphor in Frost is not localized in figure of speech but is pervasive, as spirit and method.

With Poirier's central conception of poetry I am in agreement. It is contextual, not to be abstracted, is evasive of any dogmatism, abounds in ironies and double-plays: its mode is always the conditional—a view substantially that of the New Criticism. It does not simplify, does not excite to action; its metaphors do not have the comparative permanence of those metaphors upon which religious and political parties are founded. Frost's poems, as Poirier demonstrates, abound in negatives, double negatives, ifs, and other qualifications and restrictions; and what counts is that which the poet incorporates into the poem and not his personal views outside his poetry. That Frost was obsessed by a Jamesian "will to believe," in opposition to his wife's will to disbelieve, his biographer shows; and the word God is used in some end-lines of his poems like "Bereft"; but Poirier convinces me that the poem as a whole hedges in and qualifies the final line, that Frost's private faith was less strong than the test of poetry could manage.

On Frost's rank Poirier never summarily pronounces. He calls certain poems "great"; one at least he calls "magnificent"; but it is Frost's poems, brooded over by a man of perception and reflection, which leave their weight. "What is great Poetry?" is a question the author of the book reviewed never theoretically raises; but the book, together with the necessity of rereading the poems he knew and those he didn't, left this old reviewing critic with the reluctant impression, even judgment, that he had underestimated Frost; that Frost is indeed among our, perhaps among the, great poets.

An earlier book of Poirier's has been praised for its "quiet and sustained acuteness of perception." It is this quality which makes his *Frost* so memorable. His theories are some of them dubious: his *James* and *Frost*, which have a specific center, seem to me stronger than his intermediate, more theoretical books; the theories are, however, rather suggested than argued; and one can reject or but provisionally entertain them and still be deeply grateful to their perceptive propounder.

(1978)

The Quest for Auden

The sheer bulk of Auden's writing—two substantial volumes of critical prose and a huge unwieldy *Collected Poems* in small print—makes the effort to say anything comprehensive about him seem unmanageable. One could address oneself to the task by dividing it into three essays—one on the man, one on the poetry, and one on the criticism, chiefly, but by no means exclusively, literary. But with Auden that seems unsatisfactory, for in him the three parts coexisted: he never segregated his personal life from his work (as Eliot so rigidly attempted to do), nor his critical mind from his poetic work: after his early poetry his critical mind, his acute intelligence, more and more takes the upper hand over his unconscious. He was never really the romantic poet, the Rimbaud, he used to seem, not the "pure poet" of images and rhythms either. Perhaps in a sense one should read Auden's poetry backward—the latest written, first.

After 1939 he had renounced one of the persistent grandiose conceptions poets have entertained of themselves, the conception entertained by Shelley of the immense power poets wield over human lives: that they are prophets and shapers of destiny and changers of history. Instead he assigned poetry, his own included, to the humbler position which earlier ages than the Romantic had given to literature, including poetry: that of a craft with words, which described, characterized— perhaps even, in one of Auden's favorite words and concepts, "diagnosed" —human life in its more permanent, as well as its more transient, more agebound, features. Poetry can never take the place of religion: here Auden distinguishes his position from that modified romantic Arnold or, with less rigidity, allies himself with Eliot. Poetry cannot change history or even morally reform or spiritually regenerate a single man. It can soften or refine, but cannot alter, character. It can harmlessly entertain our idle hours or, at a higher level, educate and subtilize our sensibility; it can interpret. Further the originality of the poet is not in his philosophic thought (as Eliot said long ago of Dante) but in the adequacy with which he translates a worldview into appropriate aesthetic expression.

Auden was a highly intelligent man with a wide range of interests; he was not, except incidentally, a confessional poet. When he writes about himself directly, as he does delightfully in his "Letter to Lord Byron," it

67

is a simple delivery of a case history, not as a revelation of supposed importance to mankind. A lifelong practitioner of what his friends call his "clinical" method, he treats himself with (almost) the same objectivity with which he treats others.

I shall confine this piece to attempting an answer to three questions of central importance: what kind of man was Auden; why did he leave his war-beset native England for the United States; and why, in a secularist and positivist age, did he return to his ancestral Christianity?

Auden asked his literary executors to destroy his letters, and wanted no biography of him written—this despite the fact that he was himself found of reading (and reviewing) biographies, diaries, and letters of authors as well as of composers. He separated his interest in biography from his interest in poetry: what bulked larger in one was minimal in the other, and vice versa. (But biography holds an interest of its own—partly the interest a humanist takes in characterology, partly the almost universal human interest in gossip, an appetite Auden shared with Frost.)

I never knew Auden, even slightly; never saw him; never heard his voice, coming either from the lecture platform or from the phonograph. Whether this absence of the tangible and the audible is help or hindrance I can't decide. But at any event there are as yet no biographies, and no (forbidden) collections of his letters to confuse by their plethora of detail. In what I am about to write of Auden the man I am constructing a psychograph out of abundant and adequate material already in print: from the autobiographies of his two intimate friends, Stephen Spender and Christopher Isherwood (*World within World*, 1951, *Lions and Shadows*, 1938, and *Christopher and His Kind*, 1976), and from the post-mortem memories and testimonies collected in Spender's *Tribute to Auden* (1975). These are supplemented by the autobiography in Auden's "Letter to Byron" and "The Early Years," included in *The English Auden* (1977), and by autobiographical passages in his richest book of prose, *Forewords and Afterwords* (1974).

Auden was fortunte in his family—his clerical grandfathers, his father, a physician and amateur archeologist, his university-educated and devout mother; fortunate in his boyhood home, which contained a large but largely nonliterary library, and in the freedom he had to make his own choices, undeterred by family opposition. In these respects his early life was quite different from that of most American poets, who meet such opposition and are throughout their lives so weighed down by guilt at having opposed the strong wishes of their families that they make money: they go into business, or at least take up a profession.

Nor was Auden like his American counterparts in doing well in his English classes at school and university but ill in all the other courses, especially in courses in the physical sciences. Strange in Auden's youth were his early fascination with science and his belated adolescent conversion to poetry. He has written that his early passions were for words, "the longer the better," and for mines and their machinery. "From the age of four to thirteen I had a series of passionate love-affairs with pictures of . . . waterturbines, winding-engines, roller-crushers, etc., and I was never so emotionally happy as when I was underground." Yet "a psychologist, noticing that I had no practical, mechanical gift whatsoever, would have realized that the interest was a purely symbolic one." (My quotations in this paragraph come from an earlier unpublished piece, "The Prolific and the Devourer," which Auden wrote in 1939. It is included in *The English Auden: Poems, Essays, and Dramatic Writings, 1927-39,* ed. Edward Mendelson [Random House, 1977], a collection especially valuable for its assemblage of Auden's early essays on a wide variety of subjects.)

He was sixteen when, upon a school-fellow's casually asking him whether he wrote poetry, he who had thus far never written a line "or even read one with pleasure" decided that poetry was his vocation, and that with an instantaneousness analogous to a sudden religious conversion. What could a love of long words and a love for the underground, symbolic of unconscious and generally repressed instinctive motivations, add up to except a poetic vocation? In the fragment I am quoting Auden adds: "An interest in people did not begin till adolescence." That interest occurred much later than his love of words and of mining; and this belated overlay is corroborated by Isherwood's and Spender's sense of Auden's never being quite a person, never quite human.

Unlike Isherwood, who deliberately failed to take a degree at Cambridge, Auden finished his course at Oxford, but surprised his friends by taking only a third-class degree: he conformed, but no more than he found convenient. As he told his tutor, he was going to be not just a poet but a great poet—and for that vocation he needed a wide education, one largely of his own election. He was, from youth to old age, a miscellaneous (but purposive) reader and a quick reader, one whose reading quickly passed, in a way distinctly unusual with poets, into his writing. After his death Spender remarked that now "no one is poring over the *Scientific American* and turning the article on, say, the Parasites that inhabit the human body into an extremely witty meditation in the manner of Goethe's *Roman Elegies*." At Oxford Auden read and wrote all day, in a room with the shades drawn and the electric light going; kept (as he increasingly did in later life) regular hours, with the early rising and early bed of the hard and regular worker he was.

He seemed to have little or no idea how strong was his influence on those persons whose characters, like Spender's, were less strong and less self-determined than his. If his literary generation could plausibly be called, as it soon was, the Auden generation, this was not because of any Pound-like or Amy Lowell-like deliberate assumption of leadership, any planned marshaling, but because of the precocious and prophetic way in which whatever he wrote symptomized the way the others were going to think and to write. The son of a doctor, he readily used the words diagnostician, disease, and symptom; and, as a reader of Groddeck and Homer Lane, unorthodox analysts, the adolescent Auden irritated and impressed his friends by his turning all their supposed physical maladies into giveaways of their neuroses. All disease was psychosomatic. And Auden was also early an analyst of social disease like the decay of capitalist and industrial society.

As Auden's natural self-assurance gave him a power over other literary men who in varying degrees were less sure of their identity than he, so did his range of knowledge, his immense curiosity, his dogmatic manner: though he might change his beliefs, he never changed the assurance with which he held them. This combination of powers caused some who knew him in early life to be reminded of Dr. Johnson and those who knew him in later life to be reminded of Goethe (the latter analogy not entirely unfamiliar to Auden himself).

The most memorable, most picturesque portrait of Auden in his Oxford years is given by Isherwood in the fifth chapter of *Lions and Shadows*: of Auden with his gnawed and nicotine-stained fingers, of his piano-playing (chiefly of Anglican hymns), of his abrupt manners, of his rapid progress through the imitation of one poet after another—Edward Thomas, Dickinson, Frost, E. A. Robinson, Hardy, Eliot; of his poses, of his hats (his opera hat, his workman's cap, his panama with a black ribbon—representing his "conception of himself as a lunatic clergyman; always a favorite role"—and his schoolmaster's mortar-board). These were all poses or attitudes, but all also proper decor for aspects of Auden's character which could abstractly be named.

In his youth, as in his old age, Auden was, like Johnson, a strange mixture of the conventional and the unconventional: both, shall we say, were on principle gentlemen and not Bohemians, but the distinction would be hard to make if one observed their behavior, which was eccentric or uncouth. Neither handled books as objects gently; both were habitually slovenly in their dress (famous were the carpet slippers which Auden regularly wore in his American years, in which he traveled, lectured, and recited poems); both read greedily and ate greedily. Both were habitually untidy—not only in their persons and in their living quarters—not from unconcern but from absorption in other affairs. Both were men so overpowering of character that, without meaning to do so, they intimidated their companions; but both were so sure of their views, whatever they might be, that they dogmatized. Both were lonely men who needed, but could not have, a family. Both were neurotics (this aspect of Johnson, Bate's recent biography more acutely analyzes than does any earlier work); and both aspired to be as normal as they could. Both were poets, but much more. They were also teachers and preachers: Auden was an actual successful teacher in the classrooms of English boarding schools and American universities. Both held views on all subjects of humane discourse; both were moralists and excellent writers of critical prose.

Of Auden's political views, his leftism for which he was once celebrated, I have so far said nothing. It is curious and significant how small a part he plays in Hynes's *The Auden Generation*. The two onetime Communist party members of that generation were Spender and Day Lewis; and it was they, and not Auden, who were the political tract-writers of the group, those who tried in prose to reconcile Communism and Poetry. Though Auden's poems and plays of that period *could* be read as Leftist, they could also be read as Rightist: they are about obscure plots by young neurotics to overthrow the Establishment of the rich and the aged, the Fathers—the schoolboy plots of neurotics. At no time however did Auden share the antisemitism of Pound: many of his best friends, early and late, were Jews; and when, as he has several times said, he realized that no poetic crusading has saved a single Jew, he withdrew from any effort to save the world by political means, while remaining, like his American friend Niebuhr, a liberal.

II.

Neither a recluse who refused to travel, nor yet one who made traveling his profession or vocation, Auden made an early stay in pre-Hitler Germany during the Weimar Republic, the age of Brecht; he briefly visited Spain during the Spanish civil war. On advances made by publishers he and Louis MacNeice journeyed to Auden's ancestral Iceland and produced a book; and similarly he and Isherwood journeyed to China during the Chinese civil war and produced another book. In 1957, with prize money, Auden bought the small house at Kirchstetten, thirty miles from Vienna, in which he and his partner, the American Chester Kahlman, thereafter spent their summers. From New York he returned to England to occupy for three years the Oxford professorship of poetry, the chair once occupied by Matthew Arnold; and in the last years of his life he accepted quarters at Oxford as E. M. Forster had done at Cambridge.

His life divided itself into virtual halves. In January 1939, when he was thirty-three, he settled in New York City, while his traveling companion and close friend Isherwood settled in California; and in 1946 Auden became an American citizen. What prompted this quietly dramatic decision on Auden's part? The poet had changed countries in 1939, the very year in which England declared war on Germany, the opening year of the Second World War. His action was much censured by the English press and by his literary contemporaries like Evelyn Waugh, those not of Auden's circle—to which censures Auden disdained to reply.

The reason was not pacifism. Like his American friend Reinhold Niebuhr, and like Dietrich Bonhoeffer, Auden was no indiscriminate pacifist: there were just wars, and the war against Hitler was among them. Auden's motives were purely private. He has written much about family, most often for him a metaphor for any closely knit group: a gang at public school, a group of literary allies, any group with its cozy inclusiveness and in-talk, its stock of shared memories and allusions, its sense of *we* as against *they*. If there is warm and mutual support in such a family, there is also a shut-inness, productive with certain souls of the claustrophobic. And Auden, for whom *family* was ever an ambivalent term, came to feel it exclusive and narrowing; and he "wanted out." Had he remained at home, he might have become the poet laureate which his friend Betjeman became. He would at any rate still have borne the poetic responsibility of being the Auden of the "Auden Generation," a responsibility which he desired to shun as being at once too heavy and too narrow, too insular. He wanted to develop in his own way, wanted to make his own decisions.

During the second half of his life he seemed to others, both Americans and English, unmistakably, unalterably English, despite the enlargement of his vocabulary to include many American words, vulgar and colloquial. But in fact Auden never really became, or tried to become, American. As he himself said, he was a New Yorker—that is, a citizen of the world city, *the* world city, and hence (as he never overtly said) a citizen of the world and an internationalist.

Being a New Yorker meant for him being anonymous—free, like any ordinary citizen, to live as he liked and to choose his own friends, which he did. These friends were partly fellow homosexuals, partly fellow poets, partly fellow British, like Ursula Niebuhr and Anne Freemantle, partly (I must use the phrase) fellow Germans, like his close friend Elizabeth Mayer, daughter of a Lutheran clergyman, and Hannah Arendt, the learned, brilliant, and profound German Jew to whom he dedicated *Forewords and Afterwords*. He had no family; and his friends belonged to different groups, each with its center of interest—groups which met only in him, and were otherwise disjunct. That situation was as he wished it: it left him free to be, in all its potentialities, Auden.

In the 1940s and 1950s his residence in New York meant much to younger American poets, those studying at Columbia or Princeton or natives of the city—to Anthony Hecht, John Hollander, William Meredith (one of his three literary executors), and others—partly as an influence, a conservative influence, making for adherence to more or less traditional forms as a counterbalance to confessional poetry and to the group vaguely known as the Black Mountain School and the New York School. Like Frost or Yeats and older poets in general, possessors of their own distinctive or hand-forged styles, the New York Auden was not sympathetic to new styles and trends; having in his youth vexed his elders he found himself in old age vexing the young. But he was chiefly felt as a benign representative of major poetry, the "resident poet" of New York.

For the American continent he did not much care: Robert Craft complains that while Auden was visiting Stravinsky in California, he showed no interest in the landscape nor yet, or even, in the seascape. From Olivet College in Michigan, where he spent a summer teaching, he wrote to Mrs. Niebuhr: "I do not like the provinces, especially in the USA, where they are provincial by so many thousand miles. . . . If I stay here much longer, I shall either take to mysticism . . . , or buy a library of pornographic books." Apart from that summer of teaching and a year at the University of Michigan in Ann Arbor, Auden confined his terms as a visiting teacher to institutions in or near New York—the New School, Barnard College, Swarthmore, Bennington, Vassar—never wandering from the eastern seaboard, but chiefly living in his disreputable apartment at St. Mark's Place in the Village.

Of course living in New York put him near his American publishers; and living in America gave him a financial independence he could not have had in England, so he said. He was modestly proud of the $10,000 he made in 1946, from his poetry and his reviewing and his teaching. But those tangibles were minor advantages in staying here: the chief gain was the isolated confrontation of himself against the background of a ruthlessly competitive city in the nation most "advanced" in its technological industrial society.

The essays collected in *The Dyer's Hand* under the heading "Americana" show how distasteful he found the United States as a whole. He writes at brilliant length of Henry James's *The American Scene* to conclude that a "recent immigrant" like himself is struck by "how little . . . America has changed, in any decisive way," since James's late visit; how the same features strike one, "like the magnificent boots and teeth, the heavy consumption of candy" or "the promiscuous gregariousness" and the elimination from the scene of the squire and the parson. Auden adds a "footnote": "The immigrant would like to add one element, the excesses of the climate, which is either much too hot or much too cold or much too wet or much too dry. . . . The truth is, Nature never intended human beings to live here, and her hostility . . . must be an important factor in determining the American character."

What America is, Europe and the rest of the world are becoming: "The issue between America and Europe is no longer a choice between social levelling and social distinctions." "Nothing can prevent the liquidation . . . of the individual in the collective proletariat, the liquidation of Christendom in the neutral world." "And it is from America, the first egalitarian society, that it [Europe] learned how to adapt itself."

Auden came to America to face the future of the human race, its democratic, industrial, earth-despoiling, technological, and specialist-ridden future, with whatever resources a man can face it with: a sense of the comic (which is a sense of proportion), self-knowledge, humanism, and a religion into which much philosophy has been absorbed—a philosophy imbued with pessimism about history, but faith in the Transcendent.

III.

Though Auden's grandfathers on both sides were Anglican clergymen, the real impact of a rich and personal religion came from his mother, an Anglo-Catholic who frequently made retreats in convents: her death in 1941 was a powerful blow. In his early years the poet was a choirboy and a boat-boy, one who carried the thurible from which the priest dispensed incense; when religion bored him he still enjoyed the ritualism of high mass. But when he was fifteen, he discovered that he had "lost his Faith." Absorbed in all the things which interested him—lead mines, literature, sex, psychiatry, and leftist politics—he did not miss it. But the Spanish civil war and Hitler's war shook his (as he came to feel) innocent liberalism.

No friend agrees on what brought Auden back to Christianity and even to Anglicanism. It was certainly no one thing, but many, out of which his Newmanic "illative sense" produced a convergence of motives almost amounting to approximate conviction, that rather than any sheer Pascalian or Kierkegaardian leap of faith.

Some convergent motives can be named. In 1937 he was shocked to find the churches closed in Barcelona, to feel the refuge of religion denied to the religious. At various times in the 1930s he had mystical experiences, felt himself "in the prey of demoniac powers . . . , stripped

75

of self-control and self-respect, behaving like a ham actor in a Strindberg play," and on another occasion "invaded by a power that was irresistible and certainly not mine." And in the same decade he met Charles Williams, the poet, novelist, literary critic, and lay theologian, and for the first time in his life felt himself "in the presence of personal sanctity." Some of us know how few such people there are, especially among intellectuals, and the reverence that they inspire, the kind of practical argument they offer for the faith they hold.

Auden returned to the Anglican church—the English church and not the more universal Roman Catholic church—in 1940 when he was thirty-three. It is strange that the time when he rejoined (or consciously joined) the Anglican church was when he left England to become an American citizen or a cosmopolitan, a citizen of the world-city New York.

In the 1940s there were intellectual motives which converged with his mother's death, the impression of Williams's personal sanctity, and the collapse of Auden's secular leftist tendencies. Auden read Reinhold Niebuhr's *Nature and Destiny of Man* (1941–1943), probably the most intellectually and morally impressive restatement of the Christian faith in our time (certainly for English readers and non-Roman Catholics). And he was at first powerfully impressed by Kierkegaard, of whom he later took a scaled-down and more judicious view. He was also impressed, as was Niebuhr, by Charles N. Cochrane's *Christianity and Classical Culture* (1957), which expounded St. Augustine's view of history and life. Auden felt himself an Augustinian rather than an adherent of the rational, the Thomist, tradition. Can one state the difference simply yet without undue inaccuracy? The Thomist is the Christian rationalist and systematic position; the Augustinian is the more somber, the more empathic of God's power and man's weakness, the less rational, the more voluntaristic, personal, and mystical. Yet Augustine—and Cochrane—are not simple pietists but are culturally aware, conversant with history, philosophy of history, and philosophy (as was Kierkegaard, as was Niebuhr). Auden never withdrew from culture or contemporary problems into a simplistic and obscurantist faith.

Yet Auden's old friends, English and leftists, and many of his American friends viewed his Christianity as a retreat: Hannah Arendt, a brilliant and wise secularist, spoke of his faith as "comfortable," a charitably ambiguous way of calling it an evasion of the world's real problems. It was in a sense, but not, I think, in any shameful sense, a retreat and a withdrawal. Religion was to Auden, as philosophy often is to others, a refuge to one who feels oppressed by the impossibility of any permanent solution to wars, the state of the state, social injustice—all the problems which can at best be solved only locally and temporarily.

The poet did not return to the religion of his mother or his boyhood, the tight Anglo-Catholicism represented by the convert Eliot. He remained an Anglo-Catholic only liturgically and, one could say, politically, for the best Anglo-Catholics from the generation of Bishop Gore and Archbishop Temple had been politically liberal, socialists in effect. Though Auden was not theologically Anglo-Catholic, yet he was orthodox in another looser way, like Charles Williams and C. S. Lewis among Anglicans and Niebuhr among Protestants. Like Eliot and unlike Lewis and G. K. Chesterton, he wrote no apologetics, no reasoned defense of his newfound faith. He was however a lay theologian and an excellent one. Writing in 1933, that considerable clerical thinker Dean W. R. Inge observed that "in England, and I think in other countries too, almost all serious thinking on theology is done by laymen." This statement is still substantially true.

If his secular friends were embarrassed by Auden's adoption, in mature years, of a religious position, his newfound clerical allies were also puzzled: "puzzled," says Ursula Niebuhr, "by his free use of theological categories," which they thought should not, any more than Sunday clothes, be used on weekdays.

Having "taken up" religion, Auden became interested in reading technical theological writing like that of Barth and Bultmann and C. H. Dodd, just as he had earlier taken up the physical sciences (in which he continued all his life to be interested) and then psychology and psychiatry and (to a considerably lesser degree) political science. Auden had ever a remarkable mental agility and alertness, an ability quickly to work up a new subject and take a new and comprehensive point of view. Was he not, some of his friends thought, just once more changing, and the more he changed the more being his own Audenic self? The fact that he stayed by his last stance for the rest of his life gave them pause, but it did not resolve their doubts. Auden, I think, never became a religious man in the sense that Eliot and some others, mostly converts, have been religious. His religious position was, as it often is with mature men, partly disillusionment with schemes for reforming the world; partly increase of conservatism, which always includes large elements of disillusionment and skepticism; and partly the need for the largest and deepest possible theoretical sub- and superstructure for writing about good and evil, the "origin and destiny" of man, matter, mind, and spirit. With all its uncertainties and intellectual inadequacies, religion probes deeper, aims higher, and offers more hope than any purely secular scheme.

I have just said that Auden was not really a religious man; but almost as soon as I have said it, I hesitate as I think of his unostentatious weekly communions (not liking the average sermon, he regularly attended the sermonless early morning service).I think too of his attachment to prayer and his wise remarks about it, made to Anne Freemantle, one of his few deeply devout friends, and made also in his review of Loren Eiseley's *Unexpected Universe* (1969) published, of all places, in the *New Yorker*. It would be probably fairer and more accurate to say that Auden's religion was of a singularly unsectarian and untraditional sort. He expresses to Mrs. Niebuhr his unconcern with modes of ecclesiastical government: all institutions are corruptible and bad, yet institutions are necessary.

His central line of thought in theological matters is a line which goes back to George Macdonald in the nineteenth century and comes down through C. K. Chesterton to Charles Williams. Auden has written sympathetically of all three: consider especially his introduction to Williams's *The Peace of the Dove: The History of the Holy Spirit in the Church* (1956). An admirable book by R. J. Reilly, *Romantic Religion* (1971), traces this sequence, adding to the names I have cited Owen Barfield, C. S. Lewis, and Tolkien, all literary laymen who, as Reilly says, "meet on that middle ground between *faerie* [imaginative literature, with a strong bent for fairy tale, myth, and allegory] and formal religion." These men undertake to show that "the experiences, which we severally call romantic —*Sehnsucht*, sexual love, *faerie*—are also, or can become, religious experiences."

As his lifelong friend Spender says, love was Auden's lifelong theme: and love in any mode, love as outgoingness from the self, is the *unum necessarium*. Freud and Marx and later the spiritual writers were all, for

Auden, enlargements of the meaning of love. And Auden refuses to keep separate his categories of secular and sacred, of flesh and spirit, and he could even cite the Incarnation in validation of his stance.

This "romantic religion" probably explains the most puzzling part of Auden, how he could be at once a Christian and a practicing homosexual, a "proper Anglican homosexual," as one of his friends calls him. Auden certainly was aware of St. Paul's, and the church's, attitude toward sodomy, a sin tolerated if it is one of temperament and not of performance, and if, whether thought or performance, it is sacramentally confessed. But Auden, I am sure, did not, though he may have considered the temperament a misforture, consider the acting out of the temperament a sin. One of his friends says that in early life Auden separated moral duties which he owed the world from those which he did not; and his homosexuality he doubtless viewed as belonging to the latter class.

All Auden's writing bears out this view, from the brilliant speeches in *The Orators* to his flagrantly outspoken "Papa Was a Slyboots," a review of J. R. Ackerley's autobiography, *My Father and Myself* (1969). For Auden only self-love, narcissism, is the ultimate sin, almost the only unforgivable sin; all love of others, even Ackerley's love for a bitch-dog, is venial sin or positive good: it is always better to love, love what you can, than not to love at all. If you can't love women, love men; if not that, at least have some other "object of love," a cat or dog or lizard.

Spender and other secularists among Auden's older circle have tried to define what the effect of Auden's newfound religion, to which he adhered for thirty-three years, was upon his life, its discernible ethical consequences; and they agree that he grew kinder, more magnanimous. He grew more isolated and lonely as he grew older, alienated by his separation from England and his friends, alienated by his religious position, but he grew kinder, more charitable. He was never a social or intellectual snob, and he disliked men like Evelyn Waugh and Gore Vidal who were. His older brother remarks on how free he was from race, national, or class prejudices, and the range of his friends proves that: the one exception the brother can think of is the French. Of his help to the Catholic Worker Movement its founder, Dorothy Day, has delightfully told; how, looking like a tramp, like her own "parishioners," Auden emerged from a crowd to give her a check for $250 and then disappeared.

And how dear his Austrian peasant housekeeper, Frau Emma, was to him, as were all the inhabitants of his adopted Austrian village.

I don't know which to admire more—the free and natural way in which, in his writings and, it would seem, in his talk, Auden moved from matters secular (literature and sex) to religion, or his more specifically religious essays, of which the three chief are the introduction to the anthology [edited by Anne Freemantle] *The Protestant Mystics* (1964) and the two pieces on Kierkegaard. Both evidence the remarkable Christian humanism which was perhaps, or probably, the greatest achievement of Auden's maturity.

The two essays on Kierkegaard were written sixteen years apart: the first in 1952, the second in 1968. The second is subtitled "Second Thoughts." The first is brilliant; the second is wise. Early in the second essay appear the sentences: "Like Pascal, Nietzsche, and Simone Weil, Kierkegaard is one of those writers whom it is very difficult to estimate justly. When one reads them for the first time, one is bowled over by their originality . . . and by the sharpness of their insights. . . . But with successive readings one's doubts grow, one begins to react against their overemphasis on one aspect of the truth at the expense of all the others." Auden revolted against what first attracted him to Kierkegaard (and presumably to Simone Weil): their inhumanity and intolerance in the name of truth and religion, their making it impossible for ordinary normal people to become Christians. "Ideally of course, everyone who calls himself a Christian, whether a clergyman or a layman, should be an apostle, but to imagine that at any time in history this has been, or could be, the case, is a sheer Donatist fantasy." Well versed in the chronicle of heresy, Auden goes on to charge Kierkegaard with being, in his sensibility, a Manichean, insensitive to the sheer blessing of being alive, and (like all heretics) picking and choosing among those dogmas which, in their balance, make up orthodoxy. "The Passion of Christ, for example, was to Kierkegaard's taste, the Nativity and Epiphany were not." "By anthologizing the New Testament, selecting the passages that appealed to him but ignoring their concrete context, and omitting those passages which do not appeal to him, a man can produce a Pelagian, a Calvinist, a Montanist, a Gnostic Gospel as he pleases, and claim that he has Scriptural authority."

Auden draws two conclusions: first that the church, as an institution which Kierkegaard with spiritual arrogance derided and otherwise attacked, should be defended; and second that Kierkegaard, an artist and a genius, really has a "message" only for other artists and geniuses who feel themselves superior to ordinary men, who feel, because of that fact, that "ethical and religious norms do not apply." "No person of talent who has read him can fail to realize that the talented man, even more than the millionaire, is the rich man for whom it is so difficult to enter the King-dom of Heaven." Here speaks the modest and wise Christian humanist which was Auden in his last years.

The introduction to *The Protestant Mystics* seems the most comprehensive and important statement of Auden's theology. Its title is misleading: it should read "Four Visions," or "Positive Approaches to Ultimate Reality." Auden begins by referring to von Hügel's classic analysis of religion as compounded of the institutional, the intellectual, and the mystical (which amounts to saying: the church; philosophy and theology; and personal encounter with God, the devotional life, including mysticism). He then distinguishes four kinds of "first-hand religious experience": the Vision of Dame Kind (his favorite way of naming Mother Nature), the Vision of Eros, the Vision of Agape, and the Vision of God—an ascending order. Nature mysticism, as Dean Inge and Evelyn Underhill call it, is chiefly modern, that of Traherne, Wordsworth, and Jeffreys, the "vision of the splendor of creation"; it is "the initial cause of all genuine works of art"; and though it is not particularly Christian, it is compatible with "the Christian belief in a God who created the material universe and all its creatures out of love and found them good."

Eros and agape, sexual love and brotherly love, are the kinds of mysticism open to most men, especially to Auden. He illustrates the former from Dante's *Vita Nuova* and Plato's *Phaedrus* and *Symposium*, which, though they are to be sharply distinguished, both move from the love of person to a higher love. The latter, what may be called the pentecostal vision, is illustrated by Auden's own experience of a social gathering which for two hours was transfigured by the presence of agape.

The last part of the essay, on the Vision of God, deals with mysticism as commonly understood, the "direct encounter of a human soul with God"; and, contra Reinhold Niebuhr and some other formidable Protestant theologians, Auden believes in the possibility and the validity of mysticism—though, as himself leading "an ordinary sensual worldly life," he disclaims ever having had such an experience. He further admits that his church, the Anglican, has not inspired many to "a life of interior prayer" and has given little instruction about it, though there is, as one can see in the writings of George Herbert, Lancelot Andrewes, and Charles Williams, "a characteristic Anglican style of piety, different from both Catholic and Evangelical piety," but nevertheless "genuinely Christian." (He devotes a shrewd discerning page to the characteristics of Anglicanism).

In the final seven pages of the essay, filled with many acute distinctions and discriminations, he contrasts Protestant and Catholic versions of religion and concludes them to be theoretically, as they are more and more becoming in post-Tridentine practice, complementary. Piety and social justice; faith and works; the life of the cloister and the "devout and holy life" practiced in the world; family prayers and the reading of the Bible conjoined with frequentation of the Sacrament: such is Auden's ecumenical ideal.

IV.

To approach Auden as I have been doing is to approach a poet through his self, his character, his knowledge and his wisdom, not through his poetry. In Auden's case this is not a bizarre procedure, for though he is finally to be considered as all he ever claimed to be, a poet, he is much more than the diminished thing the contemporary poet often seems to be: he is a poet on the older, larger lines of Milton and Dryden and Goethe, one whose perceptions, intuitions, and purely literary felicities do not rule out the humane dimensions of the universal man. Like the three I cite, Auden is a master of prose as well as poetry, ambidextrous. Not an original speculative mind like, say, Kierkegaard or Nietzsche, he is far better balanced and more synoptic than either existentialist (unlike these two, ever aware of the community as well as the gifted individual); he takes within his conceptual grasp and sweep Freud, Marx, and Christian thinkers; and though he finally takes his stand with the Christian thinkers, it is in no manner a sectarian way. His prose mind, trained on science and philosophical criticism, is what gives ballast and substance to his poetry.

(1979)

The Poetry of Auden

My first essay about Auden, "The Quest," came into being with relative ease. I was there in search of his character as a man, his ideological convictions, and the purport of his prose. From the start, however, I had intended to follow it with an essay on Auden's poetry; and this I have found extraordinarily hard to do. More or less of a year has gone to reading and rereading the poetry—and the chief commentaries on it, those of Monroe Spears and John Fuller, as well as the chief critical essays, as collected in Spears's *Twentieth Century Views* of Auden, an excellent anthology. The same year has produced many pages of my own script attempting to "fix" the note, the scope, the position, even the *rank* of Auden's poetry, in comparison first with the great modern Anglo-American contemporaries, Yeats, Pound, Eliot, Frost, and Stevens, but then as he, at once humble and ambitious, virtually requires, with the great European poets of all ages, and with the Romantic and Victorian English poets.

Having written this beadroll of greats, I remember Eliot's warning that the reader must first ask of poetry, *Is it Genuine?* The serious pastime of ranking comes but second; yet the two are certainly interrelated. How can I tell the genuine from the pinchbeck save by comparison? And theory of poetry must come in, too: in critical practice, there must be a constant interchange between the questions *What is Poetry?* and *Is this a poem?*

The single remark by a critic which has most pursued—and guided—me for a year was written by John Bayley in 1957: "Critics of Auden have always appeared to find it difficult to talk about his poetry, as opposed to the borrowed materials in it, and its nominal preoccupations. . . ." To myself I phrased that as the question *Where, and What is the Poetry in the poetry of Auden?* And that, in turn, threw me back to the larger question, not put to myself for years (one of those youthful, all-searching questions which professional men in their busy lives put away on the assumption either that they have been answered or that they are unanswerable)—the question, that is, *What is Poetry?*

There are two ways of honestly answering this question. One is the purely descriptive way: to draw up a definition which will cover all, in every time and place, which has ever been considered poetry. The other is the normative way: to single out some quality—verbal music, or visual imagery, or metaphor, or magic; to exclude from our definition story-telling or doctrine-expounding—the narrative and the didactic poem; to exclude the long poem and to identify poetry with the short, the moment of metaphoric insight.

Historically, Poetry has been the original verbal art, the matrix out of which, late, artistic prose developed, just as philosophy was the original intellectual discipline out of which developed ethics, political theory, and aesthetics. The history of thought and art is one of ever-increasing specialization; the generalist, who seeks to reclaim the ancient, the primitive, freedom of scope, is a suspect and endangered species. And, accompanying the specialization of subject matter and form, has come an ever-increasing specialization of audiences. Where, now, is the famous "general reader," to whom Dr. Johnson could appeal as a final arbiter? He has become as mythical as the general writer, the "man of letters."

The foregoing reflections are immediately relevant to one's view of Auden as a poet, for, if his life and work are studied as a whole, it is evident that, after his youth, so far from going with his time, he deliberately, consciously, went against it—tried to turn back the clock, not only by reverting to Christianity in a clearly post-Christian period, but by reverting to the ancient conceptions of poetry, the poet, and his audience. A comparison with Dryden comes frequently to the mind of critics, but Dryden is a relatively late example; one should, for analogues, go back to medieval poets, especially Chaucer, but also Langland, Skelton—and Dante, who is to Auden, as to Eliot, the supreme name.

Much can be learned about Auden from his remarkable anthologies, especially the *Oxford Book of Light Verse* and the five volumes of the Viking Press *Poets of the English Language* (1950), including the Introductions to each volume, which, for me, bear the internal evidence of having been written by Auden. Auden really assimilated the whole history of poetry from his ancestral Norse sagas down to Frost and Eliot, taking in oral popular poetry on the way—the nursery rhymes, the ballads, the nonsense verse of Carroll and Lear, the witty society verse of Praed, the cowboy and barroom songs of the Wild West: *nihil humanum alienum putavit.*

86

I once thought of calling this essay "The Poet Trying to Be an Ordinary Man"; for Auden wanted to reassert the old-time conception that the artist is like other men—except for his being an artist. The technical side of his art Auden loved—the devices of stanza form and rhyme scheme and alliteration and all that which only his fellow-craftsmen could identify, recognize, and acclaim—his villanelle, his elegiacs, his ballads, his terza rima, his sestina, his sapphics (all of these used in his *The Sea and the Mirror*, that "virtuoso display of Auden's technical accomplishments," as Spears calls it). Auden thought with pleasure of craftsmanship, and of the ancient Celtic schools for Bards, which survived in Ireland into the seventeenth century. In all of his copious literary criticism, however, there is almost no "workshop" analysis such as we find in the earlier critical essays by Pound and Eliot. Auden's criticism concerns matters which will interest the reader as a *honnête homme*, as a general unspecialized reader: biography, psychology, political and religious ideas, affairs of every day and of all time.

Every artist, Auden once said, should be "more than a bit of a reporting journalist"; introducing Henry James's *The American Scene*, he remarks, "Few writers have had less journalistic talent than James, and this is his defect, for the supreme masters have one trait in common with the childish scribbling mass, the vulgar curiosity of a police-court reporter"—a generally wise dictum as well as an illumination of Auden. But his journalism extends farther at both ends: it goes from fascinated observation and noting of the minutiae of daily urban life to intellectual reporting, keeping up, as an observer, with the latest modes of thought. John Bayley speaks of the "borrowed materials" in Auden's poetry: there are of course his "ideas"—which, by the way, are *borrowed* not *stolen*. Auden neither is nor makes claims to being an *original* thinker on the abstract level; and scarcely an academic scholar can be more scrupulous than he in naming his sources and acknowledging his debts: see, for example, the Notes he appended to *New Year Letter*.

There was a journalist in him, and a reporter, but he transcended both roles by making poetry out of them—trying to make poetry, and mostly, though not always, succeeding. The word *transcend* is a lofty, perhaps even pompous, word, with perhaps even magic connotations. I must therefore add again the warning that Auden did not aim at the sublime or at an unvaried "high seriousness." The immense variety of his verse forms has been remarked already; it is even more important to cite the range of his genres: that he wrote didactic poems (such as *New Year Letter*), satiric poems, verse epistles (like those of Horace and Byron, one of these indeed a *Letter to Lord Byron*), eclogues and pastorals, Bucolics and Georgics, lyrics, ballad and narrative poems (*The Age of Anxiety*), sonnets on authors (perhaps suggested by those of Matthew Arnold, to whom he devoted one), and in his old age many domestic pieces (of which *About the House* is a delightful example).

"Journalism" denotes starting with the immediacies of here and now —the details caught by the photographic eye, the fashions of thought, the ideological news of the day. But to make it into poetry is to give what is permanent, or at least more permanent, in the transient—to seize upon the symptomatic, the typical, the symbolic, to give it (in Johnson's once famous phrase) the "grandeur of generality." How often, writing about Auden, I find neoclassical phrases from Pope and Johnson recurring as relevant—not, I think, the mere accident of my own early neoclassical studies and tastes. It was toward a neoclassical—or let us just say *classical*—conception of poetry that Auden was, as he advanced in age, steadily moving—something one can best see if one will adopt the tactic, often profitable with a writer, of reading him backwards: "In my end is my beginning."

For a classicist, poetry is not to be identified with the "grand style" or with the lyric, still less with self-expression, though it may be, as occasion calls, any one of these. It does, in general, imply verse (though at no time in his life was Auden disposed to make much use of distinctions between poetry, verse, and artistic prose). But it is the mark of his classicism that, in thinking of poetry, he prefers to think of verse, and of the middle and low styles (the verse epistle, the satire, the didactic poem, the occasional poem on the birthday of a friend's son or the retirement of an Oxford professor) rather than of the epic or—what he sometimes and famously wrote—the love song like "Lay your sleeping head, my love, / Human on my faithless arm." For Auden, anything better said in verse (or art-prose) than in scientific or journalistic prose or talk is poetry.

In the preface to his 1979 New Edition of the *Selected Poems*, Edward Mendelson writes: "The surest way to misunderstand Auden is to read him as the modernists' heir [the heir, that is, of Yeats, Pound, and

Eliot]. Except in his very earliest and latest poems, there is virtually nothing modernist about him. From the viewpoint of literary history [and, let us add, literary criticism] this is the most important aspect of his work." Mendelson's whole preface should be carefully read. He puts admirably, in different language, the position to which, on the basis of my own independent studies, I have come—that Auden rejected Modernism, including whatever of the Romantic tradition survived therein, in behalf of an older, wider, wiser tradition.

This older pre-Modernist, and pre-Romantic, tradition includes the conception that the poet is the transmitter of wisdom—not, as the Romantics held, of his own wisdom, that of the ecstatic seer with his wound and his bow, but the wisdom which potentially belongs to the whole human race. This wisdom is not, to be sure, Pope's "What oft was thought, but ne'er so well express'd" (though that, perhaps, is the half-truth of orthodoxy protesting against the Romantic-Modernist heresy of prizing the unique even if crazy). This wisdom, however, which both Eliot and Auden reluctantly found in *der alte* Goethe, is a compound of common and uncommon sense, a kind of supersanity. It is not original with the poet: it is but inherited and assimilated.

In his youth, Auden was seen as, and was, a clever, witty, quite superior young man (though not "an angry young man," for recognition came to him speedily). These traits, together with his neurotic psyche, remained with him; but he felt always, if I may judge from his early prose, collected in *The English Auden,* that they were not enough; and, as he became older, he learned to use his gifts for larger purposes than self-expression or display.

The nice old man, the Prospero of *The Sea and the Mirror,* thinks that, returned to the state he deserted, "maybe it won't seem quite so dreadful / Not to be interesting any more, but an old man / Just like other old men," and asks, hopefully, "Can I learn to suffer / Without saying something ironic or funny / On suffering?" Auden is already in the early 1940s partly the Prospero who here speaks. Of Robert Frost, Auden writes that he "disapproves of all self-pity and nostalgic regret," his "Prospero-dominated poet." And what he says of Frost could be said of himself.

In her youth, Margaret Fuller made the arrogant and ridiculous remark, "I accept the universe." The sentiment was not silly but wise, for wisdom is in large measure acceptance ("Ripeness is all"), and not grudging acceptance, either, but gracious and grateful: "Let your last thinks all be thanks," as Auden writes in his last poem, "A Lullaby." After his early youth, Auden accepted the universe, beginning with himself, with his quirks and limitations; he accepted his place, too, as a responsible man in society, concurrently with his serious but never sanctimonious sense of himself and others as children of God.

Having uttered these solemn phrases, I am reminded of Auden's Phi Beta Kappa Poem, "Under Which Lyre?", which, by its serious levity, offended its Harvard audience. In this poem, with elfin humor, the poet puts the poet, the philosopher, and the other real humanists under the patronage of Hermes, the mercuric, while "Pompous Apollo" presides over "Useful Knowledge," "Commercial Thought, / Public Relations, Hygiene, Sport," the occupations of the extrovert. This sprightly and amusing poem disposes of any least suspicion that Auden identifies wisdom with the practical.

> "Thou shalt not live within thy means
> Nor on plain water and new greens.
> If thou must choose
> Between the chances, choose the odd;
> Read the *New Yorker*, trust in God;
> And take short views."

Is this final stanza of the Harvard Ode poetry? Yes, for Auden it is. The main block in the way of answering the question *Where is the Poetry in the poetry of Auden?* is that, for one reared on poetry of the generation which preceded him, on Yeats and Eliot, one has to change, to widen, his whole conception of poetry to the dimensions of what it meant to poets and readers before the Romantics—back to Pope and Dryden, back to the Elizabethans, back to Langland and Chaucer. One's mind keeps slipping away and returning to the narrowed and diminished thing poetry has largely become—often, it seems, mere wisps of fragile perception. What Auden undertook, this reversal and reversion, was a heroic thing. An aged humanist applauds the valor; endeavors to flex the muscles of his sensibility, grown somewhat stiff, and to follow the progress of this heroic, yet genial, reactionary.

90

Auden is a special case, a modern poet who rejects the modernist theory of poetry and reverts to an older position. But, in another and narrower sense, he also illustrates what happens to any poet of importance who, because he is a poet of importance, cannot bear to repeat the particular stance and style which first won him an audience. I began reading Yeats with his late poems, yet I remember a cultivated old lady who could not read them, but still delighted in the early Celtic twilight poems. And I, who had admired "Prufrock" and *The Waste Land* and had my severe difficulties in accepting "Ash Wednesday" and even "Burnt Norton," now have come to think the *Four Quartets* the supreme work of Eliot, and one of the greatest poems in all poetry. Yet I, who was an earlier admirer of *Harmonium*, still cannot see greatness in what, for me, is the facile, orotund, pseudo-philosophy of Stevens as he later flew on extended wing. Examples could be multiplied, but let these suffice. A growing poet must change; and we readers must either find him to have lost his power or applaud the change and change our own taste.

II.

I want now to give an "airman's" view of the course, the development, of Auden's poetic career. To do this, I shall have to surrender any thought of explicating particular poems or of offering detailed commentaries. This work has admirably been done by Monroe Spears in his *Poetry of W. H. Auden* (1963) and by John Fuller in his *Reader's Guide to W. H. Auden* (1970); and I can but recommend both books to the "student." For myself, I have both profited from them and been also somewhat repelled, since they leave—unintentionally, I am sure—the impression, almost the conviction, that Auden cannot be read simply for pleasure and aesthetic, intellectual, and spiritual edification. In both, the complications of Audenic bibliography and the comparison of Auden's additions to and subtractions from his own canon, his revisions of text and title, finally distract the simple reader from any goal of innocent enjoyment.

How can I, who am not an Auden specialist, nor a specialist in contemporary literature, nor myself a poet, presume then to write at all about Auden's poetry? Only, I think, by being as simply autobiographical as I can dare. I have read Auden off and on since 1935; I cared for his work enough to give an Auden course in the mid-forties, using as a text the 1945 *Collected Poems*, so irritating to use because of its arrangement alphabetically according to the first letter of each poem's title; several years ago, I acquired the *Collected Poems*, posthumously produced in 1976; and since then I have been endeavoring to settle and fix my judgment of a lifetime's work by one who, on the basis of that lifetime's work, never ceased to seem to me a major poet.

My written notes remind me of how constantly all my views, except that of Auden's importance, have kept altering, and except, too, the notion that what he is saying is as important as his craft. If critics keep, as Bayley says, concentrating on his doctrine (which one can with useful vagueness call Freudian, Marxist, and Christian), it is because Auden, though meticulously attending to his meters, really cares what he is saying and, at least after his early poems, wants to reach an audience as wide as possible.

Auden's periods I make out to be five. His earliest group, by which he made his immediate reputation, both in England and in the United States, comprised *Poems 1927–1932* and *The Orators*. The early work of Auden, collected in the Random House *Poems* of 1934, was acclaimed by Eliot in England, by Cleanth Brooks (*Modern Poetry and the Tradition*), and by Randall Jarrell. It was this first running of Auden's genius which immediately established his reputation and remains his most striking. All Auden's subsequent shifts of attitude and poetic style were attacked by some, led by Jarrell, his inveterate and severe critic, as the defalcations of a Lost Leader.

This early poetry is undeniably obscure; Auden, an Oxford man with a more or less close circle around him, his so-called Group, was, it seemed, in lieu of an established audience whom he could address, engaging in private talk addressed only to his friends. Recently, however, we have been told on the authority of his literary executor, Edward Mendelson, that these early poems were almost as obscure to his friends as to others: that he wrote them only for himself and by his own strange method of composition, which Isherwood has plausibly described. We may suppose something of both.

It is in detail that the poems are obscure, not in drift, attitude, tone. When I try to figure out the exact meaning of a line I am often baffled; but the general sense is one of impending Judgment. A justly famous poem begins with the line, in that alliterative New Old-English style of his, "Doom is dark, and deeper than any sea-dingle." The comfortable age of European and British civilization, Victorian, Edwardian, Georgian, is forever gone—the days comfortable, that is, for the landed gentry, the upper middle class, and the privileged intellectuals. The First World War, in which the fathers and schoolmasters of Auden's generation fought, ended all that; and now some new World War is felt to be imminent.

Auden's early (1932) ambitious work, *The Orators*, is a puzzler. Like his later Long Poems it is a mixture, an assemblage, of verse and art-prose, with, in its case, a larger proportion of prose than verse. Its coherence is loose, and its degree of obscurity, both in intent and in detail, large. Its author called it, in retrospect, "a fair notion, fatally injured in the treatment," and for many years refused to reprint it; and when, in 1966, he did reissue it, he said that his name, as author, "seems a pseudonym for someone else, someone talented but near the border of sanity, who might well, in a year or two, become a Nazi." The work ends with a set of odes, one of which, the fifth, he included in the *Collected Poems* of 1945 under the apt title, "Which Side Am I Supposed to Be On?"

About this poem, which has fascination for me as a critic and exegete, Spears and Fuller have suggestive and useful things to say. The former thinks the title contrasts speech makers and others articulate with men of action, doers; further, that the work itself as "An English Study," as Auden subtitles it, is not only a study of the English upper classes but a manual of English rhetoric, with examples of the argument, exposition, the letter, and the diary—which it most certainly is. The latter, John Fuller, characterizes the work as literary *avant-garde* (*i.e.,* in the mode of Stein and Joyce and, especially, of the surrealists) and thinks it contains a few fragments of automatic writing—suggestions worth pondering.

But what was the "fair notion" and how was it "fatally injured"? In my judgment, the "fair notion" is, as Spears suggests, the contrast of sayers and doers, and, I will add, the neurotic young literary man's then vast preference for the doers. It is also the eternally recurrent warfare between young and old, and is the vehicle in which one clever and mildly "angry" young man can express his hostility, and pitying disdain, toward outmoded old statesmen, country gentlemen, and school administrators—all talkers—and his sympathy for the young, "my pupils," who are called upon to act, to fight, doctrinally and also literally, against the Old Order, the Establishment.

The notion is fatally injured (I opine) because the action proposed can certainly be read as either Fascist or Communist: there may even have been a brief time during which Auden himself hesitated between positions, clearer of the need to attack than of the enemy's identity. And the central figure of the Airman remains ambiguous: a neurotic, vaguely modeled on T. E. Lawrence but partly also, I suspect, a version of Auden himself. Is he a Strong Man or a Weak (in terms of Isherwood's distinction in *Lions and Shadows*)? His *Journal* strikes me as that of a neurotic who cannot clearly distinguish between his sickness and his sin on the one hand, his health and virtue on the other—a self-analytical, highly articulate adolescent with daydreams of political and military leadership.

While Auden was writing this "Poem," he was himself a young schoolmaster, and as such (he was an excellent teacher, with a keen interest in pedagogy) he had divided loyalties, partly seeing the need of authority, partly feeling on the side of the young revolters; so, in every way, the thematics and tone of his "Poem" are ambiguous to the point of incoherence, reaching beyond the celebrated principle of "irony." A brilliant example is the opening "Address," with its Groddeckian, and Audenian, diatribe against psychosomatic ills, which suddenly comes to an end as the speaker orders the arrest of all neurotics and leaves the room, leaving the reader with a plausible doctrine undercut.

Literally, *The Orators* is full of interest. Especially engaging are the riddles, the litany (modeled on its Anglican prototype) in "Argument," Section II, and the catalogues (modeled on Ecclesiastes, Whitman's *Song of Myself*, and poems from the Old English *Exeter Book*) in "Statement," Sections I and II, but also in the opening "Address." The catalogue, a list of Types, each accompanied by a pungent, picturesque, physiological particularism, is central to cerebral Auden from youth to age; but what he later learns to control and proportion is here a conscious stylistic Euphuism. For example, in the "Address," he speaks thus of one neurotic type: "With odd dark eyes like windows, a lair for engines, suffering more and more from cataract or deafness, leaving behind them diaries full of incomprehensible jottings, complaints less heard than the creaking of a wind pump on the moor." But *The Orators* is a repertory of literary experiments, both in prose and in verse, like that of Joyce. It is the one real Modernist poem Auden wrote. It both shows what a skillful Modernist he might have been, and is a monument to a road not hereafter taken—indeed tacitly rejected.

Then comes the second, still English, period of *Poems 1933–1938*, which was also exciting but less obscure, less private, more meditative—the period of his brilliant pieces in verse, the critical portraits of Melville, Henry James, Freud, Matthew Arnold, Edward Lear, Rimbaud, and Yeats, also of "Crisis" ("Where do they come from?") and "Oxford" and—what I would without much hesitation choose as his finest single poem—the "Musée des Beaux Arts," a comment on Brueghel's *Icarus*:

> About suffering they were never wrong,
> The Old Masters: how well they understood
> Its human position; how it takes place
> While someone is eating or opening a window or just
> walking dully along
>
> . . . . . .
>
> the expensive delicate ship that must have seen
> Something amazing, a boy falling out of the sky,
> Had somewhere to get to and sailed calmly on.

The poems of this period made an especial appeal to me in the 1940s, and still deeply appeal—these sensitive, subtle, evocative, and not too obscure poems which distill the essence of an author's personality or the personality of a place into a criticism which is also a poem. I could easily think this Auden's best period, but I hesitate, remembering my own professional bias as that of biographer and literary critic.

The third period (1940–1948), the first after Auden's migration to America, is the period of his Long Poems. First comes the *New Year Letter* (also called *The Double Man*), followed by *For the Time Being* (A Christmas Oratorio), *The Sea and the Mirror*, and *The Age of Anxiety* (1947). After this, for whatever reason (he never explained his abstinence), Auden wrote no more Long Poems, though he substituted for them groups of poems, the literary equivalent of orchestral suites.

Milton was the author, as every schoolboy used to know, of Minor Poems, such as "Il Penseroso" and "Lycidas," and of Major Poems, such as *Paradise Lost*. And Virgil too wrote both the *Aeneid* and the *Eclogues* and *Bucolics*; so we might go on. The postulate certainly is that, in middle life, a major poet must write major poems—*major* meaning, to start with, long, but, less superficially, poems which have to be long because they concern themes not to be essayed unless they can be given the space for appropriate development, and because a large poetic personality, at its maturity, needs such space for expression of its opulence.

So Auden had to write Long (*i.e.,* intentionally Major) Poems. And he did. They did not wholly satisfy his, on the whole, best, certainly most rigorous, critics, Bayley and Fraser; and they do not satisfy me. The consensus is that *The Sea and the Mirror* is the best of them; I register my dissent, voting for the last written, *The Age of Anxiety*. Indeed, to my finding, these Long Poems become progressively better.

New Year Letter, in Hudibrastic tetrameter couplets, contains quotable lines, most of them in the first section, which recites the Honor Roll of past poets, the Tribunal which aspirant Auden, when he presumes to write, must face: Dante, "self-educated" William Blake, Rimbaud, Dryden, Catullus, Tennyson, Baudelaire, Hardy, and Rilke, "whom *die Dinge* bless." The second section, on sin and the wiles of Satan, reminds me of C. S. Lewis' *Screwtape Letters*, without, from the dates of the two works, any indebtedness. The third concerns America, industrialism, the need for a Just City (Auden's standard phrase forh is political ideal, which is neither an Eden nor a Utopia). To this didactic poem, an epistle, Auden appended pages of notes, quotations from the impressive reading on which, so to speak, his poem had been based—his proof texts. This, Auden's first poem since his conversion to Christianity, gives evidence of a clever convert's intelligence and zeal.

The Hudibrastic couplets do not fit the poem; heroics would, I think, have been better. Perhaps this is as good a place as any to remark on the unpredictability of Auden's success in matching verse forms and meter with subject matter and tone. In all the bulk of his criticism, Auden never attempts, as Eliot does in writing about his earlier plays, to discuss matters so ultimately technical. The verse forms interested Auden, the virtuoso craftsman, and so did his ideas, but these two often ran on separate tracks—not always, or at his best, but often.

Certainly he is never given to "imitative form," so urged by *Understanding Poetry*. Without his ever pronouncing a doctrinal position, his theory and his practice seem rather on the side of Yvor Winters and John Crowe Ransom (in *The New Poetry*): decay and limpness are not to be echoed but rather portrayed by crispness of mind and metrical regularity.

For the Time Being, an Oratorio, is an intelligent, up to its date, Christian poem, dramatizing—with interspersed lyrics and a prose speech by Herod, wittily conceived of as a Liberal—the cycle of Christmas. It is too bright, too little brooding. The Christian paradoxes of the Incarnation, familiar to any reader of Christian theology of the great tradition, and the Christian poetry of Baroque poets such as Crashaw, not being freshened up, sound tired. Auden's most overtly religious poem does not compare favorably when ranged against the poems of deeply religious men like George Herbert, Gerard Manley Hopkins, Charles Péguy, and T. S. Eliot—or the novels of Georges Bernanos. He is intelligent, and he has sincerely adopted the Christian position; but he has adopted it as, on the whole, the best available solution of the world's mysteries—not been adopted, gripped, seized by it.

The Sea and the Mirror is a kind of commentary on Shakespeare's *The Tempest*, that final play commonly interpreted as his farewell to his art, and a play ever attractive to his fellow artists, Henry James among them. Auden's work, formally hard to classify, is half a closet drama, half a philosophical poem on the theme of the artist's relation to experience, life, people—at once his subject and his audience.

The first part presents the characters in *The Tempest* as they are about to depart the enchanted isle, each given a speech. It is, on one level, a virtuoso display of Auden's technical powers at his craft, the magic of his wand; on another level, it is an exhibition of the unresolved struggle between Prospero and his "wicked" brother Antonio, who returns (a recalcitrant ego or experiential reality), not to be reconciled, absorbed within Prospero's art.

The second section, Caliban's speech, a prose epilogue to the closet drama, is a disquisition on the relation of the artist and his audience. Addressed to the audience, it points out what great art cannot do: it can satisfy neither the lowbrow, who wants something sentimental and nostalgic, nor the highbrow, who desires abstract philosophical ideals.

One curious feature of Caliban's speech, its style, is seen by commentators, myself included, as a parodic imitation of Henry James's late manner. Caliban's is, says Spears, a "faintly ridiculous style"; says John Fuller, it "partakes of the smiling drone of the unnerving bore." Both are correct, I think: Caliban's speech is far too long, and so full of subtle distinctions and ironies and illustrative examples that the reader finally gives up trying to follow the argument and just enjoys the rich Audenian satire and detail. Though by what reasoning Auden makes Caliban speak ripe Jamesian language, I cannot work out, I know that the author of "At the Grave of Henry James" was a lover of the Master who could recite whole pages from his works. I also know that we parody only styles, and persons, loved, and that love is quite compatible with seeing the ridiculous side of loved objects—for example, the prolixity and the incapacity for the simple of the old James.

The Age of Anxiety I think the most characteristic of Auden's talents and their range, and the most central. It does not prove anything, and happily does not try to: written after Auden had long been a Christian, it has nothing tendentiously Christian about it, yet nothing incompatible with the Christian faith. The final meditation, by Malin, Canadian and a medical man, like Auden's father, and the character nearest to representing Auden's own point of view, is Christian, but undoctrinal.

The poem has a satisfying formal structure. It is a modern version of the traditional pastoral scheme, as we find it in Theocritus and in *The Shepheardes Calender*: "the singing contest; an elegy; love-songs and laments, with courtship of a shepherdess; a dirge; formal, 'artificial' diction and meter" (Spears). There is *mélange* of styles: lyrics, sung to the accompaniment of the jukebox; interspersed announcements and commercials from the radio of the New York bar in which four "lonelies" find themselves gathered by chance on one All Souls' Eve during the Second World War. All the verse is encased in a continuum of prose, the most flexible and civilized prose Auden ever wrote—not Jamesian, indeed not mannered at all, just well-bred, flexible yet urbane. It is conversational without being sloppy or repetitious; it is modulated prose without any eccentricity or special hallmark. Auden has almost as many prose styles as styles in verse; in prose, too, he is virtuoso. But the prose in *The Age of Anxiety* is quintessential Audenic prose.

The prose encasement, or links, offers one continuum. The alliterative verse, after the Old English model, provides another; and, unlike the prose, which is modern, contemporary, this neo-archaic verse provides aesthetic distancing from the material—the characters and themes—of the poem. Its choice was a masterly stroke on Auden's part. His Norse heritage, or whatever, makes him a "natural" as a reviver; and his unflagging inventiveness in this seemingly limited verse form removes it from ever being boring. The disparity between matter and form is not really ironic: the sadness of Old English lyrics has something in common with the sadness of the anxious "lonelies" gathered in the bar. But there is a counterpoint.

What is baroque about this eclogue? Auden uses this word in no strict literary-historical sense, any more than Spears does when he speaks of Caliban's speech as baroque. Both mean a style which is intentionally artificial, ostentatiously artful—still more, one given to profuse ornamentation, to rich and lavish and redundant use of detail, illustration, specificity. These latter traits are reminiscent of Dickens, with whom Bayley and the Italian critic Carlo Izzo find Auden, a Dickens lover, to have such an overlap. In a loose sense, both Dickens and Henry James write baroque, and so often does Auden, even when he does not, as here, so name his work.

The characters in *The Age of Anxiety* are four: three men, old, middle-aged, and young, and one woman, an English Jewess of uncertain age. She is a disillusioned Romantic who nostalgically dreams of the English countryside, either real or fictive. The young man, the only American among them, has his memories of his typical American boyhood and his fears about his future—fears that, once the glamour of his uniformed youth is over, he may turn out to be as commonplace as his boyhood friends.

Auden is not a dramatic poet. The characters all speak alike, in Old English Audenese. They are distinguished by their type traits of sex and age, by their symbolic memories, and, most of all, by their attitudes. Medieval allegory and its eighteenth-century diminution into personification are both forms natural to cerebral-minded Auden. An instinctive generalizer, he is hence attracted to types—of character and of situation.

99

He is the conceptual in search of the illustrative concrete, not the particularizer who broadens out.

According to some commentators, the four characters represent Jung's four epistemological types: Malin, Thought; Rosetta, Feeling; Quant, Intuition; and Emble, Sensation—and their very names have been given emblematic significance. Though I do not find this reading very convincing, it points in the right general direction. The ancestral writers who come most to mind are Langland and Spenser, most of all in the interior sections of the poem, "The Seven Ages" of man and "The Seven Stages" of life. The former, fairly easy to follow, reminds one vaguely of the shorter parallel sequence in Pope's *Essay on Man*. The latter, the obscurest part of the poem, John Fuller explains as a physiological allegory, each landscape corresponding to some part of the human body (*e.g.,* the city represents the brain).

About the Long Poems, my feelings, in the mid-forties and now, are mixed. None of them, I judge, is an unqualified success. Yet to have written them augments the stature of Auden. Not afraid to fail, he is the greater poet for having attempted them. That very courage sets him apart from minor poets who are partly so because they are perfectionists. Greatness takes risks, is willing to be imperfectly large rather than impeccably small.

The fourth period (1948–1957) comprises the autumnal poetry of the much (and justly) lauded "In Praise of Limestone," that *paysage moralisé,* the fine suites "Bucolics" and "Horae Canonicae," "The Shield of Achilles," and a modern Horatian ode which I much admire, "Under Sirius," a stanzaic and rhymed poem combining wit and magic.

And period five (1958–1973) is that of the poet's premature old age (poets early become aged eagles). *About the House,* later called *Thanksgiving for a Habitat,* one of Auden's groups of poems, belongs to this last period. And there are other fine shorter pieces such as "The Horatians" and "Ode to the Medieval Poets" and "On the Circuit" and "Old People's Home." Many occasional poems, verse epistles, and greetings remind us of the eighteenth-century poets, not only Dryden and Pope but Prior, Shenstone, and all the rest.

I regret the many pages of "jottings," notebook entries, limericks and stanzas in isolation, such as a younger Auden—who, like Pope, accumulated passages for use in a future poem—might have, had he had his earlier comprehensive vigor, worked into a completed poem. It is natural that Auden went on writing till his death: no literary man earlier put down his pen. But why must he publish everything he wrote? Why must his "jottings" be perpetuated, save as workshop chips, "Chips from the Sculptor's Studio"?

This is not to say that Auden's general intellectual powers in any way failed or declined: his critical reviews, often appearing first in the *New Yorker*, and then collected as *Forewords and Afterwords*, remained firm, crisp, and coherent to the end of that lifelong distinguished critical career which, side by side, accompanied the fecund poetic creativity. In nothing was he more like Dryden than in this dual activity. Arnold's poetry stopped when he began to be first a literary and then a social critic. Eliot's poetry and criticism diverge when his criticism shifts from the review-essay to the lecture. But in Auden the relation between the two remains close.

From a fine, perceptive, and just essay on "Auden's Last Poems," those of his sixties, written by Robert Bloom for the 1974 *Harvard Advocate* Auden issue, let me quote two comparative judgments. The last poems "are deeply personal . . . yet not confessional, not embarrassingly intimate, as Lowell, or Snodgrass, or Plath can be, nor historically autobiographical, like Yeats." And again: Auden, in his old age and its poems, offers "the example of a man using all his powers to sustain a civilized existence in the midst of twentieth-century horror, brutality, fanaticism, and anarchy without resorting to the moaning of Eliot, the theatrics of Yeats, or the exotic, enigmatic oracularism of Stevens." These judgments, out of Bloom's context of delicate specificities in the perception of Auden's poetry, and his fine choice of passages to quote, sound, in their brevity, melodramatically crude; yet only crude contrasts like these can give one what one is always in danger of losing, amid distinctions and discriminations—one's ultimate critical bearings.

Unfamiliar with these post-*Age of Anxiety* poems of Auden's till a year or two ago, I am more and more coming to admire them—for their civilized urbanity, so wondrously blended with the personal voice, the "I" never stridently assertive yet never merely the socially disciplined mask. The chasm between I-poetry and we-poetry or communal poetry some-times, often, seems unbridgeable. Yet here it is done, in a community of independent and individual voices voluntarily collaborating. The achievement is a poetry of a maturely wise old age.

III.

Auden was a phenomenon, a prodigy, a poet-hero who gave his name to a group and a poetic generation in his English youth, and who, after he migrated to the United States, became a public figure, almost an anonymous famous man. To survive three or four poetic generations, generations which now move so rapidly, is to pass close scrutiny, and, as any survivor must, pass the muster of sundry, and often conflicting, points of view.

At the moment it is difficult to read him at all, for one has to face the huge, gray *Collected Poems* of 1976, a forbidding book looking like a telephone directory, now assembled with editorial care and fidelity; the sheer bulk of it is overwhelming for a reader accustomed to the spare and sparse poetic production of an Eliot or even of a Yeats, or to the thin volumes in which contemporaries like Ashbery or Merrill or Hecht bring out their work.

From the *Collected Poems*, the reader who is to enjoy Auden, not just study him, must take up the *Selected Poems*, the New Edition of 1979, an intelligent three-hundred page sampling, probably as good as could be made, with a brilliant, illuminating preface by Edward Mendelson, the same literary executor who has edited the *Collected Poems*.

Auden does not lend himself to close-reading exegeses. Nor does he lend himself well to brief illustrative quotations, such as, throughout writing this essay, I have wanted to produce: partly because the sentences in his poetry are characteristically long, as though, like Milton, he was deep-lunged; partly because he is not given to phrases literally memorable either for their verbal music, their visual image, or their epigrammatic condensation. His syntax carries him along, and his sure sense of style, which persists even through passages which are briefly flat, diffuse, or obscure. He must be taken in quantity and at speed, this mode of reading alternating with slower speed and in selection.

Have I answered my question, *Where is the Poetry in the poetry of Auden?* Well, it is everywhere—or nowhere; it is not to be found in segregation. *The Letter to Lord Byron*, a long and entertaining verse epistle, originally published in that not very interesting *olla podrida*, the *Letters from Iceland*, is poetry, in the form of light verse. So is Caliban's artful prose discourse to the audience. So are the "Musée des Beaux Arts" and "In Praise of Limestone." Poetry is, for Auden, well-nigh synonymous with literature, if one will take literature in its richest and, still more, its most archaic sense. It is literature restored to its ancient liberties —as well as its traditional formalities.

As the tone of this essay must have made clear, I feel deep sympathy with the whole career of Auden and the aims which motivated and directed it: with his intent to give not only youth but middle age and old age their appropriate expression, but even more with his wish to restore poetry to a wider readership than one of other poets, academic specialists in poetry, and the professionally literary. Says Edmund Wilson, "If he is not precisely a 'family poet' like Longfellow, Wordsworth, and Tennyson, the fact that he is one of the most *edible*, one of the most *satisfactory* of contemporary writers in verse, is proved by the sales of his *Collected Poetry* [1945] which have reached in the United States [by 1956] the almost unprecedented figure of over thirty thousand copies."

Though the sale of books is not a very precise measurement of readership, to be sure, sales prove something. Certainly any ordinary reader who looked into Auden, even cursorily, might well agree with Wilson that he is not only a "great English poet" but also "one of the great English men of the world," not only an artist but a humanist, who has something wise and well-worded to say on almost every topic of general concern.

Auden is not, either by temperament or by Christian cosmology, a tragic poet, but he is a serious one. The Just City, "Society the Redeemed Form of Man," is not to be reached by apocalyptic reversal and can never, on earth, be perfectly realized, but it is not to be despaired of by impatient, romantic utopians and other idealists. And—very unromantic of him—Auden practiced and preached a chastened cheerfulness. It was this, as well as his art, which endeared Horace to Auden, who in 1968 linked himself with that poet:

103

You thought well of your Odes, Flaccus, and believed they
would live, but knew, and have taught your descendents to
    say with you: "As makers go
    compared with Pindar or any

of the great foudroyant masters who don't ever
amend, we are, for all our polish, of little
    stature, and, as human lives
    compared with authentic martyrs

like Regulus, of no account. We can only
do what it seems to us we were made for, look at
    this world with a happy eye
    but from a sober perspective."

This charming poem, which I have quoted primarily for the sake of the two final lines, does not sum Auden up, but it expresses the final phase of him.

As Yeats says, man is "forced to choose / Perfection of the life or of the work"; it is impossible to be both literary master and a saint: each vocation requires an utter concentration. To be sure, Abraham Cowley addressed his contemporary, Richard Crashaw, as "Poet and Saint"; but the author of the "Ode on the Epiphany" was scarcely major at either of his vocations. Of Auden, my considered judgment is that he was, to a high degree, both a robust, loyal, and generous man and a major poet, equaled in modern times only by Yeats, Frost, and Eliot. Not such a perfectionist as the later Yeats or as Eliot, he has written no work of length which I can rank with the *Four Quartets*; but he is larger in his range and scope than either Yeats or Eliot, an ampler and richer representation of the Anglo-American genius in poetry. His civilized, and civilizing, legacy remains, to challenge and to bless.

(1981)

Homage to Allen Tate

It is customary, when eminent scholars reach seventy or thereabouts—that is, retirement form their academic chairs—for their former students, their colleagues, and others to produce for their honorification a *Festschrift*, a collection of articles on topics within the scholar's area of specialized concern. Quite properly, the custom is paralleled, when great and distinguished poets and other men of letters reach the same approximate age—though not the same retirement, for writers never retire—by the publication of what might well be called an homage, a collection of essays the contributors to which, chiefly admirers, but admirers of weight and discrimination, characterize the person of the author, analyze, and evaluate his lifework. Such an homage to Allen Tate has recently appeared.

Its editor, Radcliffe Squires, is a fine meticulous poet and an excellent critic of poetry. After books on Robinson Jeffers and Robert Frost, he published in 1971 a *Literary Biography* of Tate which is a model in kind—tactful, appreciative—indeed admiring but never uncritical, abounding in fine perceptions, discriminations, and evaluations.[1] In general, conservative in his taste, Squires is not of any recognizable "school of poetry" and is not an old Vanderbilt friend or, indeed, a Southerner; he brings to bear what seems exactly the right proportion of sympathy and detachment.

Squires's collection of essays runs to over three hundred pages, followed by a bibliography of Tate's work and of articles, reviews, and doctoral dissertations on Tate. This valuable assemblage calls to mind and into comparison Tate's own *T. S. Eliot: The Man and His Work* (1966) and William H. Rueckert's *Critical Responses to Kenneth Burke* (1969), which prefatorily acknowledges helpful suggestions from Tate.

The three books differ somewhat in method, structure, and proportions. In the Eliot book there are more memoirs than critical essays. In Rueckert's *Burke*, there are no memoirs or other biographical pieces; the

---

[1]Radcliffe Squires, *Allen Tate: A Literary Biography* (New York: Pegasus, 1971). Radcliffe Squires, editor, *Allen Tate and His Work: Critical Evaluations* (Minneapolis: University of Minnesota Press, 1972).

critical essays and reviews form a single series, arranged in strictly chronological order. Rueckert's book includes "pieces that are both for and against the man and his works so that the dialectical polarities might be clear. . . . No secret disrespect is intended by this inclusion of the opposition; so tough and skillful a veteran of the dialectical wars as Burke could not feel honored by the exclusion of his adversaries." Burke's friend Tate is another such tough and skillful veteran. He has been a champion of causes and an opponent of others, a polemicist and "strategist" (that military metaphor dear to all the Southern critics from Ransom down) since first, more than forty years ago, he appeared in print; he attacked Eliot's teacher and mine, Irving Babbitt, and his New Humanist followers with considerable violence and even rudeness. I have some feeling that Squires's critical anthology should have given at least a few pieces of anti-Tate polemics by New Humanists, Communists of the thirties, and positivists of the forties—such pieces perhaps as Sidney Hook's, referred to in the *Literary Biography*. (In general, I think Tate fairly represents the position of the causes he attacks—including that of Charles Morris, the Chicago positivist.)

The pieces in Squires's anthology are divided into four categories. The first is "The Man," a set of memoirs by John Crowe Ransom, Andrew Lytle, Malcolm Cowley, Robert Lowell, and others (including a valuable analysis of "Tate as a Teacher," written by a former student of his at the University of Minnesota); then "The Essayist"—that is, primarily the literary critic, but also the stylist and the "man of letters" (this phrase, more common in France than in English-writing countries, Tate often uses as a description of himself as well as a general concept); then "The Novelist" (four altogether admirable essays on *The Fathers*); and, finally, and properly longest, studies of "The Poet."

These four categories do not quite cover the ground. I would like to have seen some consideration of "The Biographer" (dealt with briefly by Squires in his *Literary Biography*; is there yet, I wonder, a dissertation or other monograph or a critical essay dealing with the Confederate biographies written by Tate, Andrew Lytle, Robert Penn Warren, and their allies?). Perhaps, too, "The Social Critic" might be distinguished from the literary critic—and even the practicing literary critic from the literary theorist. Tate is, of course, all three kinds of critic. But the distinction between the subgenres of criticism might be pedantic in the case of a man who passes so readily, often in a single essay, from one to the other.

Another category I would gladly have seen added, even though I see how difficult it would be to discuss it in an essay, is Tate as a literary friend, correspondent, or prefacer. Squires touches upon this in his "Introduction," in speaking of the thousands of letters written to Tate which are already in the University Library at Princeton, and how they testify to Tate's "kindness and generosity to others," the "moral action" behind this generosity, the disinterestedness of both the action and the generosity. "That is because Allen Tate has always conceived of the profession of letters as a service to something more important than self," his "serious and dispassionate objectivity."

Evidence of his devotion to his literary contemporaries is so abundant that one can choose almost at random. He early entered into close relations with Hart Crane: he wrote the preface to Crane's first book, *White Buildings*. In the correspondence with Donald Davidson, recently published in *The Southern Review*, we see him defending the work of Hemingway against Davidson's strictures. These are early examples. As an elder statesman of letters, Tate (like his great exemplar, Eliot) is the writer of many prefaces to books by other writers, either younger than himself or less known, inadequately recognized men of letters approximately his coevals—John Peale Bishop, for example, or Francis Fergusson. He also writes the best "blurbs" I know (presumably sentences from letters to the author or publisher); they are at once generous and precisely worded—never vague undefined good will, not to be borne down upon.

To return from categories not set up to those so generously provided and filled with such rich *exempla*: of the memoirs, the first and chief is properly by John Crowe Ransom, Tate's senior by ten years and once, when Tate was a Vanderbilt freshman, formally his teacher of writings.[2] This is an utterly delightful piece of Ransomianism—easy, candid, and elegant. (Apropos of the friendship between him and Tate he refers to the treatment of that virtue in "an old book . . . a sort of pagan bible," Aristotle's *Ethics*.) "Allen's personality," he writes, "was always more

---

[2]Ransom's memoir and Cowley's, presently to be referred to, first appeared in "Homage to Allen Tate . . . [on] his Sixtieth Birthday," *Sewanee Review* (Autumn 1959).

harmonious than mine, and un-folded more surely and happily. At twenty his mind was further on its road than mine when I had passed thirty"; and again, "His personality is as whole and undivided, and it is as steady, as it is vivid." "*As steady, as it is vivid*" is an apt coupling; and the almost oxymoron seems to me accurate.

Of the relation between teacher and taught, Ransom describes how he used to put his freshman writers through elementary exercises. But Allen "would have none of that." He "had decided to start his writing at the top." And in his reading he took his own advanced experimental line, studying on his own as an undergraduate Baudelaire (whose "Correspondences" he early translated) and Mallarmé; he had "literary resources which were not the property of our region at that time." It was Allen who read Eliot's early critical books and warmly reviewed them in *The Fugitive*, which published almost no criticism; it was Allen who first introduced Eliot's criticism and then his poetry to Ransom. Ransom does not add that this introduction did not convert him, though he found the "classical" criticism more acceptable than the modernist poetry, especially *The Waste Land* (about which he wrote his former teacher with "much agitation"). Ransom's taste in poetry was, and remained, more conservative than Tate's—remained more in the English tradition, from Skelton to Hardy. And he certainly shared to some extent Paul Elmer More's dismay at the seeming discrepancy between Eliot's criticism and his poetry, in which chaos was reflected by fragmentation; he would have none of the "expressive fallacy" that style should mirror content instead of going its own regular metrical way. On this subject Ransom stood with Yvor Winters while in his following of Eliot's method and practice, Tate was followed by the Brooks and Warren of at least the first edition of *Understanding Poetry* (1938).

It is an easy academic mistake to suppose that it is always the younger man who is influenced by the older man. In the case of Ransom and Tate we are dealing with two strong minds, wills, and personalities, more profitably distinguished than identified. Close friends and allies in general, each has influenced the other, but only up to a certain point. And Ransom is speaking from self-knowledge when he speaks of Tate as having followed the steadier course. By his Kenyon years, the elder man had given up allegiance to institutional and traditional religion, defended in *God Without Thunder*, and in 1945 he publicly withdrew from the

Agrarian cause. To some degree, he has made peace with positivists and naturalists, accepted indeed that "modern world" which Tate has been said not to accept. Tate's "reasoned conservatism" Ransom professes to admire but does not profess to share. But Tate has developed consistently from the time of his earliest appearance in print. Though he did not become a Roman Catholic until he was fifty, he writes, in 1929, "I am more and more heading towards Catholicism." And from the early thirties on, he has been at once a regionalist and an internationalist, by which I mean not one who seeks to syncretize Western and Eastern cultures, as in different ways Irving Babbitt, Ezra Pound, and Aldous Huxley attempted, but one who seeks firmly to attach American civilization to its traditional *fons et origo*, Greek and Latin European or Mediterranean culture.

In 1929 Tate wrote to Davidson, "Ransom and Eliot are more alike than any other two people alive. . . . It is very hard for me to distinguish the influences they have had upon me; they merge." That early statement would require much modification and many distinctions, yet they have remained, I think, the two men whom Tate has most admired and whose general approval he has most coveted—whom he has cherished first of all as men of high personal integrity and then as spirits naturally conservative and orthodox. Of the two, it is surely Eliot who has been the chief influence. Tate's published tribute to Eliot is chiefly personal; yet the large and strong relationship has been literary—both poetic and critical —and in general social or cultural doctrine. In connection with Tate's social essays, one should reread Eliot's *Idea of a Christian Society* and especially *Notes Towards the Definition of Culture* (1939 and 1948) as well as the earlier *After Strange Gods* (1934), first delivered as lectures at the University of Virginia. In the very first of these lectures, Eliot speaks with interest of *I'll Take My Stand* and defines and commends regionalism; and a footnote links Chesterton's "distributism" with the regional-Agrarian views of "Mr. Allen Tate and his friends."

One other memoir, Malcolm Cowley's, should be mentioned for the sake of the important period in Tate's career which it commemorates. The Nashville friends—especially Davidson, the most conservative—distrusted New York City, the American metropolis, the center of the American publishing trade and on these accounts the preferred residence of many, if not most, American literary folk. But Tate became a convinced regionalist only after first testing his mettle, and that triumphantly, against the talents and the talk of his best literary contemporaries from wherever in the States.

In 1924, after two years of planning, he made his first trip to New York, and there he met and formed friendships with Hart Crane, whose correspondent he had been for some time, and with Cowley, Matthew Josephson, Kenneth Burke, Edmund Wilson, and, a little later, Mark Van Doren. He met Ford Madox Ford in 1927; Caroline Gordon became Ford's secretary in 1927–1928, and in 1928 Ford persuaded Henry Allen Moe to award Tate a Guggenheim Fellowship. He spent four years in New York, earning his living as a free-lance writer, reviewing for the *Nation* and the *New Republic*, then at their height, and composing his life of General Jackson. He could, like his *Fugitive* friends, have followed from the start an academic career. He had belief in his writing talent and the bravado to try to support himself by free-lancing.

New York, the national literary capital, was, a few years later, succeeded by two years in Paris, the literary capital of the world—at least in the days of Tate's "expatriate" and "lost" generation, about which Cowley has written his classic, *Exiles' Return*. Here and elsewhere in France Tate met Gertrude Stein, Hemingway, and renewed his close friendship with Ford Madox Ford. Briefly in London, he began there his lifelong friendship with Eliot and Herbert Read.

It was these years of the twenties in New York, and the two in Paris, which gave Tate his permanent and distinctive stance. He gained the assurance that he was at least the equal of his ablest literary contemporaries. And here, against the background of the world city, he came to define himself as a regionalist and at the same time to become an international man of letters—an adherent both to culture and to Culture.

The essays chosen to discuss Tate as an "Essayist"—that is, as a critic, show how difficult this criticism is to discuss. It is partly the wide range of the essayistic operations, some of which belong to literary theory, some to practical criticism, some to social or cultural criticism—the latter commonly with reference to the artist or poet or man of letters in his relation to society or to the subsidiary regional topic of the man of letters in relation to Southern culture. It is partly because the essays collected were written over so long a period of time—now "four decades"; and while there is a remarkable steadiness and coherence of central point of view, most of the essays were written for occasions and the many polemic pieces were written in specific polemic contexts which need now to be historically restated. I have in mind such an essay as "Literature as Knowledge," which, with its generally exciting topic, chiefly expends itself on a particular controversy.

The Forlorn Demon (1953) seems to me the best single volume of Tate criticism because the essays brought together there were all written within a limited space of time—the early fifties, the early years of his first tenured teaching, as professor at the University of Minnesota—under the unifying influence of conversion to Catholicism, and with, as a distinct center, the two poles of Poe and Dante, of the solipsistic and "angelic" "forlorn demon" and "superman" Poe and the symbolic, culturally responsible, spiritually mature Dante. It contains also one of Tate's best unpolemic single essays, to which I frequently return, "The Man of Letters in the Modern World," and a fine essay in the kind of historical criticism at which Eliot excelled, "Johnson on the Metaphysical Poets."

But in general one should take Tate at his own judgment, that as an essayist he has year after year "conducted his education in public," speaking in order to find out what he thinks on matters of central concern to him. Elsewhere he apologizes for the "toplofty tone" of some of his essays—that tone which appears also in the earlier essays of Eliot. But to write and publish at all can be considered an act of aggression; and the more modest, tentative, and exploratory a man is, the more (appearing in public, there to conduct his self-education) he finds it necessary to don some armor—of belligerence or extreme courtesy, or both.

The most substantial and closely reasoned of the essays on "The Essayist" is "The Criticism of Allen Tate" by Monroe Spears, sometime editor of the *Sewanee Review*. This piece pay tribute, in conclusion, to what he calls Tate's "greatest virtue," his "masterly . . . analyses . . . of specific poems," which "stress heavily the element of meter, rhythm, music"—one should certainly add *imagery*—"most critics tend to neglect." Mr. Tate "relates this element to the whole meaning and effect of the poem, and discusses it with an intelligence and sensitivity that are, as far as I know, unique." He add that Tate "does not reduce his critical apparatus to a formula, as even such excellent critics as Ransom, Brooks, and Winters tend, in varying degrees, to do." This is just praise.

The bulk of the essay, however, pays Tate a different kind of compliment—that of addressing to him some objections to questions about basic matters of literary theory, which concern the relation of literature to religion and to society.

These questions and objections are well stated, at least as they apply to Tate's earlier work. The first question is, in effect, how, before he became a Catholic convert, could Tate conscientiously say of attempts like Irving Babbitt's that they were not enough to take the place of religion? Or, more generally, how can one deplore the "deep illness of the modern mind" if one holds, as Tate then seemed to do, some modified cultural determinism like Spengler's? The answer to these questions is that whether one has a personal solution or not, and whether individual conversion is at all the same thing as participating in a Catholic culture in a Catholic age, one can still deplore "Modernism," and think the traditional view (embodied in the Christian mythology) a deeper and truer view of human nature than any modern positivist scheme. This view can be maintained out of insight backed up by history.

The second question has to do with "Literature as Knowledge," though Spears's prime quotation comes from "Narcissus as Narcissus." Spears partly objects, as I am disposed to do, to what appears a semantic quibble over words. The "knowledge" poetry gives is not what ordinary language means by knowledge (*i.e.*, scientific or other factual information); it would seem more appropriate to call it wisdom or insight or aesthetic experience. But more importantly, Tate seems to mean by his knowledge the "absolute experience; the contemplation or vision or revelation . . . sought usually in philosophy and religion." And is that not "making art a substitute for religion"?

That the "true value" of literature seems to both Ransom and Tate to be "cognition" is their way of defending aesthetic value as at least on a level of importance equal to that of science and philosophy. What Ransom, at least, is defending with his "precious objects" and "world's body," and Tate, too, with different language, is the value of particular individual things, objects and persons, and the value of concrete experience as distinct from, and in opposition to, abstractions; and they find in literature, specifically in poetry, what might be called the institutional representation of these concretions.

But surely it is not only in art that we experience the concrete; we experience it every day, or should, or might. And, on the other hand, no literary theory can identify literature with particularity alone. From any large point of view, literature offers "concrete universals"; and it is a matter of literary period whether the typical or the individual receives stress.

Again, a poem communicates an experience, or a meaning, tied down to and identified with a specific verbal structure or construct. You cannot participate in that experience, or receive that meaning—indeed, the poet could not arrive at it—without going through the verbal process. This is that specific knowledge which a poem is or gives. But to "know" poetry, I must read many poems and not only analyze but compare them; and it seems that knowledge in the ordinary sense emerges only when we get beyond the particular poem and begin to compare (*i.e.*, to relate the particular poem to other poems).

Spears's third and chief charge is that there is a "fundamental antiquity" in Tate's thought about art and society: that his "two goals" —great art and a traditional society—ultimately conflict, since, according to Tate, "great art is produced not by traditional societies but by the breakup of such societies." More precisely, great art appears, whether in Jacobean England, or in the New England of Hawthorne and Emily Dickinson, or in the South of Ransom and Faulkner, at the moment of transition from an unquestioningly accepted orthodoxy and a fixed society to a "liberal" or anarchic or valueless or skeptical world. (Even Dante came toward the end of medieval orthodoxy.)

I don't know how Tate would answer this charge. The dilemma is surely a painful one for a poet or a critic. Tate does not attempt to represent Poe's antebellum South as a climate favorable to poetry (politics and its literary form, oratory, engaged the articulate and the ambitious); nor, I shall add, was New England during its two Calvinist centuries when orthodoxy and farming gave stability and continuity to society.

Frank Kermode supplies Tate with an answer: "He sought a way of life, having the kind of order that is now found only in art; and order available to all, and not only to the estranged artist." But this sounds closer to the Agrarian Utopianism of New England Transcendentalism than anything I can imagine Tate's assenting to.

113

Kermode, one of today's best critics, is one of the four contributors to the section "The Novelist"—the section I find the most wholly satisfactory. The essays on *The Fathers* are led off by that of Arthur Mizener, the biographer of Fitzgerald and Ford Madox Ford. Indeed, the three essays which follow it, one of which is Kermode's, were prompted by the English reissue of the novel, for which Mizener's essay served as introduction. But the British critics add much. They see both the novel and the South with at once informed intelligence and sympathy and with illuminating detachment.

The English writers "compare and contrast" Tate's novel with Scott's historical novels, especially with *Waverley*, also concerned with "the last days of an order." (The influence of Scott's novels upon the Old South's conception of itself is an old commonplace of literary historians.) They repeat the generalization about the difference between British fiction—say that of Trollope and George Eliot, with their sense of "weight and thickness of social pressure around the characters"—and the poetic quality, meaning in depth, and "underlying pattern of moral fable or covert allegory" of Hawthorne and Melville. They compare the American Civil War with the English.

I would like to add a few reflections of my own. First, Tate's single novel seems the book which most brings all his parts and powers together: in it, both the essayist and the poet collaborate and fuse. It is a poet's novel, yet not a poetic novel or a piece of prose-poetry. It is a critic's novel, but not the kind of didactic, ideological novel, the *Bildungsroman*, which the academic critic is likely to write as his sole novelistic venture. It is a historical novel, but all the set pieces of history, the battle scenes and the debates, are left out: the public history, including the war, is seen only from around the corner and is seen and felt by characters who are not historical principals. It is an autobiographical novel in the sense that Tate's study of his genealogy (out of which he earlier began to write a novel of three generations, to be called *The Ancestors*) prompted it, but not in the sense that it *is* Tate's own life story. Lacey, the narrator, torn between his manner-molded but archaic father Major Buchan and his brother-in-law, George Posey (for whom

114

Tate's extrovert brother Ben is said to have offered the requisite degree of prototype), is Tate only in the sense that he is also the meditative loiterer by the graveyard gate in "Ode to the Confederate Dead."

Mr. Squires writes, in his *Literary Biography*, that *The Fathers* "is a novel of extraordinary strength. It has some indebtedness, some echoes, but, taken as a whole, there is nothing quite like it in its genre." This is a provocative remark. I can think of nothing in the novel so definite as echoes unless Squires is thinking, as I would, of certain thematic resemblances in the powerful Part III, "The Abyss," to Faulkner's *Absalom, Absalom!*—less miscegenation, rape, murder, and suicide than a general sudden speeding up of the course of things, a melodramatic ending after a long brooding meditative prelude (and the Quentin of *Absalom, Absalom!* is a kind of Lacey). The "indebtedness" mentioned is perhaps intended to refer to Henry James and his technique of the "point of view" in narration, which the novel so skillfully and subtly uses. But I am unable to guess what the "genre" is within which no other member of the genre seems "quite like" *The Fathers*.

I would find it easier to say, "There is no other novel quite like it," and stop there; I cannot point to any generally recognized and accredited genre. Tate's own statement of his intent seems to me carried out in execution: "I wished . . . to make the whole structure symbolic . . . in terms of realistic detail, so that you could subtract the symbolism, or remain unaware of it, without losing the literal level of meaning, . . . but if you subtract the literal or realistic detail, the symbolic structure disappears." True—the attempt, and the success, are at a symbolism firmly based on history, or fact, and everyday reality, even some old-fashioned narrative structure; something which is neither "realism," as practiced by H. G. Wells and Arnold Bennett or William Dean Howells, nor symbolism, as practiced by Maurice Maeterlinck or Virginia Woolf. But do not all works of art we recognize as great meet Tate's requirements for himself; do not writers as different as Dante, Hawthorne and Melville, Proust, Mann and Joyce?

Tate never attempts in his work to create characters who give the illusion of being lifelike. A professional reader of the manuscript appears to have complained that Tate "never comes to grips with the characters." Quite so. They are seen as types, as ways of life, as modes or qualities of being; in this respect I am sometimes reminded of Lawrence's *Women in Love*—and that not merely because Birkin is, like George Posey, a type of the willful unruly modern man. A word ever hovering before me is "allegory," a word currently in ill repute but undeservedly so. Of course, Tate's novel is not a systematic allegory; but when one remembers the novel, even at no great distance of time, it is the allegory—the contrast of types of life, of types of virtue and vice which one remembers: the characters do not walk out of the page and assume separate life. They appear within their frames.

To what genre does *The Fathers* belong? If I cannot answer that question with any fixed traditional generic pattern, I can—and find it engaging to—think what books and authors it presents a degree of analogy to, and to cast a fairly wide net, thinking of such features of a genre as theme and fictional technique but also even of such matters which finally count aesthetically as length. This is a fairly short novel, rather in that respect like *The Great Gatsby* or *The Spoils of Poynton* or one of Hawthorne's, and unlike the Victorian three-decker novel or the novels of Dostoyevsky and Tolstoy, which James once referred to as "those loose baggy monsters." One of the British critics evokes, as I should be disposed to do, the name of Turgenev, even without his specifically evoking *Fathers and Sons*, which has also thematic relation to *The Fathers*, the hiatus between generations. The Hawthorne novel which presents most analogy is *The House of the Seven Gables*, with its contrast of Hepzibah and Clifford, archaic gentlefolk, and Holgrave, the "new man"; Clifford is a partial parallel to Mr. Jarman, Tate's recluse.

There are fine *aperçus* in the novel, almost *sententiae*, from which every critic of the novel has quoted, from Mizener down. "The Poseys were more refined than the Buchans, but less civilized." "Excessively refined persons have a communion with the abyss; but is not civilization the agreement, slowly arrived at, to let the abyss alone?" "Our lives were eternally balanced upon a pedestal, below which lay an abyss. . . ." And there are orderings of concepts—the code of landed gentlemen with their ritual communions through manners contrasted with the sheer unpredictability and violence of unlanded, deracinated (even though still Roman Catholic) city dwellers, living off their inherited means without responsibility to a family or a community—"isolatoes," personal and violent. A critic is likely to remember, perhaps most of all, these *aperçus*, the covert allegory of the novel. But when one turns back to the novel to

116

locate these *schemata*, he sees how difficult they are to find: the remarks, and the distinctions, grow out of pages of naturalistic detail; they are incarnate in incidents like Posey's suit for the hand of Susan or his behavior at the tournament.

The final sentence of the novel I find baffling, the more so that it must have been carefully considered. Lacey concludes, as he goes back to fight, "If I am killed it will be because I love him more than I love any man." How can he love the man who killed his brother, who drove his sister insane, who was the antipodes of his gentle and gentlemanly father? How can he love the whirlpool or the abyss? Likely this is Tate's way of identifying Lacey with the man at the gate of the graveyard in the "Ode" and ultimately with himself—a man in tension between the old and the new, regretting the fragility amid its stability of the old order, but with pity (for this is what Lacey's *love* must partly be) for the solipsism, "personality" and violence of the new, stumbling along without regard for precedents.

Tate likes to characterize himself as a "man of letters" rather than a poet. This he does, I can suppose, partly out of modesty and partly because, as a matter of fact, he is more than a poet: outside of the poet's linguistic aptitude he is an unspecialized man, a general intelligence. But there can be no doubt that he cares most about his poetry and would wish to stand or fall by it.

He is, in all his periods, a difficult poet. John Bradbury intelligibly writes that Tate lacks the "ease of the natural poet, of a Yeats or an Eliot or an Auden"—we might add, of a Poe or a Ransom. But his difficulties and obscurities are partly willed. The kind of poetry he willed to write is alien to the Southern tradition of politeness and rhetoric, which he permits himself, sometimes excessively, in his prose. With Yeats, he believes that rhetoric comes from our quarrel with others; poetry out of our quarrel with ourselves. His poetry also refuses to aim at the American goal, the goal of the media, communications; it is not for those literate illiterates who are the characteristic products of contemporary American —shall we say "modern"—education. They are in some modified sense

117

sacred texts, to be grasped first as wholes intuitively, then to be pondered, made subject to exegesis, then reassembled by the intuitive intelligence.

It is true that not all of his poems are equally "dense" and intense, nor are all parts of all poems. Many of the critics in Squires's symposium quote, or cite, the opening lines from "The Meaning of Life":

> Think about it at will; there is that
> Which is the commentary; there's that other,
> Which may be called the immaculate
> Conception of its essence in itself.
> It is necessary to distinguish the weights
> of the two methods lest the first smother
> The second, the second be speechless (without the first).

The discursive lines quoted are commentary; the anecdote which follows is what is so strangely called "essence"—"strangely" because the word, and the words before it, are so *abstract*, while what is intended seems *thing*, "precious object," myth, or vision, the concrete datum of immediate experience, linguistically rendered with precision. (I apologize for all my own abstractions, but they are the words of a critic.) The commentary is speech; the essence is vision.

Most connoisseurs of Tate's poetry prefer his poems of "speechless" vision, to judge from the testimony offered.

Because Tate aims at making a verbal object to be pondered, a construct not aimed at immediate intelligibility but at utmost literary richness, he must be read before he is studied, then studied, then reread, and so on indefinitely. Because he is difficult, it is appropriate and profitable, at the intermediate stage of study, to take advantage of the labors of earlier qualified and devout readers such as are well represented by the fourteen essays on Tate as "The Poet." In what follows, I have grouped the essays according to their kinds and attempted a preliminary digestion of them.

First come two short general essays, the first of which, properly, is Cleanth Brooks's discussion in *Modern Poetry and the Tradition*, published in 1939; this is excerpted from a chapter which also considers the poetry of Ransom and Robert Penn Warren. Brooks writes both of Tate's themes and of his linguistic-literary structure and texture (themes as well as style appear almost necessarily in every discussion of his poetry). Memorably, Brooks writes of Tate's "structure of violent synthesis"; and, of the "surface of the poem," he notes its "apparently violent disorder. . . . Almost every adjective in his poetry challenges the reader's imagination to follow it off on a tangent"—a remark that might have been made of "Death of Little Boys" but is in fact illustrated from "Ode to the Confederate Dead."

Miss Chapin, writing for the *New Republic* in 1965, seems independently corroborating Brooks when she observes that the "vehement emotion which underlines so much of his [Tate's] writing is reflected in the intensity of his style."

Three essays consider Tate's poetry by a method which might have been further extended. I might use as a topic sentence here the one beginning Sister Bernetta Quinn's "Allen Tate's Inferno." She writes, "Certain critics have called the verse of Allen Tate Augustan, pointing out in particular his affinity to Pope; others have labelled it metaphysical, after the poetry of Donne's age; still others, in the tradition of the Graeco-Roman classics." After which prelude, Sister Bernetta finds Tate's "basic concern especially as revealed in *Poems: 1922-1947*, to be medieval"—by which latter she means Christian and Catholic—a basic concern with "the struggle of Everyman to win beatitude and to escape eternal reprobation." Her position is obviously based on themes and worldview, not, as in the critical positions just cited, on style or poetic method.

Miss Feder's piece, "Tate's Use of Classical Literature," is substantial and valuable; a little less than fully literary criticism, it is considerably more than a mere accumulation of notes. Her essay is accurately named. Primarily, we are given a systematic discussion of what used to be called "classical allusions." For example, "muted Zeno and Parmenides" is explained; so is the relation of "The Mediterranean" to the *Aeneid*, from which its epigraph comes, and that of "Aeneas at Washington." But there are also good generalizations: "Tate uses the classical past in his poetry to represent a unified society, in which man's conduct is directed by a heroic code of conduct." Probably her primary aim is to show that Tate's use of historical material, his appeal to history (which, I will add, he opposes to philosophy as the concrete to the abstract) is not limited to the revocation of the Old South. And this is an important point to make. Here again we see Tate's double recourse—on the one hand to the regional and on the other to Graeco-Roman-Mediterranean culture—something which transcends the United States, the higher culture in which, so far as we have one, we participate.

There are also some preliminary remarks on Tate's classicism in the sense not of thematic material or allusion but of aesthetic theory and method. And at this point I may introduce the third essay in this group, that by Vivienne Koch, which argues that Tate is a "poet of romantic sensibility . . . who has tried to compress himself into classical form," but who is at his best when his "romanticism gets the better of him." Even in his earlier years she finds his poems "alternating violence and absolution," to show a romanticism in discrepance with his criticism; and she judges the much admired "Death of Little Boys," written when its author was twenty-six, as "romantically experimental" as the poems of the same period by his friend Crane. (It sounds, indeed, much like Crane, surely one of the "influences" on Tate.)

Miss Koch thinks, with some justice, that *The Winter Sea* (1944) "projects an almost complete break with Tate's earlier work." "Seasons of the Soul," first published in that book, she praises as "a major event in Tate's career as a poet. It is lyrical, sensuous, and tragic. It is, for whatever meaning that chameleon term may still carry, romantic." In other words, in his forties, Tate's "romantic sensibility" was allowed, at last, to cast off its classical and metaphysical constrictions and to express itself in "lyrical" poems—poems unlike "Death of Little Boys" and "The Subway," which might be called sensuous and tragic, but certainly could not be called lyrical.

A literary theorist will distinguish, with such terms as "romantic," "classical," and "baroque," between their use to designate literary periods and their use to name recurrent types of sensibility and style. Indeed, one has to be very careful in his use of these terms; they are so easily "chameleon" that one ought always to follow his use of the word with some parallel gloss, some *ad hoc* definition of what one here intends by the term. Obviously, none of these terms are used by Tate's critics in a historical sense; they are all references to style. In this loose sense, one can speak of Tate *in toto*, or with reference to a particular poem or group of poems, as "expressionist" (a word Tate half accepts in one of those letters to Davidson I have earlier quoted) or "symbolist" (in the tradition

120

of Baudelaire and Rimbaud) or metaphysical or baroque or classic or romantic: quite an array of possible characterizations.

In Tate's career as a poet, there have certainly been change and development (as well as continuity). Such development there is in every poet who keeps alive. The case of self-renewal is patent in two of Tate's masters and precedents, Eliot and Yeats. I could wish Squires's book contained an essay on Tate's poetic periods or stages; but here, as elsewhere, when I find gaps I have to reflect that presumably no such essay already existed for the anthologist to use.

Miss Koch is correct, I think, in seeing a new turn with *The Winter Sea*. The next, and apparently final, turn was taken by the *terza rima* poems, "The Maimed Man," "The Swimmers," and "The Buried Lake," written in 1952 and 1953 (poems discussed by Squires in the admirable final essay of his anthology, reprinted from his *Literary Biography* of Tate), poems which are parts of a projected "long poem," tentatively planned to consist of nine parts. Every twentieth-century poet of stature wishes to end with some "long poem," some "epic" or philosophical poem which, compressed and elliptical as no poem before his century was, shall still make the effect of largeness and inclusiveness. These parts of a long poem are discussed by Squires in an admirable, closely written essay. Squires sees Tate's "long poem" as "autobiographical"; but is it more so than Eliot's *Four Quartets*? He sees it also as a "break" on Tate's part with certain aspects of Eliot's poetry. In more than his use of *terza rima*, Tate seems to be emulating Dante, not only the *Commedia* but the *Vita Nuova*.

I turn now to a group of essays, in varying proportions histories and exegeses of single poems of Tate's—as it happens, all early poems, composed and revised in the late twenties and early thirties. They are "Ode to the Confederate Dead," "To the Lacedaemonians," and "The Cross"; the critics discussing them are Louis Rubin, Donald Davidson (Tate's fellow-Fugitive and fellow-Agrarian), and R. K. Meiners, author of *The Last Alternatives* (1963), an important, serious book on Tate's work. All are valuable.

The first two poems, still printed together in the latest collection of Tate's poems, can both be loosely described as "about" the Civil War, or "about" the soldiers of the losing side; but, of course, they are really both about now—in relation to then. The Confederate veteran in the second poem is speaking to his comrades, whether still surviving or dead, while he looks dizzily around him at the "progressive" South—"eyeless with eyesight only, the modern power," at a South where "All are born Yankees of the race of men / And this, too, now the country of the damned." And the first, the famous—"Ode" (the piece always evoked by mention of Tate's name, the piece translated by the Maritains into French, the piece which gives the title to Rizzardi's Italian translation of Tate's poems)—this is really about the solipsist who is aware that he, a twentieth-century Narcissus, cannot properly respond to the challenge put by the "ragged arms, the ragged heads and eyes": all is fugitive, like the leaves. The very word "Ode" is ironic, calling up as it does some public poetic address, like Timrod's, and, if Pindar comes to mind at the word, some celebration of triumph. Tate had originally called it, literally, an "Elegy," and that might perhaps have served if one could trust to the memory of Gray's most famous poem in which the lament is more for the poet who meditates in the graveyard than for those who lie buried there.

The "Ode" is a fine, sensitive, and musical poem. But I can agree with Rubin, its exegete, that it has often been praised for the wrong reasons, even on a misunderstanding of its theme (an assumed Southern poet's celebration of the Old South) perhaps also because Tate (set onto his task by Norman Pearson, who was going to include it in his *Oxford Anthology of American Literature*, and felt he, or the lay reader, needed some help with it) wrote on it his single essay in explication of his own poetry. For my part, I am embarrassed to record that I too need the essay and am left with two grave doubts—the first, whether I could now read that poem with adequate fullness without it, and the second, whether all the features delineated in the essay find actual objective correlation in the poem. And, since Squires says that few readers except Davidson have liked "To the Lacedaemonians" let me say that I do like it, that I think it a remarkably fine public poem—(it is the only poem Tate has composed for an occasion and for oral delivery on the occasion). It is thinned-down Tate, to be sure, but it is not thin: Tate can, upon occasion, stand some thinning down and still remain richer than most poets.

"The Cross," written in 1928, is the subject of Meiners's essay—a painstaking discussion of a powerful but painful poem—discussed also by Sister Bernetta, and by M. E. Bradford, in his essay entitled "Origins and

Beginnings" (also by Squires in his *Literary Biography* and by Robert Dupree in the October 1972 issue of *The Southern Review*). The exegetes are not in entire agreement about the meaning of this poem, which Squires calls "his best poem of the period." I agree in general with Squires: "it is not a 'Christian' poem so much as a psychological poem, documenting the nearly unbearable strains of Christianity, the very strains Nietzsche felt Christianity had imposed upon Western man. . . . The speaker of this poem would as gladly lief be rid of religion as he would be immersed in it." It expresses the doubts and difficulties of a man contemplating conversion, drawn to it but feeling rather the burden and the peril of the religious life than anything like relief or redemption. It is Jansenist, Calvinist, Manichaean even, in its somberness. The Cross introduces sin into the world and the grave possibility of damnation as well as the possibility of real life instead of mere existence. Hence the powerful ambivalence of the poem and its plays on *life* and *death*, on *light* and *darkness*. There is in the poem no word of the Cross as a symbol of triumph, and no intimation of St. Paul's "But where sin abounded, Grace did much more abound." Related at once to the "Ode," with its lament over solipsism, and to "The Cross," with its fright over the prospect of conversion, but going a step beyond both, is "Last Days of Alice," written in 1931, which reads

> O God of our flesh, return us to Your wrath,
> Let us be evil could we enter in
> Your grace, and falter on the stony path!

All the discussions of "The Cross" are conducted at a serious and responsible level. It is clear that with the poetry of Tate, a poetry condensed, rich, and hence often obscure, there is need of many more such exegetical studies of particular poems, as well as of responsible extended treatments like those of Meiners, of M. E. Bradford (whose forty-six page book, *Rumors of Mortality* [1969] is excellent), and of Squires.

We are grateful to have Tate's reading of his "Ode," and we learn with interest from Squires's book that Tate seems (on the basis of letters now in the Princeton Library) to agree in general with Meiners's interpretation of "The Cross." But is important to reaffirm that commonplace of the now old New Critics that the meaning of a poem is not the author's—not what he meant before he started to write the poem, nor what it means to him now, years after, as he rereads his own work. The meaning is the poem's—and the poem is a verbal construct intermediate (as Eliot says) between the poet and the reader, existing in its own right, and having what Wellek used to call its "ontological situs."[3] To read it fully, or approximately, or adequately, is first of all a problem in literary theory and in hermeneutics, the art of interpretation, and then a matter of what Richards called "practical criticism"—which requires both method and sensibility, first and last, the latter. We are far yet from a set of responsible readings of Tate's poetry, poem by poem; and only on that can any serious general discussion of it, and of its meaning and value in relation to and in comparison with the poetry of other poets, be attained.

A fine perceptive general essay on Tate's poetry, which I have been unable to group with other essays, is that of the poet Howard Nemerov, which was published in 1948 as a review of Tate's *Poems: 1922-1947*. This piece shows sympathy with Tate's worldview, his antipragmatism and antipositivism as well as with his kind of poetry; and it discusses both his themes and his "composition"—his structures and styles. The second part of the essay is the best analysis I have ever seen of the recurrent symbolic imagery in Tate's poems—of Blood and Cave—of liquid and solid, fluid and rigid—the polarity so strikingly pursued under sundry metamorphoses.

I want to conclude this essay by setting down some quotations from three Italians whose essays are reprinted. This conclusion is variously appropriate. In his later years, his fifties and sixties, Tate has been, both officially and informally, a cultural ambassador of the United States, lecturing in India, England, France, and Italy. He was Fulbright Visiting Professor at Oxford and at Rome. In Italy, where contemporary American literature, both the novel and poetry, has been much translated and warmly received, he was especially welcomed and appreciated. There is an international perspective on Tate's career given by the Italian pieces, the first of which, by Pier Francesco Listri, is based upon a Florentine

---

[3]Wellek's masterly essay "The Mode of Existence of a Literary Work of Art" was published in *The Southern Review* (Autumn 1942) and republished under the title "The Analysis of the Literary Work of Art" as the basic chapter in *Theory of Literature* (1949).

"Encounter," or interview, of 1970. Listri writes of Tate that "his cultural world is double-stitched. One thread secures him to Europe, the other to the defeated South." In a meaningful as well as eloquent sentence, he calls the visitor "a magisterial poet, perpetually discomforted by the global power of his country"; and he continues that, though shocked by what is happening to America, he "affects no wild rage"; he is "armed only with the grandeur of his despair and the grandeur of his language." His despair is not only for his country but for American poetry, as he sees the younger poets so "extremely subjective, so occupied with their own sensations," believing no longer in the possibility of attaining objective or sharable truth.

In an excellent short general essay, "Culture and Technique in Tate," Francesco Mei first comments on the mistaken tendency of Europeans to think of an American writer as a "genial barbarian, talented but without critical conscience or intellectual maturity," though the

> idea that the American writers lack university education and know little or nothing of European thought, history, and literature is simply a myth. . . . Most American poets today are also critics, often university professors. Far from being immediate and spontaneous, theirs is among the most difficult forms of poetry ever produced, the most dense with erudition and with thought, the most disciplined technically. Our own [Italian] Hermetic poets, by comparison, represent a prodigy of simplicity.

Mei discusses both the poetry and the criticism. In the poetry, he finds both Europe and the South—"the influence of the Latin poets, especially in his spirited and stinging satire, basically political, in the mode of Persius and Martial," and that of Dante and Donne, on the one hand—on the other, of the "hallucinated" world of the South, in which sphere he moves with "the other symbolist writers of the South, such as Faulkner and Poe." Of his literary theory, he notes that Tate does not defend the autonomy of art "on the basis of a sterile aestheticism, like that of a Wilde or a Mallarmé, and not even on the grounds of an abstract idealism, like that of Croce," but on the basis of "the classico-Christian tradition, which is traceable to Aristotle and St. Thomas, and which has been taken up again by the French philosopher, Jacques Maritain." And of his practical criticism (he cites the essays on Donne, Keats, Hardy,

Emily Dickinson, and Crane), Tate "sees the author, with exemplary historical insight, as an inseparable part of the spiritual experience of the civilization in which he lives."

The fine essay by Alfredo Rizzardi, which served as the introduction to Rizzardi's translation of Tate (*Odi ai Caduti Confederati e Altre Poesie*), is an essay on a poet by a poet. It is perceptive, closely written, not to be summarized or paraphrased. Its prime value, for me at least, lay in its comparative references to other poets, its partial analogues never intended to designate "sources," and its impressionistic characterization of Tate's style. I note the characterization of "Last Days of Alice" as "one of Tate's tensest and most outspoken pieces" and his comparison of such dramatic monologues as "Sonnets at Christmas" to the "terrible" sonnets of Father Hopkins and the Holy Sonnets of Donne, and his evaluation of "Seasons of the Soul," "one of his most taut and lucid poems," as equal to "the most inspired pages" of Yeats and Valéry. The "mechanical vitality" of the modern world is "rendered with expressionist violence" in "The Wolves," "Subway," and elsewhere: "Mankind presses against the bars of these poems as a modern bestiary." "Death of Little Boys" is Hopkinsian in its "rhythmic urge" and Dickinsonian in its "exotically lucid imagery." For a final quotation: Tate has written poems "in a quasi-discursive mode, where the poet employs a line modeled on Eliot's dramatic monologue (of the Prufrock type); and there are others where traditional meter combines with a strongly elliptical language, compressing the syntactic structure to the point—at times—of impenetrability."

As I now reach the end of this commentary and ponder how to round it off, the thought of a once famous critical essay comes, unbidden, to my mind. It is Eliot's "Tradition and the Individual Talent." As I took it up and reread it, it seemed as germinal and seminal and magisterial and fresh as ever. It is a kind of essay on the "apostolic succession" in poetry, on the originality which consists in reception and transmission. We have a tendency, Eliot says, to

> insist, when we praise a poet, upon those aspects of his works in which he least resembles any one else. . . . We dwell with satisfaction upon the poet's difference from his predecessors. Whereas, if we approach a poet without this prejudice, we shall often find that not only the best,

but the most individual parts of his work may be those in which the dead poets, his ancestors, assert their immortality most vigorously. And I do not mean the impressionable period of adolescence, but the period of full maturity.

As a poet, Tate has always been learning from others—and not merely from the "dead poets" but from his contemporaries as well; he seems to have had one of his first teachers in his exact contemporary Crane (even though they had shared teachers in Baudelaire and Rimbaud). He long and variously and richly learned from Eliot (and learned directly and indirectly from Donne). He later shows the influence of the master of the great style, Yeats, and still later, of Dante. This poet, Tate, who seems so arrogant (and without arrogance one can scarcely be a poet at all today), is a splendid example of loyalty and gratitude toward his ancestors, at a time when such gratitude and loyalty are unfashionable.

In that famous essay, Eliot spoke of personality and impersonality. "Poetry is not a turning loose of emotion, but an escape from emotion; it is not the expression of personality, but an escape from personality. But, of course, only those who have personality and emotions know what it means to want to escape from these things." Tate did not fear or need to fear, whether he had emotions and personality; they were his endowment. What, in the "Postscript" to *T. S. Eliot: The Man and His Work*, Tate wrote of *il maestro di color che scrivonno*, is true of his own case: "his theory of the impersonality of poetry met no contradiction in the intensely personal origins of the poems."

Tate became in turn a transmitter of the poet's discipline and authority. Roethke and John Berryman were once his literal pupils. In their early years, Robert Penn Warren and Robert Lowell were unofficial beneficiaries. To how many more has he been unofficial teacher, guide, accomplice, and friend? And, all the while, this admirable poet has also been, for responsible critics of literature and society, and readers who take both seriously, a prime and fortifying representative of culture—the man of letters in the modern world.

(1973)

A Survivor's Tribute to T. S. Eliot

Though I have written several times about Eliot, most recently in *Connections* (1970), my writing about him has been concerned with his prose—his literary criticism and his "sociological" books: *After Strange Gods*, a defense of Regionalism, *The Idea of a Christian Society* and *Notes towards a Definition of Culture*.

Attraction to the prose and thought of Eliot came to me naturally. At Harvard, in 1921–22, I was a student and ardent disciple of Irving Babbitt, who converted me from my adolescent Romanticism to his doctrinal Classicism. At Princeton, where I did my graduate work, I once called on Paul Elmer More, Babbitt's closest friend and ally, whom, some years later, I came to know well and with whom I carried on a considerable correspondence. But I felt closer, as a critic, to Eliot than I did to his two older friends, finding him more literary, more "aesthetic," than either.

When, in 1930, I was appointed by my Princeton mentor, Robert K. Root (a devout Anglican and the director of my dissertation on *Pope as a Critic*), to a year's fellowship at the British Museum, I had as my chosen topic of investigation Richard Crashaw, the religious poet on whom Eliot had briefly written in *For Lancelot Andrewes*. During this year in London I did not limit my "research" to Crashaw or his period, but also went on with a study I had begun on the elder Henry James, the Swedenborgian father of the novelist and the philosopher.

I carried no letter from Babbitt or More introducing me to Eliot. Instead I wrote Eliot, already at Faber and Faber, around the corner from the small Bloomsbury hotel where I spent the year, telling him of the Crashaw project and asking him if I might meet him. He replied immediately, with that generosity to younger writers for which he has justly been renowned, inviting me to call at his office. That call—the one at which, I think, he introduced me to Mario Praz, the young Italian who had written a book on Crashaw and Donne—ended with an invitation to have lunch with him. The subject of our talk was chiefly the late, or later, Henry James; after all these years I recognize that Eliot's talk during the meal about *The Sense of the Past* and *The Ivory Tower* was apropos of what Eliot, confusing father and son, thought I was writing about.

When we met, Eliot, who was about ten years older than I, that is about forty, no longer was the handsome, elegant young man familiar from his earlier photographs: he now was spectacled and his teeth had become carious. His intonation was distinctly British. He looked the man of affairs, not my image of a poet or literary man.

Eliot graciously asked me if there was anyone I would especially like to meet, and I immediately said "Evelyn Underhill," whose *Mysticism* had been one of my favorite spiritual guides. Eliot said he had never met her but would like to, and could easily arrange a meeting. He got up a luncheon for the purpose of this introduction, the other guest being Miss Underhill's cousin or brother, who had been Eliot's confessor. The luncheon frankly disappointed me; in my naïveté I had expected the table talk to be mystical or at least theological: it was neither. Evelyn Underhill and Eliot politely talked personalities; asked each other in a gingerly, tactful way I have never forgotten, "Is he a nice person?"—a question to be answered by delicate characterization.

Reticence and urbane reserve were the notes I encountered when I thought to meet embodied poetry (in Eliot), or mysticism (in Underhill). But I stood in awe of both and did not presume—an obscure young scholar, not then even a critic—to judge this absence of free discourse.

To my surprise, Eliot sent me a Christmas card after I had returned to America in 1931; but when, in 1932, he came to Boston to deliver the Charles Eliot Norton lectures at Harvard, I did not presume to look him up or to invite him to my apartment. What I, then professor at Boston University, did was to attend the lectures Eliot delivered at the Sanders Theater; and I missed not a lecture. In saying this, I am merely saying that my primary attachment to Eliot was not to his poetry but to his criticism.

To Eliot I owe my interest in metaphysical poetry (Donne, Herbert, Crashaw, Marvell); and my interest in the seventeenth-century sermon (Donne, Andrewes, Jeremy Taylor); and Eliot's *Homage to John Dryden* and his general respect for neoclassicism reinforced my early, self-begotten taste for Pope.

To Eliot I certainly owe, in part at least, lifelong concern with my own prose style; Eliot's markedly Latinate diction was akin to the taste of the former Latin major at Wesleyan; and Eliot's precision and his utterly unjournalistic urbanity both strongly appealed to one who loathed the oh-so-American Mencken. Of the senior Humanists, Paul Elmer More wrote well but was far too inclined to pseudo-poetic phrases like, "I know not what." Babbitt was too breezy and vernacular. I am sure Eliot was the model for my own prose. I aimed at being a stylist of a somewhat archaic sort; never indeed tried to write like one of my own generation—Scott Fitzgerald or Ernest Hemingway. Until I read Eliot, my literary rearing was in the prose of the nineteenth century, especially Arnold and Newman. Later, Eliot and his style and my own taste drew me back to earlier prose writing, like that of Browne and Dr. Johnson.

In "To Criticise the Critic" (1965), Eliot makes it clear that his early, most influential criticism was that of a poet working out what his poetry should be like, that it was a craftsman's working criticism. I see now that, including the essays on Elizabethan drama (essays that did not much interest me), it was. But I see as well that the early essays, which I much prefer to the looser, more liberal later essays (*e.g.,* on Tennyson and Kipling) owe much of their merit to their rigidity and dogmatism: those of a man writing to define and defend the kind of writing he means to write, his own literary position.

Coming to Eliot by way of Babbitt and More, I never wholly diverged from these older men's view of Eliot's poetic career. More wrote an essay called "The Cleft Eliot," in which he professed the sincere admiration he felt for Eliot's criticism while disapproving of his poetry—indeed, baffled to reconcile its modernistic and experimental style with the classicism and traditionalism of the criticism. More had particularly in mind *The Waste Land*, a poem which might be described as a jumble of fragments and recondite allusions, a chaotic poem about chaos. Too timid and too loyal to the critic Eliot to say so in print, or even orally in the classroom, I certainly shared More's view; nor was I reconciled by Eliot's defense of his two styles to More: that prose can express ideas and ideals, but poetry has to be about the world as it is. I agreed with Yvor Winters, with whom I generally was in disagreement, that disorder can be seen from the point of view of order and chaos from the point of view of coherence; and that is what Eliot should have done.

I think "The Love Song of J. Alfred Prufrock" and "Gerontion" are the two achievements, triumphs, of the early period, with minor successes in such Ariel Poems as "Animula" and "Marina." *Ash Wednesday,* the first of Eliot's religious poems, I find a convert's rather boring experiment but not much more. The real triumph in Eliot's poetry comes in 1943 with the *Four Quartets*, especially the first and perhaps the last. These Pindaric odes, as Dame Helen Gardner suggestively calls them, are philosophical poems of the highest order; and it is on them that Eliot's claim as a poet must finally rest. They seem to me indeed the greatest poems of the twentieth century.

"Prufrock" and "Gerontion" are clearly Eliot's masterpieces in his first manner or style, that symbolized by his early attachment to French poetry, especially that of Laforgue. Written, it is said, while still at Harvard, "Prufrock" might well take its setting and character from either Boston or London, as is also the case with "Portrait of a Lady." It is a city poem, and Eliot is generally a city poet, his city being either upper class or lower class, sometimes both in the same poem, as they notably are in "Prufrock."

The theme of "Prufrock" is indecision. (The problem of indecision is indeed the center of Eliot's work.) Romantic sensibility as such is indecision: shall I, shan't I: eat a peach, marry, take holy orders—and so on. Eliot was himself lifelongly tempted to indecision; the reasons for any one action never seemed adequate. In his important essay on Pascal and elsewhere Eliot speaks of the element of skepticism necessarily present as a component part in any deep religious faith. But finally there must be a decision to be a Christian or not; and it is characteristic of Eliot that he did not merely become some vague kind of Christian, but an Anglican, an Anglo-Catholic, an acceptor of the dogma of the Incarnation.

Prufrock is a middle-aged bachelor, a dilettante. Like the "aged eagle" of *Ash Wednesday*, Prufrock is one version of Eliot himself, an empathized version of what he feared he might turn into himself if he made no decision to *be* or *do*, made no commitment to either a loved person or a precious cause. Eliot tended always to think of himself as old and wrote brilliant psychological and philosophical meditations on old age in several of his *Four Quartets*.

I relish "Prufrock" and keep returning to it. It is an ironic, satirical poem about a sentimentalist; it is the portrait of one whose chief suffering comes from his self-awareness, his sense of how at once comic and pathetic he is.

The background of the drawing room, the women talking of Michelangelo, represents the art-chatter of the cultivated who talk of the art of the past, who are not creative. They—and Prufrock—represent an effete, and decadent, and decayed world in which women—and men—talk instead of acting and loving.

"Gerontion" (1920), a brilliant, subtle, elliptical poem, shows in its style the strong influence of late Elizabethan and Jacobean dramatic verse. The poem is a soliloquy, that of a symbolic little old man who lives squalidly at the end of a culture. In it, there are images of decayed religion, of some surviving sacrament celebrated by men and women of many nations. Then comes Christ the Tiger. Is "Gerontion" ultimately a Christian poem? No more so than *The Waste Land*. One can say of all poems of decay, waste, and death that their very negations, the hollowness of the hollow men, the wasteness of the Waste Land, all imply at least the need for positive antitheses of fertility and faith. Reading Eliot backwards, one can certainly make such a reading; but it is a reading back. Eliot himself has said of *The Waste Land* that he was being drawn toward Buddhism when he wrote it.

The *Four Quartets* (which I reviewed when they, as a collection, appeared in 1943) are meditative poems, especially my favorite, "Burnt Norton," the first to be written. Only the fourth, "Little Gidding," can be called a religious poem, almost an ecclesiastical one. The famous dialogue in terza rima, I (and most literary men) admire; but the poem as a whole I like least of the *Quartets*; it is too neat, too much of an attempt to bring together, especially in the final paragraph, the themes and motifs of all that has preceded.

"Burnt Norton" I still read over and over again with deep admiration. Sections I and V particularly appeal. I like the pronouns, the "they" especially, the hovering sense of others, former owners of the estate, or spirits, or. . . .

II.

Eliot's conversion was the central act of his life. He was congenitally an ascetic. I do not think he was homosexual, but that all sex was more or less repellent to him. *The Waste Land* shows indeed how distasteful most

133

of life was for Eliot. He was spiritually a New Englander, and a Puritan, conscience-ridden.

His conversion is best understood in terms of his essays "Religion and Literature" and "Pascal"; and his approach to religion is what his friend, Paul Elmer More, in his book of that title, calls the skeptical approach. Newman's *Grammar of Assent*, referred to in the essay on Pascal, serves also as an important clue. The conversion was finally, I think, an act of the will, in which all sorts of concomitant motives took part, the concomitance of which was perceived by Newman's "Illative sense."

Eliot says that prose may express ideas but that poetry can only deal with actualities. In this sense, theology is, I think, a combination of prose and poetry, and Eliot's is partly one of sensibility. He never goes beyond what he can feel or has experienced. For example he occasionally mentions the Incarnation, but it and other theological terms appear rarely in the *Four Quartets*, while the *Bhagavadgita* (which Eliot judged second only to *The Divine Comedy* among philosophical poems) is quoted in "Dry Salvages." We know from philosophical reviews which Eliot published a few years before his conversion that he had difficulty in accepting the concept of a personal God, and after his conversion he doubtless continued to have such.

It is at the center of my admiration for Eliot that he is intellectually so honest, and of such integrity, that he cannot feign belief; in a sense acknowledges that such and such a dogma is *de fide* and is not to be contradicted but is also not to be celebrated unless he also feels it.

"Thoughts after Lambeth" at least partly answers a question which "thinking Christians" (a phrase sometimes used by Eliot) must raise—why, becoming a Christian, did Eliot not (like Evelyn Waugh, Dame Edith Sitwell *et al.*) become Roman Catholic? He himself remarks how surprised Anglicans were to have him seek baptism and confirmation. The answer seems, at least in part, that Eliot accepted the Church of England as "the Catholic Church of England," but I find that formula too facile to settle the Anglo-Roman controversy. To Eliot, I cannot but feel, it seemed falsetto that a New England type of American should get nearer to Rome than Anglicanism. Eliot also takes an Anglican line on some practical points like birth control. A close reading of the much dated

"Thoughts" shows Eliot his usual cautious, discriminating self, even in accepting a faith and a Church.

III.

After pondering which should be the noun and which the adjective, I call myself a liberal conservative. I really belong to the Chesterton-Belloc-Tate school of thought, called Distributism, a line of economical and political thought which is neither communism nor capitalism, is indeed represented by no actual political party. I am a regionalist (not only for myself) and an internationalist as well; it is the national state (that nineteenth-century invention) which I abhor.

This position I essentially owe to that cautious, conservative Eliot, whose *Notes towards the Definition of Culture* I admire. Though in an earlier pronouncement Eliot called himself a Monarchist, he elsewhere made it clear that he was not a believer in the Divine Right of kings, or even of installing kings where kings no longer exist. If at one time Eliot seemed to lean towards Fascism in its Mussolinian form, in due time he drew back from all such: seemed merely in favor of a strong, traditional central government which admits regional language and culture.

In his quarterly, *The Criterion*, Eliot sought to take a Pan-European position, representing the best German, French and Italian writers of the time—along with British writers and American. His conception of tradition certainly started with the ancient classics, especially Virgil; and the greatest of writers was for him Dante, upon whom he wrote so memorably.

But Babbitt, it is to be remembered, sought to appeal for sanctions to the Orient as well: for Humanism to Aristotle and Confucius; for religion to Jesus and Buddha (himself more to Buddha). Eliot would certainly object to the latter coupling, for, as a "thinking Christian" having weighed the alternatives, he had chosen not Jesus the ethical Jewish prophet, but Jesus the God-Man, and Christianity an institution with a Church, a theology and a form of worship. But Eliot had studied the Sanskrit religious writings, and the Hindu religion is always referred to with respect. Eliot's treatment of comparative religion claims my own respect. Though Christianity is the supreme religion and also, happily, the form of religion natural to the West, it is not the only "higher religion."

IV.

The figure of Harry in *The Family Reunion* is a figure whom Eliot later rejected as a "prig." The whole character of Harry seems to me, however, Eliot's self-portrait, and his condemnation of himself is characteristic of his guilt-ridden temperament. Did Harry kill his wife or only think he did? This is surely Eliot's feeling about his first wife. Harry's mother, Amy, whom Eliot said later he thought the best character in the play, is a family woman, one who wants to keep her family and its estate intact; she is sorely disappointed, indeed dies of shock, when after being back at home for only three hours, Harry leaves again. When he wrote the play, Eliot obviously thought of himself as, centrally, what he was all his life: a solitary man, a follower of the Negative Way. Like Harry, he had a mission, a vocation.

Ten years after his first wife's death Eliot married again, a devoted woman, his former secretary, much his junior. In his second marriage Eliot was blissfully happy, and he wrote two slight last plays, *The Confidential Clerk* and *The Elder Statesman*—the latter, I think, a heavily veiled autobiographical confession. He had been old as a boy and as a youth; in later years he became, in such a style as an old man can manage, young.

The Church teaches there are two ways of life, two modes of salvation: one is the monastic or celibate life ("if thou wouldst be perfect"); the other is family life with all its responsibilities—life in the world. The early Eliot, indeed almost the lifelong Eliot, was a solitary and an ascetic, and he celebrates the martyrdom of St. Thomas and Celia, who have "chosen the better part." In Eliot's creative work there is marriage but there are no children. We hear their laughter, remembered, but they are corporeally absent, and so is happy family life. The general sense and tone of Eliot's work is somber and austere.

Eliot reaches the heights of his literary criticism in *Selected Essays* (1932; 1936): his best essays are written as essays and not as public lectures. He is at his best when he is most privately pontifical; best when he is the unknown young critic behind the typewriter, not when he is the eminent public figure giving an address before a learned society or a university.

His Christian Humanism does credit to Eliot as a man: like his later literary criticism and his poetry it allows for more than one way of salvation. But, both as a critic and as a poet, Eliot excels when he does not try to transcend his natural asceticism and his natural literary fastidiousness. Eliot was a perfectionist; and it is for his most richly rigid and immaculate work that I venerate him.

(1985)

Pondering Pater: Aesthete and Master

The aesthete is a late-appearing, a decadent type of man—a man who, having the practical basis of life provided, the economic basis, and security, not for the day or the year but for a vague perpetuity, is free to enjoy. The aesthete is one kind of hedonist, of man who can, and does, live for pleasure. But his pleasures are not of the cruder sort, such as gluttony or debauchery, are not indeed sensual, but sensuous—the pleasures of discrimination (Huysmans's *À rebours*), the epicure's pleasures, those of the gourmet in any form, but most especially the pleasures of the connoisseur of the arts of painting, music, ballet (addiction to which is almost a hallmark), of "pure poetry," of art for art's sake. The aesthete is the specialized consumer of the arts, who may spend his daytime resting in order that he may be fresh to receive in all their delicacy the impressions an evening performance, of whatever kind, may give.

Definitions of the aesthete are best neither too brief nor too rigid. There are exclusions, but there are also linkages and overlaps. The aesthete as such is not an artist, a maker, a craftsman, a producer of the beautiful, but a consumer; yet of course the same man may be producer and consumer—*e.g.*, the readers of a writer's writer (a term that today means chiefly a writer regarded by critics as serious) are other writers: Joyce is almost entirely a writer's writer.

Sexually the aesthete generally proves to be a lover, passive or active, of his own kind—a lover of young men. He is an introvert as well as an invert; an indoors, and most likely also a nighttime, man (night being the time when ideas and dreams best flower, with the exclusion of extroverted sunlight and the optional addition of alcohol and drugs).

The aesthete is a dandy in dress and manners (Baudelaire, Wilde, Max Beerbohm); a dandy in literary style even if not in personal décor (Wallace Stevens: the dandy as a poet; Firbank: the dandy as writer of daintily elegant dialogue). And the aesthete's dandyism is pride, not vanity: he dresses, talks, writes, performs for his own mirror-image, his own delectation. He cares no more to impress than to instruct or edify.

The aesthete is, proudly, a dilettante. He shrinks from being professional—which means partly being so good at something that one can earn his living by it. If that is how one defines a dilettante, then obviously most of the serious writers of our time are dilettantes: they earn their livelihood by editing or teaching or the reading circuit, not by their writing.

The aesthete is often identified with the hedonist—that is, one who identifies the good with pleasure, not with, say, duty, or with social usefulness or utility. But the aesthete may hold out for eudaimonism—for happiness as his goal. He is likely to be a solipsist, for whom the only demonstration of existence is his own consciousness, his own sensations and ideas.

He loves artifacts rather than Nature, thinks indeed that it is the artist who gives value to Nature; we see only what art has taught us to see. He is likely to collect artifacts (books, pictures, phonograph records) and to find the meaning of his private existence, his leisure, his solitude, in selecting from among his treasures the single work upon which he is, at this time, to concentrate.

Perception, appreciation, vision, contemplation: these are, in ascending order, the names for the aesthetic experience. As Pater said, it is not the fruit of experience (the generalization, the moral, the wisdom) but the experience itself that is to be prized.

So much for a type portrait of the aesthete, the man who lives for, and in, his sensibility; and whose sensibility is most gratified not by natural objects, but by objects of art and persons. Of course no one is ever perfectly the type; and those aesthetes whose names occur to me are, in addition to their enjoyment of the beautiful, also either collectors and patrons of art and artists, or art experts and curators like Bernard Berenson and Sir Kenneth Clark, or critics of art like Roger Fry and Clive Bell, or writers about art (the highest category) like Ruskin and Pater. Ruskin was also a moralist and an economist, rather a good one; and Pater was a thinker and writer of high distinction, a master in kind.

Now, I turn from the type to Pater, first as a Man and then as a Writer, two portraits that almost merge yet gain from being not quite merged.

Pater as a man is best outlined in the early (1908) two-volume life by Thomas Wright, a stupid, crude, and essentially hostile book, yet one that preserves early stances of Pater otherwise unnoticed: especially the adolescent Anglo-Catholic ritualistic and orthodox piety, that of his Canterbury schooldays, and of his friendship with Dombrain and MacQueen, schoolfriends whose very existence was unknown to A. C. Benson, Pater's authorized biographer; then the Oxford undergraduate period of religious skepticism followed by the young Oxford don's period of flippant yet serious gibing at Christianity in social gatherings of faculty and their wives; finally Pater's late return to ritualistic religion, a religion without the dogma, but flamboyantly represented by Pater's acquaintance with Richard C. Jackson and the St. Austin Friars.

Pater signally tried to suppress, cover up, the overtly, sophisticatedly skeptical period in his life. No critic before me has remarked that; and indeed in *Marius the Epicurean*, the intellectual outlines and the destined patterns of Pater's own development, there is no skeptical, no *blasé* period. Nearest would come the friendship with Flavian (who is called "corrupt"—in unspecified ways); but this friendship is at least dominantly aesthetic, literary. And—a correlative observation—the wit and irony which characterized Pater's conversation in early middle life are completely absent from all periods of his writing. He never learned how to unite the two sharply separate sides of his nature; perhaps he was even repelled by the idea of doing so. This is not a late development but true from the start; the writings, even the earliest ("Diaphanéité" and the early essay on Coleridge), are utterly serious and sincere. This is perhaps to be regretted: a tincture of Wilde's levity would have helped a prose that can become clogged and sweetly cloying, as that of *Marius*, for example, sometimes becomes.

The boy Pater was strict and pious (he loved to play the priest, and to arrange holy processions; and he loved "holy lights, flowers, and incense," his sacred trinity). In "The Child in the House," the first and the germ of his Imaginary Portraits, he sketches the sensitive, chiefly solitary boy he was, perceptively aware of delicate impressions, of light and shadow and fragrances. And he notes the two dominances that go through his life and his writings: beauty and pain, or beauty and death—notes the fugitive character, the fragility of all beauty. In Pater's nature, as we see increasingly in the late writings like "Denys l'Auxerrois" and "Apollo in Picardy," there is an element of algolagnia, the love of pain, a sadomasochism, one side of his passive sensibility. What in Swinburne (an early teacher of Pater's) is overt—what Mario Praz calls the Romantic

Agony—is so clearly present that I cannot doubt Pater's awareness of this element in his nature. At any event he certainly makes no effort, in those latest "portraits" of his, to try to conceal it.

About Pater's sexual nature I think there can be no doubt. He was by temperament a lover (in the Greek style of Socrates, another physically plain man) of young men, especially young athletes and soldiers (like Emerald Uthwart and Cornelius). It is highly improbable that he was a practicing homosexual: in the Oxford of his time, that would have been virtually impossible, and so retired a nature as his would almost certainly, at that point or any near it, have shrunk from such a display of appetite. Another of this kind was A. C. Benson, whose 1907 book on Pater I think far superior to the current estimate of it. David Newsome's excellent *On the Edge of Paradise: A. C. Benson, the Diarist* (1980) makes clear how much the men had the same problems. Benson is never (save for the limits of his period and his profession) evasive. Of Pater, if Benson speaks with great reserve, it is on his own account as well as Pater's—but, as he says accurately, Pater's "secret is told for those that can read it in his writings."

The set, the pattern, the direction of Pater's mind was unique. It was little attracted to things or models English—that is, to literary or artistic monuments. He likes a certain kind of almost dumbly inarticulate and unconscious young Englishman of character (Emerald Uthwart, or the type of Shadwell, the model for "Diaphanéité"); Santayana felt the same attraction: compare his *Soliloquies in England* and *The Last Puritan*. But how strangely absent from Pater is any attraction to the English cathedrals, or to places like Bemerton or Little Gidding, or, for that matter, to men like George Herbert who were at once unneurotic and unique, artists particularly English.

For Pater, devotee of Culture, the models were—as they were, intellectually, for Arnold also (in some ways, along with Ruskin, Pater's distinguished predecessor as proselyte and prosateur)—Germany and France. To them Pater significantly adds Italy—not, however, the Italy of the present but of antiquity and the Renaissance, and not the Italy of literature but of painting, sculpture, and architecture.

Pater began as a scholar of philosophy, centrally of Hegel (so often quoted in the initiatory essay by Pater, the long one on Winckelmann). But then he breaks dramatically, almost histrionically, with the abstractions of philosophy. "Winckelmann," the nearest to an intellectual autobiography Pater ever wrote, describes that predecessor and guide of Goethe as he turns away from the few "colorless books" upon which he has "hungrily fed" at school, and turns toward the plastic, the concrete, the particular, and the sensuous. *Plato and Platonism* (1893), the last book by Pater to be published in his lifetime, is a strange attempt to press even Plato (whose dialogues grow more and more abstract and bloodless) into the cause of the concrete. Pater pleads that the only value of abstractions is to know the relief granted their greyness and bleakness by the delicacy of a rose petal.

The new developments of the physical sciences, including Darwinian evolution, certainly played a significant part in shattering Pater's early development. He read Huxley, Renan, and Comte; became an unawed positivist and contributed to the *Westminster Review*. He also became aware of his solipsism: that man can never really get outside his own consciousness. As he wrote in his famous Conclusion to *The Renaissance*,[1] "experience, already reduced to a group of impressions, is ringed round for each one of us by that thick wall of personality through which no real voice has ever pierced on its way to us, or from us to that which we can only conjecture to be without." His solipsistic conviction finally destroyed for him the validity of any metaphysical system. Epistemology and Ethics remain to him; he is in effect an existential philosopher, to be grouped with Kierkegaard, Nietzsche, and William James: it is to me strange that Pater has not so been recognized. His writings are not—are far from being—just exercises in style; Pater is always painstakingly, painfully saying something really momentous about consciousness and conscientiousness, or observation and meditation.

Pater intensely meant all he said, and meant it with an intensity hard to take in, since his "message" is not something doctrinal, and is even less some call to action. (Action is as absent from Pater's contemplative and solipsistic world as dialogue, except dialogue with oneself.) When Pater calls himself an aesthetic critic and calls for the production of such criticism, he is sharply dissociating himself from any moral or social

---

[1]Title of the first edition (1873) was *Studies in the History of the Renaissance*. Subsequent editions were called *The Renaissance: Studies in Art and Poetry*. See 1893 text.

criticism, with the call of such criticism to do or reform something. Aesthetic criticism expresses the critic's "enjoyment" of a work of art and seeks to share that enjoyment.

Pater also overtly contrasts aesthetic with historic criticism: the former detaches from a work done by past standards its current value, what we can call either its timeless value or its value for the present moment. Pater stresses the latter element, feeling that as soon as one talks about the timeless, as a classicist is wont to do, one is likely to stray away from the immediate direct confrontation of and delectation in the work of art. Pater's aesthetic essays, like his *Marius*, are all, amazingly, written from *now*, and the reader is not allowed to forget that.

To see an object as it is (the Arnoldian phrase quoted in *The Renaissance*) is to see and feel a work of art as Pater, in his time and with his sensibility, sees it. He is dealing with impressions, facts to sensibility; and his desire is to find, in his turn, a "formula" that will sum up in speech the unique quality that his refined sensibility discovers in a painter or a poet or a painting or a poem.

The search for the unique: that is almost the central term for Pater's quest. Of uniqueness he is a connoisseur. Habits and routine dull our perceptions. In this brief life we have time beyond our minimum duties (in Pater's case the don's reception of his scholars and their essays) only for the unique of this moment—a completely hedonistic doctrine. The end of these unique precious experiences is not to use them: "not the fruit of experience but experience itself."

The most famous part of *The Renaissance* (1873), the freshest, most boldly written, brilliant, and influential of Pater's books, is the Conclusion. Though half of the reviewers did not mention it, it struck the attention and the discussion of Sidney Colvin, for example. Before long the chaplain of Brasenose College, John Wordsworth, wrote Pater a frank letter telling him that the Conclusion was contrary to all Christian doctrine and would have a bad influence on the young who read it. The book, especially the heretical Conclusion, was ill received in Oxford, and Pater's Oxford reputation suffered. He was passed over in all the relevant academic promotions, including the professorships of poetry and the fine arts. Pater professed not to feel pain at his rejection; such professions his personal decorum required; but of course he felt them keenly, as he did the satire of him as Mr. Rose in Mallock's *The New Republic* (1876).

What had happened? Was he unaware what bold doctrine he had avowed? Could he possibly have supposed that his real meaning would not be grasped? Had he been brave without properly counting the cost to his academic career? I cannot answer clearly. He had never fitted well into the academic world; later he moved to London to further his other and dearer pursuit, his literary career. But London life didn't quite suit him either: he was too literary for Oxford, and too donnish for London.

Pater withdrew the Conclusion from the second edition of his book, fearing that it might "mislead" some of the young men who read it; his subsequent note, when it was returned to later editions, stated that he had, in *Marius*, made his original meaning clear. This is untrue. In *Marius* a different doctrine is preached. For hedonism is substituted eudaimonism, the search for happiness as the chief goal; and that happiness, that completeness of experience, is indeed so interpreted as to include an undogmatic reception of religion.

Published in 1885, *Marius* was the work of six or seven years, and shows it. Benson, who in his milder way shared something of Pater's dilemma, has written much the best exposition and appraisal of this overlong and overlabored book. Pater meant it as a correction and wiser statement of the bold doctrine he, in his thirty-year-old self-confidence, had brilliantly blurted forth in *The Renaissance*. Pater intended *Marius* to be his masterpiece, but I think it is not. This sensitive and brilliant essayist could not manage a long book. Why should he? The very delicacy, subtlety, and precision with which he writes a sentence, or a paragraph, or at the most a chapter show his talents misplaced in this ampler genre.

Try to summarize the arguments of *Marius*, his book-length essay, and you fail to reproduce all that is characteristic of its best perceptions, thinking, and writing. Even the four parts are too crude as divisions: part 1, Marius's boyhood ancient (pagan) religion, his schooling at Pisa, his early literary preciosity ("Euphuism"), and his friendship with Flavian, the young poet, who (like a true Pater hero) dies young; part 2, Marius's secretaryship to Marcus Aurelius—his Cyrenaic phase, his study of the emperor's Stoicism; part 3, "Second Thoughts," about the adequacy, as life-guides, of the two philosophies—the reaching toward wisdom; part 4, the movement to the way, Christianity.

145

In *Marius* Pater carries on two historical sequences at once. As he says, early in "Second Thoughts," *Marius* is about Marius-like young men at the end of the nineteenth century, whether they be in Paris, London, or Rome. Pater is not a historicist; he is a cyclical thinker, who is drawn to interpret his own time, a *fin de siècle* time of termination and transition, in terms of parallel times in the past: if he did not anticipate a Fall of the British Empire to parallel the Decline and Fall of the earlier empire, still he did see the parallel religious situation, the slow transition from paganism to Christianity (in Pater's time, the reverse was beginning to take place), the many intermediaries and relations. In Elizabethan euphuism he sees the parallel to his own fine art-writing (artistic prose).

It seems impossible to follow securely Pater's serpentine wanderings and reflections. Does Marius cease being an Epicurean (1) as he has "second thoughts" or (2) as he almost becomes Christian? Though I can't answer either question with certainty, I am inclined to say No to both. And (3) in *Marius* has Pater changed his position from that of *The Renaissance* or has he, as he asserts, merely stated more fully what he had meant in the earlier work? Though again I waver in my view, I think Pater has changed—at least widened or amplified his position. "Transcend by including" is, I'm sure, what Pater thought he was doing. In all this there was a certain insincerity or hypocrisy, whether Pater recognized this in himself or not. Certainly Pater, the brilliant young don, had falsely estimated what he could get away with at Oxford, and was pulled up short. But I think that he was really led to reconsider his brash hedonistic Conclusion to *The Renaissance* and to substitute "enlargement of consciousness" for intensity of single vivid experiences.

Part 4 of *Marius* ends with a version of Pater's own final ritualism. From reading his two biographers, Benson and Wright, I cannot decide whether Pater really returned to the faith of his high-church childhood, which would mean that he went to the altar rail in Brasenose Chapel and received the sacrament, or whether he just sat in his decanal stall, or kneeled at least ceremonially, reverently. Most probably the latter. I infer that Pater never regained—never after he became an adult held—any intellectual literal faith in the Apostles' Creed, never accepted the dogmas (existence of God, Incarnation, Trinity, personal immortality). Such an inference is quite compatible with supposing (as I do) that Pater's whole attitude toward religion and the "historic Church," as he characteristically calls it, did substantially change, over the years—after the writing of *The Renaissance*.

Pater observed to a friend that *Marius* was written "to show the necessity of religion." And to Violet Paget, who had written an article outlining three types of rationalistic unbelief—optimistic, pessimistic, and humanitarian—Pater testified that writing *Marius* was "a sort of duty" to him, because "I think that there is a fourth sort of religious phase possible for the modern mind." This fourth phase one might call reverent and hopeful agnosticism—agnosticism which does not close the door to a faith which it cannot prove.

Tradition would be the best single word to express what, in popular culture—and to a certain extent in high culture also—Pater valued. *Continuity* would be another word, and *comprehensiveness* another. This whole tendency in Pater seems inconsistent with his early emphasis on the intensity of an individual aesthetic experience; it represents change and development. They are united only by being (both) aesthetic—in one aspect sensuous. Liturgy, the Christian ritual, is, like the pagan ritual of Marius's childhood, like the ritual of Pater's boyhood, a matter of processions, lights, flowers, and incense. (Why not add music? Apparently because, despite his generalization in aesthetics that all arts aspire to the condition of music, Pater himself lacked interest in music.)

Pater's view of the relation between ritual and religion can almost be summed up as this: Let the ritual persist, while the myth behind it can, may—and will—change. The continuity of society (precious to those sensitive souls who need for their well-being even an external continuity) means stability of the social order, security quite compatible with shifting of dogmas or (those less potent things) philosophical systems.

It is common—and natural—to accuse people who like ritual in church (candles, incense, flowers, colored priestly vestments, and altar hangings) of being, at best, concerned with the externals of religion; and if you think, as Arnold did, that religion is only morality "touched with emotion," these ecclesiastical trappings may seem even antireligious: in one way this is the age-long fight between the prophet and the priest. But there is, I believe, an aesthetic approach to religion which is not only valid so far as it goes but the only one available to some, probably many, people. In his "Symposium" Plato teaches the ascent from beautiful bodies to the idea of the beautiful; through intermediate degrees the sensuous can lead to the supersensuous, the Idea of the Beautiful. And Catholic Christianity is sacramental and incarnational: the divine is incarnate in man; in the sacraments an ideal reality assumes material manifestation. What is the whole religion of symbolism but an expansion, an extension, of the sacramental system? Every material object is a correspondence of some spiritual essence. The soul never appears, is never known, naked: it is always clothed, vested. We approach the soul through the body, through the senses.

I put all this flatly, matter-of-factly. But to Pater all this was flaming, fighting doctrine. Having started his intellectual life a student of Greek and especially of German philosophy, and having then (probably during that memorable first tour of Italy) turned from the philosophy of Germany to the visual art of Italy, he felt a kind of anger at having been so long misled. When Pater returns, from his youthful skepticism and irony, to some kind of acceptance of religion, he thinks of religion as an orderly sequence of sensuous objects dimly symbolizing spiritual truths, but not to be skipped over as though they were mere signs.

Why could Pater not entirely dismiss the Church and churchly religion for very long—not for more than ten or fifteen years? First of all I have to think of the solipsistic doctrine so painfully put in the famous Conclusion—that memorable passage about how walled in, how insulated each of us is. We can't prove the existence of anything outside of our own consciousness—not even the "existence of other selves" (to cite F. H. Bradley). Solipsism is an epistemological problem: how do we know, how can we know, anything outside the self? And, as Hume will add, how do we know there is a self beneath all our momentary impressions? But solipsism is more than an intellectual problem: it names the emotional chill of feeling isolated, not by passing circumstances, but by the very nature of things.

Pater's deep sense of isolation, of inability to communicate, reaches out for community; and the "historic Church," through its ritual, gave him at least the illusion of belonging to a group, a sense that, for him, neither State nor University offered. And in part 3 of *Marius* we see this "hero" reaching out toward a theistic belief that he is not alone in the world, that there is an Unseen Companion (a kind of spiritual double) walking beside him. And then in part 4 I note Pater's emphasis on the "blitheness," the cheerfulness, the gaiety, of the Christians he meets through Cornelius, the ideal young soldier, and the life of Hope which pervades the Christian community. Though Pater never reached that Hope, he envies it, and connects it with the Christian church.

Pater knew of attempts—on the part of the Anglo-Catholic clergy as well as men like Maurice and of course the positivists—to preach and initiate social reform. And, since Pater read and almost began his own career as an aesthetic critic by reading Ruskin's *Modern Painters*, he must have been acquainted with Ruskin's later teachings in *Unto This Last*—and must have known something about the social teachings of William Morris, to whose poetry he had devoted an essay. But really Pater has nothing to say to, or about, economic and social equality. He seems to take it for granted that the poor will always be with us, and he is concerned only with giving the poor the temporary relief of beauty—a flower or a stained-glass window. Pain cannot be abolished: it can only be temporarily assuaged, alleviated.

Pater is so much of an elitist that he never seems to feel any guilt at his standing, however modestly, on what Forster in *Howards End* calls "the gold island," that island on which people who attend concerts and read highbrow books and frequent picture-galleries obviously must stand (unlike Leonard Bast, who vainly hungers for "the best that has been thought and said in the world"). To be sure, to be an aesthete you don't have to be rich (at no time in his life was Pater that), but you have to have a minimal start in the world even to be an Oxford man on a scholarship.

The intellectual progress, the argument, or the dialectic (no one of these terms fits) which occupies the middle section of *Marius* (part 3 particularly) is the most serious and engaging part of the book. It's a philosophical discussion of an existential sort. Pater is an antiphilosophical philosopher (like Kierkegaard and Nietzsche): once attracted by philosophy, he seems to feel that it wasted his time, misled him. He now is the foe of abstraction. But you can't talk about silence except in words; nor can you attack philosophy except by being abstract. Pater never really solves this problem: he ends up an amateur.

Pater's *Guardian* reviews—of Amiel's Journal, and of *Robert Elsmere* —try to define what he meant by a fourth phase, a sophisticated modern view which could be taken toward religion. This view invokes sympathy with—a reverent, sympathetic agnosticism toward—"the historic Church," as Pater repeatedly called it. (This reminds me of the phrases I used to hear about the "historic episcopate" and the "historic creed.") The word *historic* here is a weasel word that does not assert the truth or validity; it only suggests a certain—and valued—continuity.

There is a minor but real relation between Pater and Newman, a generation earlier. Like Arnold, Pater admired Newman—as a stylist certainly; but also—for Pater was a thinker as well as a literary man—he admired Newman as a type of original thinker. In his early *Westminster* essay "Coleridge as a Theologian" (1866) Pater speaks of Newman: "How often in the higher class of theological writings—writings which really spring from an original religious genius, such as those of Dr. Newman—does the modern aspirant to perfect culture seem to find the expression of the immortal delicacies of his own life, the same yet different." Christian spirituality "has often drawn men on little by little into the broader spiritualities of systems opposed to it—pantheism, or positivism, or a philosophy of indifference." That earlier meaning he found in the sacred we find today in any artist or philosopher.

A possible relation may exist between the *Apologia* and *Marius*: for *Marius* is Pater's reply to the attacks on *The Renaissance*, in which he tries (Newman-like) to review the habits of thought and of feeling that underlie, and lead up to, what seems put dogmatically and too briefly in the famous Conclusion (which in a way stands like the dogmas to which Newman subscribed). In Newman's case Kingsley doubted his sincerity; we may not doubt Pater's, but Pater expressed himself with an uncharacteristic and melodramatic bravado.

Pater's uninvitingly named *Miscellaneous Studies* (1895), a posthumous collection, gives the best idea of his scope: Pascal, Raphael, Art Notes in Northern ("cis-Alpine") Italy, but also the delicately autobiographical "The Child in the House" and "Apollo in Picardy." This book one can pick up at any time and read a few pages in, opening even at random. What does that tell one about Pater, and his characteristic virtues? Much, I think. His characteristic virtue is closeness of attention, concentration, on what he is saying and (but only incidentally) on how he is saying it. (To call him a stylist seems to imply that he has nothing to say, which is untrue.) But what he has to say is not a broad generalization which can be taken in as you speed-read it. The Conclusion, I'm afraid, can—even if improperly—be so read; but it is uncharacteristic.

150

The kind of thing Pater wants to say is a fabric, a tissue, of qualifications, hesitations, reserves, modulations, hints—something said half, but only half, restricted to what can be said by nuances.

This makes Pater in much of *Marius*—say, in "Second Thoughts," perhaps the deepest and subtlest chapter of the book—hard to understand. Pater ponders. It is thought-feeling, or felt-thought, intellectual sensibility which is his *métier*. But I apprehend all along that he is trying to be precise, not vague—aiming at precision, though the materials with which he works are filmy and fragile.

Pater teaches one attention, concentration, the scrupulous analysis of one's own mental and affective states. Continuity, the broad long straight line, is not Pater's strength. How can it be? He has the defects of his virtues, his virtues being for the minute, the delicate, the detailed.

Walter Pater was a man born with a Word to utter, and he uttered it. Almost from the start he knew what he wanted to say and how to say it: groping and fumbling are amazingly absent, after he had destroyed his early pious poetry. It is perhaps to be regretted that he didn't find some way of incorporating his satire and irony, his sharp, wry, negative note, into his harmony, but only perhaps. His tone is pure rather than rich, though here words "slip and slide," for in another sense he is a cloyingly rich and sweet writer. This purity, or singleness, was of a richness that had to exclude the tart and the acid. That is his formula, his essence.

(1983)

William Law: Ascetic and Mystic

In many ways, the eighteenth century was like our own. Joseph Butler wrote, in the "Advertisement" to the first edition of his famous *Analogy* (1736), "It is come, I know not how, to be taken for granted by many persons that Christianity is not so much as a subject for inquiry, but that it is now at length discovered to be fictitious. And accordingly they treat it as if, in the present age, this were an agreed point among all people of discernment and nothing remained but to set it up as a principal subject of mirth and ridicule, as it were by way of reprisals for its having so long interrupted the pleasures of the world."

In England, the eighteenth century was the age of the "Enlightenment," of "reason," of common sense and easy compromise. And the Church was the profession for a gentleman, the younger son of a landed family, who needed no other qualifications for his office than an education at Oxford or Cambridge and the absence of an openly scandalous life; it involved no claims or aspirations to devoutness, still less to sanctity. The Anglican priest was an official of the state, just as the Anglican layman was an Anglican precisely and only because he was a loyal Englishman. "Enthusiasm," the being "filled with God," was viewed by clergy and people alike as being un-English—fanatical or at least whimsical and "peculiar," like the Papists, the Methodists, the Quakers, and those "lesser breeds," the Seekers, the Anabaptists, and the Ranters.

In such times, the danger to the Church is not persecution by pagans or atheists but the flattery and compliance of the world. No longer beheaded or otherwise martyred, "Christians" are publicly honored for their compromise with Caesar and Mammon, with the powers that be. The enemies of the Church are within. Those Christians who are loyal to their principles are spiritual heroes and saints, admired by almost all, though followed by very few. Such men in the eighteenth century were Bishop Butler, Samuel Johnson, John Wesley, and William Law, Anglican saints who kept the faith in difficult times. It is not strange that these men, especially Butler and Johnson, were somber, even melancholy, of temperament; that Law was an austere and religious moralist till he became a mystic; that all were sober and cautious thinkers. And, living when they did, these men had to be "inner-directed," quietly independent thinkers who had, like Pascal, Kierkegaard, and Simone Weil, to examine the very foundations of their faith.

William Law (1686–1761), born in King's Cliffe, a village of Northamptonshire, was a graduate of Emmanuel College, Cambridge, which, in the reign of Elizabeth, had been a nursery of Puritanism, English and American, and which, in the early seventeenth century, had been the center of the Cambridge Platonists—Whichcote, Cudworth, Henry More, and John Smith. It is strange that Law never mentions these men of an earlier generation at his own college. The reason is probably their churchmanship, which was Puritan while his was High Church; for, being moralists, and, two of them, mystical philosophers, they should have had a strong appeal for him.

A serious young man, Law, before he set out for Cambridge in 1705, drew up a set of "Rules for My Future Conduct" which reminds one of the "Resolutions" young Jonathan Edwards drew up for himself. Among Law's "Rules" are these: "To avoid all concerns with the world, or the ways of it, except when religion requires." "To remember frequently, and to impress it upon my mind deeply, that no condition of this life is for enjoyment but for trial; and that every power, ability, or advantage we have are all so many talents to be accounted for to the Judge of the whole world." "To avoid all excess in eating and drinking." "To be always fearful of letting my time slip away without some fruit." "To avoid all idleness." Time must not be wasted. If he says nothing about money, it is probably because he then had none; but in *A Serious Call*, waste of money becomes almost as important as that of time: "voluntary poverty" becomes a definite part of his mature scheme for Christian living. The "Rules" continue: "To think humbly of myself, and with great charity of all others." "To think often of the life of Christ, and propose it as a pattern to myself." "To spend some time in giving account of the day, previous to evening prayer: how have I spent this day? What sin have I committed? What temptations have I withstood? Have I performed all my duty?" Characteristic words are "sin" and "idleness," "duty" and "Judge." These are ascetic notes, all essentially negative. "The fear of the Lord is the beginning of wisdom." But where are the peace and joy of the spiritual life? They lie far ahead, but eventually they are to be attained.

Law took his B.A. in 1708. In 1711 he was elected to a fellowship of his college, but in 1716 he resigned it, finding himself conscientiously unable to take the oath of allegiance to the Hanoverian George I. He was ordained a priest by Nonjuring Bishop Gandy in 1711. Law belonged to the second generation of the Nonjurors, that group of High Church men who, believing that the Stuarts were by Divine Right the legitimate monarchs of England, refused to take the oath of allegiance to William and Mary and to the Hanoverian Georges. This Nonjuring schismatic Church, far more Catholic-minded in doctrine and liturgy than the Establishment, continued in England and especially in Scotland, where Jacobite sympathies were strong, well into the latter part of the eighteenth century; and it was the bishops of the Nonjuring Episcopal Church of Scotland who, in 1784, ordained Samuel Seabury as the first prelate of the American Episcopal Church.

This stance, at once political and religious, of the Nonjuror, made it impossible for Law to hold any university or church appointment. Like other Nonjuring priests, he had to earn his living as a tutor, private chaplain, or writer. Between 1716 and 1740 he was all three. For ten years, he was the tutor, at Putney in Surrey, of Edward Gibbon, the father of the great historian. "In our family," writes the sceptical historian, "he left the reputation of a worthy and pious man who believed all he professed and practiced all that he enjoined."

About 1740, Miss Hester Gibbon, the historian's aunt, and Mrs. Hutcheson, a rich and pious widow, took a house in Law's native village, King's Cliffe, and the celibate Law joined them as their spiritual director and chaplain. This small household, a kind of "Protestant nunnery," resembled the family community of Nicholas Ferrar at Little Gidding and continued that seventeenth-century experiment in "holy living" into the eighteenth century, forming a link between it and the revival of the monastic life after the Oxford Movement of the nineteenth century. The members of the household at King's Cliffe pursued a "regular" and methodical regime, assembling three times a day, morning, noon, and evening, for corporate prayers. With money given him by an anonymous benefactor, a grateful reader of his writing, Law had earlier founded a school for poor girls, who were taught to read, knit, and sew, and to study the catechism and attend church service regularly. Mrs. Hutcheson added another school and almshouses. Of their large joint income they

155

lived on a tenth and gave the rest away. The three gave clothes and soups and money to the poor. They were, indeed, so generous in their charity, and so uncritical of the merits of applicants for it, that King's Cliffe gained, it is said, a reputation for attracting the idle and the worthless. The time of the little community was divided between pious exercises and "works of mercy."

Law rose at five, and spent much of the day in a small study occupied at his reading and writing. He was already absorbed in writing meditations on the works of Boehme, which he had begun to read some seven years before. But he possessed, besides these works, a large and choice library of other mystical books. He wrote, "I thank God I have always been a diligent reader of those mystical divines through all the ages of the Church, from the apostolic Dionysius the Areopagite down to the great Fénelon, Archbishop of Cambray. . . ." Deeply attracted to the Desert Fathers, he owned *Les Vies des Saints Pères des Déserts* and the *Spiritual Homilies* of Saint Macarius of Egypt; he owned also the medieval mystics, Ruysbroeck (his copy of the *Opera Omnia* is underlined and evidently much read), and Tauler (both in Latin and German), and the *Theologica Germanica*, which he valued highly and recommended to the more advanced among his disciples. He knew well the *Imitation of Christ* and Saint Francis of Sales's *Introduction à la Vie Dévote*, the Catholic counterpart of the *Serious Call*. His spiritual life was nourished by the books of his spiritual ancestors, and by what nourished them as well as him, a life centered in prayer and meditation.

Though Quakers, actual or virtual, can find warrant for their views in Law's writings, Law lived and died an Anglican. Ready to find testimony to the truth in Papist and Protestant writings, and at the end an ecumenical spirit, he was unwilling to separate himself from the specific regional church into which he was born. And though as a matter of private conscience a Nonjuror, he took no part in the characteristic Nonjuring activities, which were markedly liturgical enrichments or attempted reunion with Eastern Orthodoxy. Instead, with the two ladies under his direction, he attended all the services at the parish church of King's Cliffe, this despite the fact that he and the resident rector were not on personally friendly terms.

Law's *Serious Call* (1728), his second book, which was written at Putney, has received all manner of encomia. When Samuel Johnson went to Oxford, he picked it up "expecting to find it a dull book (such books generally are) and perhaps to laugh at it. But I found Law quite an overmatch for me." Boswell, who reports this saying, adds, "From this time forward, religion was the dominant object of his thoughts." Dr. Johnson later pronounced the *Call* "the finest piece of hortatory theology in any language." In 1789 John Wesley speaks of it as a "treatise which will hardly be equalled in the English tongue, either for beauty of expression or for justice and depth of thought"; and in his *Christian Liberty* of fifty volumes, published in 1749, he included abridged versions of both *Christian Perfection* and *A Serious Call*—as well as, later, in 1768, two volumes of extracts from Law's later writings, including the final *Address to the Clergy, The Spirit of Prayer*, and *The Spirit of Love*. But the highest tribute is probably that from Leslie Stephen, who in his *English Thought in the Eighteenth Century* says *A Serious Call* "may be read with pleasure even by the purely literary critic"; but its "power can only be adequately felt by readers who can study it on their knees."

This book is substantially as readable and as pertinent today as it was when it was written. The most entertaining parts are the "characters" which portray permanent human types: The shrewd businessman, the man of fashion, the easygoing clergyman, the literary scholar, the cultivated dilettante, the worldly and unworldly women are all still with us. In these portraits, and in the literary skill with which Law draws them, Law was in a great tradition going back to the Greek writer Theophrastus and down through the French La Bruyère, to whom he has been likened, and the English "character" writers, Overbury, Earle, and Thomas Fuller— especially in his *Holy and Profane State*; Law's "characters," like those of La Bruyère, carry Latin and Greek names as signs of their being traditional types—Miranda (wonderful), Flavia (extravagant), Calidus (cold and wasteful), Penitens (penitent), Mundanus (worldly), Faltus (sanguine), Succus (dispirited), Eusebius or Eusebia (reverent), Paternus (fatherly). Among these, there are few persons downright evil, and but a very few who are wise and saintly; most of them are at neither pole but in between, compromisers between the Spirit and the World, the Laodiceans of Revelation; and it is these compromisers, ordinary, normal, well-adjusted members of society, who are Law's chief and most effec-

157

tive butts. The keen knowledge of the human types which Law displays was based upon his years at the Gibbon estate at Putney—the family and their middle-class guests, businessmen and their wives; on his visits to nearby London (where he later lived for a few years); on his memories of the university, with its assembly of Fellows at once scholars and clergymen; and lastly on his knowledge of his own heart.

"Enter in at the strait gate" is Law's virtual maxim and motto. He admits no comfortable distinction between the Counsels of Perfection enjoined by the Sermon on the Mount, by which monks are to live, and the accommodations permitted by Roman Catholics to lay people living in the world, who are to keep the Ten Commandments of the Mosaic law and the commandments of the Church but nothing more rigid. Law knows of no "two ways" of life. He takes the Counsels of Perfection as applying to all who "profess and call themselves Christians," and makes no real distinction between priests and their parishioners except what might be termed an occupational one: All are alike called to holiness. "Be ye perfect, even as your Father in Heaven in perfect." Law seems ever mindful of him whom he calls "the young gentleman in the gospel"—the rich young ruler who came to Jesus in search of eternal life, the ruler who, having kept the Commandments from his youth up, was still lacking peace, but, because he could not bring himself to sell all his goods, went away sorrowful. Law does not interpret this as dividing those called to the "religious" life (with its poverty, chastity, and obedience) from those who follow only the Commandments but as dividing true Christians from nominal adherents.

No more than Jesus will Law allow compromise between God and the world. "Ye cannot serve God and Mammon." "No man can serve two masters." There can be no peace of mind for the half-hearted, for those whose eye is not single. Law takes his stand upon such texts from the New Testament; and though he quotes the Epistles of Saint Paul, chiefly from the mystical passages, for example, "Not I live, but Christ liveth in me," he chiefly quotes the sayings of Jesus—the sayings, not the narrative of his life, or his miracles, or the facts of his birth or Resurrection; and he seek to exposit and apply the spirit of Jesus' unequivocal teaching.

A Serious Call is written in a style plain, manly, and "nervous" (in the eighteenth-century sense of sinewy), to be paralleled, among Restoration writers, perhaps by Isaac Barrow; among his contemporaries, by Swift; among his successors, by Johnson in his *Rambler* essays. Law writes like the clear and forcible thinker he is. He is often witty, never for show but for point. Thus he speaks of "Mundanus" as always busy improving the "clearness and strength of his understanding," yet still praying the same "little form of words" which, when he was six years old, he was used to say, night and morning, at his mother's knee; and, of "Classicus," that, though he is so versed in "the best authors of antiquity" that he can "very ingeniously imitate the manner of any of them," yet "the two Testaments would not have so much as a place among his books but that they are both to be had in Greek."

A "devout and holy life," Law makes clear in his very first chapter, is not primarily one of churchgoing or pious exercises. "Prayers whether private or public are particular parts or instances of devotion. Devotion signifies a life given, or devoted to God." "It is very observable that there is not one command in all the gospel for public worship; and perhaps it is a duty that is less insisted upon in scripture than of any other. The frequent attendance at it is never so much as mentioned in all the New Testament. . . . Our blessed Savior and His Apostles are wholly taken up in doctrines that relate to common life."

There are three classes of people whom Law addresses—the clergy, aristocrats and gentlefolk, and "tradesmen"—the bourgeois; and Law never wearies in pointing out that the same general principles apply to the life of them all, though he addresses advice to each class. "Let a clergyman be . . . pious, and he will . . . no more talk of noble preferment than of noble eating or a glorious chariot." The "gentlemen of birth and fortune . . . does not ask what is allowable and pardonable but what is commendable and praiseworthy." "Let a tradesman have this intention, and it will make him a saint in his shop." But all must, if they would be true Christians, live by method and rule, wasting neither time nor money. "You see one person throwing away his time in sleep and idleness, in visiting and vain diversions. . . . You see another careful of each day, dividing his hours by rules of reason and religion. . . ." Certainly "scrupulous anxiety" is wrong, but we should have "a just fear of living in sloth and idleness"; he "that has begun to live by rule has gone a great way toward the perfection of his own life." And for a summary epigram, "It is better to be holy than to have holy prayers."

159

It is the world which, more than the flesh or the Devil, is the chief enemy of true Christians. It "was the spirit of the world that nailed our Lord to the cross." "The world, to be sure, now professes Christianity, but will anyone say this Christian world is of the spirit of Christ?" Indeed, the world "has, by its favors, destroyed more Christians than ever it did by the most violent persecutions." Law applies this practically by remarking how afraid a man is of not advancing his wealth and his ownership of great houses and fine clothes "lest the world should take him for a fool" and how "many a man would drop resentment and forgive an affront but that he is afraid, if he should, the world would not forgive him."

As a spiritual teacher, Law is a master of Christian seriousness, in this respect at least the equal of Kierkegaard, whose *Training in Christianity* has been called the closest parallel to *A Serious Call*. Law is, like Kierkegaard, the exposer of the futility—and danger—of compromise in all its manifold forms. But while Kierkegaard affords extrareligious pleasure, by his brilliant analysis of such neurotic states as anxiety and by his little parabolic narratives, and flatters the pride of the reader who can follow his subtleties, Law affords no such flattery; he lays bare and flays one's innermost motives, the motives by which one lives. He recalls a man to his adolescence, when right and wrong, sin and holiness, seemed sharply differentiated and there was no either-or; he exposes equivocations and half-truths, saying "but one thing is needful."

And yet: with all his genuine ecumenism, his revolt against sectarianism, his catholic elevation beyond and above even the distinction between "Papist and Protestant," between which Western Christendom is divided, he is still too narrow to be truly catholic. One cannot but contrast him with Bishop Jeremy Taylor, who, in his *Holy Living* and *Holy Dying*, quotes almost as much from the Greek Stoics as from the Jewish Scriptures, Old and New; and with the Cambridge Platonists of the English seventeenth century; and with their greater ancestors, the Christian Platonists of Alexandria; and with the Russian Orthodox thinkers who, writing in the nineteenth and twentieth centuries, are debtors both to speculative philosophy and to a long tradition of liturgical and mystical piety; and with Fénelon, Maritain, and Baron von Hügel— all great Christian Humanists. What is Christian—or spiritual—Humanism but the reconciliation of three deeply essential movements of man's spirit, at every time likely to split asunder: learning, or erudition; poetry, or culture; and high religion? It can't honestly be claimed that the Jesus of the Synoptic Gospels reconciled these three; yet the author of the Fourth Gospel and Saint Paul began to do so, and a rich and long-continued tradition holds that the wisdom of "pagan" aspiration is completed and fulfilled, but not cancelled, by Christian "revelation."

It is in the light of this Christian Humanist tradition that Law seems an obscurantist. He abrogates human reason, human learning, and human culture (literature and the arts) in the name of true religion. Not a Fundamentalist in the sense of an adherent to an infallible Bible literally read, he is one in his attitude toward humanistic culture, the servant and complement of religion.

According to the traditional wisdom of Christian Humanism, in things religious and moral, some things are commanded, some recommended, some permitted, and some forbidden. Between the commanded and the forbidden, there is, for Catholic casuists, a middle ground governed by the old classical principles of decorum and moderation. Pascal accused the Jesuits of laxity in what they permitted; Jonathan Edwards and Law are rigorists for whom there is really no middle ground between virtue and vice. The latter find, too, no middle ground between industry and sloth, no "innocent" amusements or "play"; and, in so ruling, they virtually rule out the fine arts—not only the theater but painting, all music except hymn tunes, and literature—poetry and the novel: in a word, culture. And they rule out card and all other games, and dancing, and sports and other athletic exercises, performances, and entertainments. The bow must always be taut, never relaxed.

The impression must not be given, however, that Law is either a dour fanatic or an advocate of ascetic extremes. He is very English in his sobriety. He does not advocate, like the Shakers, universal celibacy. Marriage is to go on, and families are to be reared. Virtuous women have their choice of marriage or a "virgin state." His ideal of family life seems that which became familiar in the nineteenth century among Quakers, Wesleyans, and other Non-Conformists, and some High Anglicans. Nor does he want to attack "right reason" (the rational) or "happiness," but indeed to show, as he undertakes to do in chapter 11 of *A Call*, that great devotion fills our life with "the greatest peace and happiness," while their enemy, the "passions, in rebellion against God and reason, fill human life with imaginary wants." The holy life is also the happy life.

If one asks whether Law's picture of the holy life seems a happy one, an attractive one, the answer must be that such a life cannot be viewed, still less judged, from outside. To a neurotic, a normal life seems commonplace and dull, without excitement; a neurotic, under therapy, fights to retain his anxieties, without which, so he thinks, he will not feel alive, will not feel himself: He is asked to find a new center. To a man of the world, a life either of study or of good works is a boring one. Both the neurotic and the man of the world must be converted, turned around, born again, before they can judge of the happiness proposed by a holy life. To both, the saints in the *Paradiso* are far less individuated and less piquant than the sinners in the *Inferno*. Sanctity has its own leveling, a leveling, however, at the highest elevation.

Law's two practical and devotional treatises, *Christian Perfection* (1726) and *A Serious Call* (1728), were preceded and followed by polemic works, published between 1717 and 1740, good accounts of which are given in the critical histories by Stephen and Elton (see the bibliography). In 1717, in *Three Letters to the Bishop of Bangor* (Dr. Hoadly), Law defended the apostolic succession of the bishops and the spiritual authority of the Church against an Erastian prelate asserting the ecclesiastical supremacy of the state. In 1723, he attacked Mandeville's *Fable of the Bees*, which proclaimed that "private vices were public benefits." In 1726, he maintained *The Absolute Unlawfulness of the Stage-Entertainment*, the theater of the Restoration. In 1731, he replied to Tindal's Deistic book *Christianity not Mysterious* with his *Case of Reason and Natural Religion Fairly and Fully Stated*. And lastly, Dr. Trapp being the enemy addressed, he assailed that fellow-Anglican's book *Folly, Sin and Danger of being Righteous Over-much*. In short, Law took on all the enemies of the orthodox Anglican Church, whether theoretical or practical; and he is credited with having argued forcibly and with acute, persistent logic.

But meanwhile Law was himself undergoing a deep change. He lost faith in the use of the external historical evidences for Christianity, which

162

at best reached the reason and left the heart unaffected. Even intellectual orthodoxy came to seem an affair not at the center of things, any more than correct ritual. What mattered was a change of heart, a new and regenerate holy life; and having reached this conclusion, he gave up arguing and addressed himself to testifying, persuading, converting. It is a commonplace that polemic works date rapidly, while ascetic and mystical works remain fresh. And, though Law was without literary ambition, this has happened to his own books.

In his years of controversy, between *A Serious Call* and *The Spirit of Prayer* and *The Spirit of Love*, Law accepted the standard "evidences" of the Christian apologist, the fulfillment of Old Testament prophecy and the miracles wrought by Christ and His Apostles. But these finally came to seem to him external, as not touching the inner reality of the spiritual life. One could know all the arguments, defend them intellectually, and still live like other people. As Jesus says of giving presents to your friends (as we all do at Christmas, the reputed date of his birth), "Do not even the Gentiles do the same?" The mark of the Christian is that he gives to the undeserving and to those hostile to him.

All of Law's mystical writings were composed at King's Cliffe in that semimonastic retirement into which he withdrew at the age of fifty-four. There, living in a country village, he continued to live by rule and method, alternating study and meditation and writing with his practical office as almoner, writing letters to a few spiritually-minded friends, seeing a few friends like Dr. Byrom and Mr. Langcake. His later writing, in all of which he expressed his admiration for and indebtedness to Boehme, alienated him from former admirers like John Wesley, who attacked him in a printed *Letter*, and Dr. Johnson, as well as, in our century, from that great French historian of Christian spirituality Fr. Louis Bouyer, who says of these books that, though they "contain passages of high spirituality, Boehme's bizarre genius here turns into a very British kind of mild dottiness." On the other hand, Aldous Huxley, author as well as compiler of that remarkable book *The Perennial Philosophy*, who probably quotes more passages from Law than any other writer—passages of "high spirituality"—holds the later writings in highest esteem and regards their author as "not only a master of English prose" but as "one of the most endearingly saintly figures in the whole history of Anglicanism."

Law certainly damaged his general reputation in his own time by his loyal and dogged adherence to Boehme, who he variously calls "illumined" and "blessed"; of whom he says, in *The Spirit of Love*, "the mystery of all things [was] opened by God in his chosen instrument Jacob Boehme." What is to it be "illumined"? What status did Law assign to Boehme? Not of equal authority with scripture, we may safely suppose. Why then was he of more authority than any other mystic, such as Fénelon's friend and inspiration Mme. Guyon, whom on one occasion Law also called "illumined"? The word had a special technical meaning in the seventeenth and eighteenth centuries, shifting though that meaning was. It signified one with claims to esoteric knowledge through "openings," visions, or private revelations. Boehme had three or four such openings, during the earliest of which he said he learned more in a quarter of an hour than he could have learned in all the universities. It was on the basis of these brief openings, and the insights they gave him, that he constructed his philosophy.

To accept these visions and their authority, Law was already prepared by a lifelong sympathy with mysticism. What such sympathy requires is belief in two things—the possibility of union with God, temporary or permanent, in this life, and the belief that religious inspiration or revelation did not stop with the end of the New Testament, but continues, as the Holy Ghost discloses truths which the world was not earlier ready to understand. Both of these beliefs Law appears to hold.

He is said to have begun his reading of Boehme—or Behmen, as he calls him—about 1734. Why did Law so avidly seize upon the writings of the seventeenth-century German shoemaker when all his life he had been acquainted with the great line of mystics from Dionysius the Areopagite down to Fénelon, the apostle of pure love?

My first answer is that it was exactly the humble status of Boehme and his supposed absence of book learning which attracted Law. I say "supposed," for modern studies show that, thanks to the erudition of his more highly placed friends, Boehme was versed in Paracelsus and the spiritual alchemists and in pietisic theologians like Weigel. But Law must have thought of him as taught directly by God through his own intuitions, a mystic in the most exact sense, and thus the direct opposite of the bishops and scholars like Hoadly and Warburton, who, exegetes and reasoners, spoke by hearsay.

Most deeply, however, Law was attracted to Boehme because the shoemaker combined Evangelical theology with speculative theories about ultimate realities, and Law felt the need of a framework for his own thinking—a framework both intellectual and imaginative which can be called either a myth or a system—a framework indeed conceptual-imaginative. He needed a philosophy of religion, and this Boehme provided him with. Though he did not like his views called a "philosophy," such they were.

The system of Boehme can here neither be given adequate exposition nor yet entirely omitted; it can but be sampled. Its speculative theology is divided, by his most thorough modern expositor, into "Good beyond Nature and Creature: Theogony," "Eternal Nature," and "Temporal Nature"; only after these do we reach "Man" and "Redemption." It is in the first two of these that Boehme is most original. God begins as the Godhead, an Abyss, an *Ungrund*; then develops a Will; then comes a Trinity of Persons; then a fourth person is added, Sophia, or Divine Wisdom, a female principle named and characterized in *Proverbs* and the *Wisdom of Solomon*. Between these persons there is a "love-play": Wisdom acts as a mirror in which the ultimate God comes to consciousness.

Nature, first imagined, becomes actual through the operation of the Seven Natural Properties, so often dwelt upon or mentioned by Law—a dark ternary and a light ternary, the intermediate fourth between the two ternaries being fire, the lightning flash. First comes Desire, or contradiction, which is harsh and hard; then Movement or expansion; then (born out of the conflict of the first two) Anguish or rotation. The lightning flash, or contact between Nature and Spirit, transfigures the dark ternary into the light which consists of: the fifth property, Wisdom or love-fire; the sixth, intelligible sound; and the seventh, Essential Wisdom. Law is concerned only with the first three, which characterize the unrest of the physical world and the unrest of man's restless, desirous nature.

This is heady stuff but it satisfied the hitherto undeveloped speculative part of Law, though he did not immediately find it easy going. He writes: "When I first began to read him [Boehme], he put me into a perfect sweat. But as I discerned sound truths and glimmerings of a deep ground of sense even in passages not then clearly intelligible to me, I found in myself a strong incentive to dig in these writings, I followed the impulse . . . till at length I discovered the wonderful treasure that was hid in this field." The reader of Law's later writings will remember this passage and take heart.

Most of *The Spirit of Love*, like its predecessor (to which Law calls it an "Appendix"), *The Spirit of Prayer*, also nominally in dialogue form, is difficult to read, not taken sentence by sentence, or paragraph by paragraph, but as a whole. In contrast to the *Call*, these works lack any clearly defined method of organization or logical progression. Called "dialogues," they come nearest to being monologues of a rhapsodic kind. Later, Law lived for the most part a quiet and solitary life. His habitual companions were two women and a few men, not his equals in character or intellect, his disciples, to whom he discoursed. This absence of method, associated in his mind perhaps with his increasing distrust of reasoning and criticism, makes his later works prolix and repetitious; and it is doubtless for that reason that they are better known today in the form of selected passages (such as those anthologized by Scott Palmer and Hobhouse, and Aldous Huxley) than they are as a whole. Yet at least one of them, and preferably the shorter, *The Spirit of Love*, should be read as a whole for the sake of the ecstatic flow of Law's own spirit, which desires to break all its trammels, to move at will among the grandest themes—the fall of man, or man's redemption, the creation of the universe and its apocalyptic reunion and transfiguration.

In literary style, the Law of these later works was what literary historians used to call a "pre-Romantic." His prose style still largely uses abstract words, but he uses them to different effect; and nature breaks into his consciousness, even though he lacks the specific natural imagery which is so characteristic of Romantic poets. His sentences become longer and looser, one clause or phrase added to another; all rigidity dissolves. The man is less talking than meditating, and addressing himself rather than any audience, willing to be overheard but adapting his discourse only to those who (unlike the readers supposed by the *Call*) are already eager to hear, and near conversion to the "heavenly doctrines" the master proposes. The modern reader should endeavor to let Law glide into his soul; put the book down for a time when he finds it boring; take it up again. The total effect will be larger than the sum of such intermittent reading.

166

We speak of the mystical writings of Law. What was their authority? Law made no claim ever to immediate inspiration, to visions or auditions such as those of Saint Paul, Saint Teresa, or Julian of Norwich. He had no known period of ecstasy like that after which Saint Thomas Aquinas wrote no more on his *Summa Theologica*. I see no clear evidence that he was an actual mystic. Yet it is difficult to relegate him to the rank of literary mystics like Richard Crashaw and Evelyn Underhill, persons widely read in mystical authors, the composers of poetry with mystical overtones: Even in these cases, we cannot be sure that they were not themselves mystics using the language of their predecessors out of modesty rather than coining a new terminology. Law speaks with authority, and in a language and a sentence structure his own. He sounds like no one else.

His deep sense of being an interpreter of Boehme needs interpretation beyond lists of parallel passages between them, such as Hobhouse has collected. The general sense of commentaries on their relationship would have it that Law selects from Boehme, omits the too esoteric, and gives a simplified version of the system; and I think this is by and large true. But the doctrine of Boehme, chiefly, when stripped of its alchemy and theosophy, is good Evangelical Protestant mysticism (cf. Boehme's "Of the Supersensual Life: Two Dialogues"). In my own judgment Law professed and felt an indebtedness and a reverence for Boehme which was partly adventitious, and he attributed to Boehme much which he had already read in the earlier mystics but was earlier not ready to accept—his "pride of intellect," his logical powers, and his sheer English common sense had first to give way.

The Spirit of Love is divided into four sections—a "letter" to a friend who is having difficulties with Law's teaching, who finds his "doctrine of pure and universal love" too refined and imaginary (fanciful), and who cannot reconcile that doctrine with the scriptural accounts of God's wrath. These are the problems which continue to engage us through the whole work; but after the letter follow three dialogues in which Law, or Theophilus, is replying at great length to the objections of his companions. These men are Eusebius, easy to be convinced of the doctrine, which, because of his affectionate nature, he embraces with open arms, and Theogenes, who is shocked to find, despite his progress in the doctrine, that "all the passions of his corrupt nature [are] still alive in him." One

167

is too easily made glad; the other, too discouraged by the fight he has before him. Law has to distinguish firmly between accepting the doctrine and putting it into practice, and, using characteristic mystical imagery, he reminds Eusebius that if he really possessed spiritual love he would know "how many deaths you had suffered before the spirit of love came to life in you."

In this whole book, divided into sections only to give semblance of reality to the dialogue-device of conversation, Theophilus is always the master, never doubting that he is in possession of the truth, and the other two are his students or disciples, men seriously in search of religious truth but with their intellectual difficulties as well as their difficulties in putting even what they see into practice. Their responses are of two kinds: Eusebius complains in the Second Dialogue that "your censure upon us seems to be more severe than just," and, in the same dialogue, Theogenes says "I could willingly hear you on this subject till midnight." The topics discussed run through all four parts, though Law says the Third Dialogue is to concern itself with "the practical part of the spirit of love, that so doctrine and practice, hearing and doing, may go hand in hand."

In actuality, Law's mind, even in the First Dialogue, goes back and forth constantly between theory and practice, between cosmic metaphysics derived from Boehme, and concerned with the seven properties of nature, and controversial references to current doctrines of the Calvinists and the Methodists and objections (unacknowledged) to his own earlier teaching in the *Call* about methods of life. And these same subjects are also discussed in *The Spirit of Prayer* (which is the spirit of love) and in the *Way of Divine Knowledge*. All Law's late works constitute a continuous meditation; he delights to repeat, with variations, these same motifs over and over, as does Boehme, so that if one has read one book attentively, and repeatedly, one has the system.

Law neither here nor elsewhere undertakes to prove the existence of God, an existence not denied even by Deists, who rejected revelation but held to "natural religion," which they maintained was "as old as creation" and "not mysterious." The existence of God was for Law certainly "proved" by scripture; yet he did not, I feel sure, rely upon scripture, but upon the negative argument, the presence of evil in the natural world— storms, hail, floods, and earthquakes—and the sin of man, and especially his desire, his restlessness, and dissatisfaction. As Saint Augustine said, "Our hearts are restless till they find their rest in Thee."

There is a striking passage in Newman's *Apologia* which contrasts the certainty of the being of "God, as certain as his own existence," and the dismal sight of the world and the confusion and futility of human history. How account for the contrast? Newman answers: "*If* there is a God, *since* there is a God, the human race is implicated in some terrible aboriginal calamity. It is out of joint with the purpose of its creator." So too felt Boehme and Law.

This "aboriginal catastrophe" for Boehme and Law was the fall in prehistory, first of Lucifer and the other rebellious angels, and then of man, who in Adam was created perfect (and so, like the Godhead, androgynous). This double fall brought into being the physical world as we know it: The fall of the angels brought into being matter; and the creation described in Genesis is really a second creation, that of a material world in contrast to the first creation, which was of ideas and forms in the imagination of God. The fall, first of the angels and then of men, has disordered God's intention. But at the end of time, the universe will be restored to its original order and harmony. As Saint Paul wrote, "We know that the whole creation groaneth and travaileth in pain together until now"; and "the earnest expectation of the creature waiteth for the manifestation of the sons of God." The end of the return movement is the "glassy sea of unity and purity in which Saint John [in *Revelation*] beheld the throne of God in the midst of it" (the phrase "the glassy sea" is dear to Law and is repeated over and over like a kind of mantra). But before that redemption, creation must pass through its seven properties of nature. "Nature can have no rest but must be in the strife of fermentation, vegetation, and corruption, constantly doing and undoing, building and destroying, till the spirit of love has rectified all outward Nature." These passages come from the first section of *The Spirit of Love*.

Both Boehme and Law, in his later period, were obsessed with the problem of evil, a problem cosmically antecedent to and inclusive of sin. How not to end up by attributing evil as well as good to God, or to postulate, like the Manichaeans, two gods, one good, the other evil? Boehme in effect solves this partly by removing the Deity by intervening stages from his creation, partly by supposing in God the principles both of love and "wrath." But Law seems to reject both of Boehme's solutions, and to take his stand on a God who is "pure love."

As Law does not undertake to prove the existence of God, so he does not attempt to prove that God, the supreme principle of the universe, is love on the basis of New Testament texts such as "God is love" or "God so loved the world"; he proclaims it, explains away all texts to the contrary, which chiefly come from the Old Testament, and then develops the implications of the doctrine that God is Love, unmixed and pure and therefore incapable of "vindictive wrath." And "the Spirit of God and the spirit of goodness are not two spirits," while wrath and evil are but two words for one and the same thing.

Though he never discusses figurative exegesis, Law's attitude toward the interpretation of scripture requires some comment. Jesus' ethical teaching in the Sermon on the Mount he took with the literalness of the later Tolstoi; but the "history" in the Bible, and in general the Old Testament, he treated with an unacknowledged but generous allowance of figurative "accommodation." At the beginning of *The Spirit of Love*, he quotes a correspondent as objecting to his "doctrine of pure and universal love" on the ground that so much is "said in scripture of a righteousness and justice, a wrath and vengeance of God that must be atoned"; that scripture seems to deny a "Being that is all Love." This objection Law never directly answers or rebuts; but from what he indirectly says it is clear that, like Swedenborg, he interpreted the wrath of God, his anger and jealousy, as not in God but in us, who are angry at God, who see God as made in man's image. Whatever the Old Testament may say, the New Testament proclaims a God of love. Says Law, speaking of both man and God, "The spirit of love can only love . . . it knows no difference of time, place, or persons, but whether it gives or forgives, bears or forbears, it is equally doing its own delightful work, equally blessed from itself."

Like Boehme and the older Protestant mystics, Law strongly opposed all forensic theories of the Atonement, those commercial and legalistic theories that Christ paid upon the cross our debt to God the angry Father, thus freeing us from our debt of guilt; and he opposed, too, all theories of Christ's righteousness being "imputed" to sinners. In *The Spirit of Love* Law writes: "The whole Truth . . . is plainly this. Christ given for us is neither more nor less than Christ given to us. And He is in no other

170

sense our full, perfect, and sufficient Atonement than as His nature and spirit is born and formed in us, which so purgeth us from our sins that we are thereby in Him, and by Him dwelling in us become new creatures having our conversation in Heaven."

Law does not accept the Calvinist doctrine that fallen man is totally corrupt: There is in man "a seed of life"; there is "a smothered spark of heaven in the soul of man," "The Christ of God" lies "hidden in every son of man," for the very desire for a heavenly life argues "something of Heaven hidden in his soul." That man is not wholly corrupt is "proved," for Law, by the fact that Adam had two sons, Cain and Abel—Cain, who murdered his innocent brother; hence, both principles must have come from Adam; and similar pairs appear in Ishmael and Isaac, and in Esau and Jacob: such "strife and contrariety" appeared in the sons of the same father. Nor does he accept, in their Calvinistic form, the doctrines of election and reprobation. He denies that they are eternal decrees relating to "any particular number of people." They relate, he says, "solely to the two natures that are . . . in every individual of mankind"—his bestial nature and "the incorruptible seed of the world, or the Immanuel in every man."

Of Wesley and the Methodists, who owed so much to the earlier Law but broke away from the latter, the mystic, Law seems to be thinking when he says that men should judge their "state of love" by "these angelical tempers, and not by any fervor or heat that you find in yourself."

Law attacks bibliolatry in a fashion that caused Eusebius to say, "It seems to me to derogate from scripture." What Law is concerned to do is to distinguish between the written word and the Word. If Saint Paul could say of the law that "it was a schoolmaster to bring us to Christ," then "one thing can be affirmed of the letter of the New Testament; it is our schoolmaster unto Christ, until Christ, as the dawning of the day . . . arrives in our hearts."

At the end of the third, the "practical" dialogue, one of Theophilus's disciples requests of him some rules or methods for attaining perfect love, or holiness. The earlier Law might have proposed some recipes, but not the later. Mrs. Stow says of Jonathan Edwards, of whose late treatise *The Nature of True Virtue* Law and his *Spirit of Love* strongly remind me, "he knocked out every rung of the ladder [to heaven] but the highest, and then, pointing to its hopeless splendor, said to the world, 'Go up thither and be saved.'" Both these rigorists felt mankind to be in search of easy ways. But the "one true way of dying to self is most simple and plain; it wants no arts or methods, no cells, monasteries, or pilgrimages. . . ." "Covetousness, envy, pride, and wrath are the four elements of self . . . or Hell." What is the cure—"the way of patience, meekness, humility, and resignation to God. This is the truth and perfection of dying to self."

In *The Spirit of Love*, Law is impatient of advice about not wasting time and money. He is forgetful of how many years he lived methodically in the Purgative Way, and now calls for total surrender of the self without "aids to devotion." He does not believe in instant conversion to a second birth, but wants to fix the mind of the spiritually minded only on that one end, the abolition of the carnal self. "Work out," as Saint Paul says, "your own salvation—with fear and trembling."

The teacher of love died on April 9, 1761, with appropriate "last words," recorded by his companion, Hester Gibbon: "He said he had such an opening of the divine life within him that the fire of divine love quite consumed him."

There is no shift in Law's uncompromising position, his rigorism, from the first of his eighteen books to the last; the deviation is in methods and tone, which depend on the audience addressed and the purpose. Like that other rigorist, Jonathan Edwards, he is the controversialist, the preacher to the many (in Edwards's case through actual sermons; in Law's, through his written homily the *Call*), and finally, in both cases, the mystic and the apostle of disinterested benevolence or pure love. In the *Call*, he addressed all professed Christians, summoning them to take their profession seriously, to "come up higher"; and he give variety to his book by alternating straight instruction and illustrative portraits, not devoid of entertainment. The later books are addressed to a smaller audience, men presumed already in the Purgative Way, who are eager to be enlightened in the higher reaches of the spiritual life.

Law never makes the relation between the two stages that his books represent as clear as it might be, and the modern reader needs the help of the traditional Catholic wisdom in spirituality to comprehend the relation between asceticism and mysticism. The higher stages presuppose the lower. Reared in the Church, nourished by the sacraments, a lifelong reader of the mystics, Law forgot the ladder by which he had himself climbed to his spiritual altitude.

Law seems never to have been read so much as in the last hundred years—that, I think, because we live now in a post-Christian period, as Bonhoeffer has called it, when, as in the eighteenth century, the truth of Christianity can no longer be taken for granted, and when the practical inefficacy and the sham of nominal Christianity is everywhere apparent. Law appeals to fundamentals, and the religion he preaches makes men take sides. So his appeal today is to Quakers, members of the Charismatic movement, and Evangelicals, but also to the spiritually minded, both within and without the Church. Like the Christian Humanist Fénelon, although unlike him in temper, he has an ecumenical audience. Law speaks to all as a writer of almost unique force, penetration, and insight.

(1978)

Selected Bibliography on William Law

Bouyer, Louis. *Orthodox Spirituality and Protestant and Anglican Spirituality*. English translation of *Histoire de la spiritualité chrétienne*. New York, 1969.

Elton, Oliver. *A Survey of English Literature, 1730–1780*. London, 1928.

Grainger, M. *William Law and the Life of the Spirit*. London, 1948.

Hobhouse, Stephen. *Selected Mystical Writings of William Law*. 1938. 2nd rev. ed., New York, 1948.

———. *William Law and Eighteenth Century Quakerism*. London, 1928.

Hopkinson, Arthur W. *About William Law*. London, 1948.

Hoyles, John. *The Edges of Augustanism: The Aesthetics of Spirituality in Thomas Ken, John Byrom and William Law*. The Hague, 1972.

Hunt, Dave. *The Power of the Spirit* [an adapted version of Law's last book, *An Affectionate Address to the Clergy*]. Fort Washington PA, 1971.

Huxley, Aldous. *The Perennial Philosophy*. New York, 1945.

Inge, William Ralph. *Christian Mysticism*. London, 1899.

———. *Studies in English Mystics*. London, 1905.

Law, William. *Complete Works*. London, 1762; reprinted by "G. Moreton" (G. B. Morgan), 9 vols. Brockenhurst, Hants. and Canterbury, Kent, privately printed, 1892–1893.

Overton, J. H. *The Nonjurors, their Lives, Principles, and Writings*. London, 1902.

———. *William Law, Nonjuror and Mystic*. London, 1881.

Palmer, W. Scott (M. E. Dowson). *Liberal and Mystical Writings of William Law* (with an introduction by William Porcher du Bose). London, 1908.

Pepler, Conrad, O. P. *The English Religious Heritage*. London, 1958.

Spurgeon, Caroline F. E. "William Law and the Mystics," *Cambridge History of English Literature*, ed. Ward and Waller, vol. 9 (1912): 305-328.

Stephen, Leslie. *English Thought in the Eighteenth Century*. 2 vols. London, 1876.

Stoudt, John J. *Jacob Boehme: His Life and Thought*. New York, 1968.

Stranks, C. J. *Anglican Devotion*. London, 1961.

Talon, Henri. *William Law: A Study in Literary Craftsmanship*. London, 1948.

Walker, A. Keith. *William Law: His Life and Thought*. London, 1973.

Walton, Christopher. *Notes and Materials for an Adequate Biography of the Celebrated Divine and Theosopher William Law*. London, privately printed, 1854.

Whyte, Alexander. *Characters and Characteristicss of William Law*. London, 1893.

Appendix A:
Our Colonial Heritage

Everett Emerson, editor, *Major Writers of Early American Literature*. Madison: University of Wisconsin Press, 1972. 301 pp.

It is a rare pleasure unreservedly to recommend a book; this pleasure I have with *Major Writers*, assembled and introduced by Everett Emerson, the editor of the recently founded scholarly journal, *Early American Literature*.

The figures considered in the book are Bradford, Anne Bradstreet, Edward Taylor, Cotton Mather, William Byrd, Edwards, Franklin, Freneau, and Brockden Brown. The contributors of the essays on them are all specialists—monographers or editors. Thus Donald Stanford has produced the authoritative edition of Taylor; Lewis Leary the standard book on Freneau. The writer on Edwards, D. B. Shea, Jr., is the author of *Spiritual Autobiography in Early America* (1968), which concludes with an excellent chapter on Edwards and his "Personal Narrative." David Levin, who considers Bradford, is the author of a *Defense of Historical Literature*, that is, of history as nonfictional narration, as an art. The essays now collected are not, however, reprints from the contributors' existing publications but written expressly for this volume; and, while varied in style and tone, they show evidence of a common agreed-upon purpose and of skillful editing.

The book constitutes an introduction to American literature of the first two centuries, expert and up-to-date, addressed not to specialists in the Colonial period (though they can read the book through with profit and pleasure), but to a larger audience, to Americanists who work primarily in later periods, to graduate students, and even to that not altogether mythical "general public." In this aim it remarkably succeeds. The essays are scholarly yet unpedantic. They combine intellectual history with literary criticism. They give adequate, never excessive, characterization of the personalities behind, and in, the books. Especially worthy of note and praise is the freshness of almost all the essays, even those on the best known and most written upon of the authors; this, it should be added, despite the fact that the experts are discussing subjects on which they have before written.

175

Where all the essays are so excellent, it may seem invidious to single any out for special commendation; yet I shall venture to do so. Easily the masterpiece of the collection is Sacvan Bercovitch's essay on Cotton Mather, which Mr. Emerson rightly terms "the fullest yet written on Mather as a man of letters." It is indeed the best single essay on the difficult figure of Mather I know—balanced and just, rich and deep in its philosophical perspective, brilliantly written. Next come, I think, the essays on Franklin, by Le May, and Edwards, by Shea—the former offering much new information, also witty and humorous; the latter allusive and perceptive: both revivifying treatments of the two *most* major authors of the period.

In Mr. Emerson's introduction, appropriate honor is done to Moses Coit Taylor, the first serious student of early American literature, whose well composed books are still not entirely superseded, and to the great twentieth-century scholars Perry Miller, Kenneth Murdock, Howard Mumford Jones, and Louis B. Wright. It is a pleasure to see a new generation arising so competent to continue their succession, and to see that strictly intellectual history is now yielding to a history more concerned with formal values.

A reviewer, even when a warm commender, is expected to offer a few demurs or raise a few questions, and so I do, though my objections are slight. I would have preferred to have such a study end with the Colonial period, excluding Freneau and Brown, who (according to one's literary-historical system) belong to the early Nationalist period or the Pre-Romantic; perhaps I would have similarly substituted for "Early American" either "Colonial" or "Baroque and Neoclassical." And, lastly, I am made uncomfortable by the adjective "major," so relative a term that one has to qualify it by "more" or "less." I remember too, that the continuity of literature as an institution runs rather through the "minor," more strictly characteristic, writers. There is still no proper "literary" history of American poetry in terms of period, style, and genre, treated, as our Colonial poetry in particular should be, from the perspective of comparative literature. It is to be hoped that the Early American group will soon undertake such a study of the Colonial centuries, in which figures like the Connecticut Wits and the Philadelphia poets, Evans and Godfrey, can be analyzed in terms of their period-styles.

(1973)

Appendix B:
Modern Literary History

Sergio Perosa. *Henry James and the Experimental Novel.* **Charlottes-ville: University Press of Virginia, 1978. 219 pp.**

American literature has been eagerly translated and studied in Italy since the late twenties, both by creative writers like the novelists Pavese and Vittorini (engaging critics of our literature) and scholars like Emilio Cecchi and Mario Praz. Italian universities now have chairs of American as well as English literature. Perosa, who is professor at the University of Venice, has published (1965) in English translation a book, a good one, on Scott Fitzgerald; is the author of *Le Vie della Narrativa Americana* (1966); and has translated into Italian *The Sacred Fount* (1963). His present monograph on James, which "grows out of an interest of many years," is written in excellent idiomatic English, but it bears the marks of its European origin in two ways: first, the display, impressive, even prodigal, that its author has kept abreast of the books *on* James which have prolifically appeared from American graduate schools and university presses in the fifties and sixties; and, second, the frequent, and relevant, quotations (in French) from apposite French creative critics, the de Goncourts, Zola, Sartre, and Camus.

Perosa's book is essentially not criticism (the value-judgments are few and are chiefly cited from others, whose opinions fill the footnotes); it is "literary history," a term which the author several times claims as his genre but does not define. By it he means approximately the history of literature, or of an author, as art, as aesthetics, as structure and style. Biography and social history and "ideas" are excluded; and while "themes" are admitted, they are admitted only as *motifs* in the art-work, not as separate parts.

The book bears some evidence of being a collection of separate studies, connected by the word and the themes *experimental*. One rather isolated chapter, "*The Whole Family* and the Lonely Author," discusses at overlength James's strange participation, at his own request, in a collaborative novel that serially ran for a year (1906–1907—that is, a year after the completion of his trilogy of mature masterworks) in *Harper's Bazaar*—a collaboration in which his fellows were such as John Kendrick

Bangs, Elizabeth Stuart Phelps, and Henry Van Dyke. James's chapter, twice as long as any other and written in his richest late manner, effectively brought the action of the novel to a standstill. This venture, however, was scarcely experimental, save as a last, and misguided, attempt to reach a popular audience.

The substance of the book is divided into two parts, the first of which deals with the twenty-year period (1881–1902) between *The Portrait of a Lady* and *The Wings of the Dove*; and this period in turn is bisected by James's dramatic years (1889–1895). His first experiment, partly inspired by Zola, was to attempt the naturalistic novel (in contrast to his earlier realism in the vein of George Eliot), and he explored new themes, like the proto-lesbianism of Olive Chancellor and the London anarchism of *The Princess Casamassima*. After his unsuccessful venture into the theater, he made his brilliant experiments with the new techniques first used in *The Spoils of Poynton* but carried out more boldly in the dialogue-limited *Awkward Age* and in the unique *What Maisie Knew*, in which the limited consciousness is combined with dramatic tightness of structure. Over these experiments the French well-made play and the plays of Isben hovered as influence. What Perosa has to say in the early part of his book is chiefly excellent summary of the already known.

His chapter on *The Sacred Fount*, the baffling book which ends this period, summarizes all the conflicting statements that evince both James's own embarrassment about the book and his desire to throw inquirers off the track and also the mutually contradictory interpretations offered by commentators on this puzzle; but here Perosa has a theory of his own to add: that this "novel" is really a critique of the novel and an anti-novel, a precursor of the *nouveau roman* of Robbe-Grillet and Nathalie Sarraute; it is a novel of appearance, of phenomena, and it shows its unnamed first-person narrator and protagonist (assumed to be, though James never so designates him, as either a writer or a writer *manqué*) to be trying, as any realistic novelist must, to give coherence and "plot" to the relationships between his characters. "And isn't possibly the very aim of James's novel to question the possibility of a fictional organization of experience by means of the novel itself?" Yes, "possibly." This reviewer, who lacks a theory of his own, was interested but unconvinced. Certainly James was not, for he immediately went on to write *The Ambassadors*.

Much the freshest part of Perosa's book is his discussion of *The Sense of the Past* and *The Ivory Tower*, two novels left incomplete and published posthumously, each "completed" by the author's Scenario of the whole, which Percy Lubbock published in 1917. Both novels were composed after James's visits to the United States in 1904–1905 and 1910–1911 and, thematically, exhibit his reengagement in weighing the claims not only of two worlds but of two time-periods, pronouncing a hesitant vote for America and the Modern. The chapter on *The Ivory Tower*, James's very last writing, is Perosa's most illuminating; it brilliantly analyzes the final relation between James's Scenario, "an unparalleled sequence of working notes by a master-craftsman," and the completed three chapters of the novel—how the transition from one to the other "is characterized by a process of abstraction, by a gradual blurring and exclusion of facts and features." He quotes Enrique Gomez, who wrote in 1918, upon the progressive devouring of the novel by the rapacious " 'scenario,' " and adds, "Not only the scaffolding, but the story line and all actions between characters tend gradually to disappear. We are given only hints and guesses. . . . People talk but do not converse —their utterances brush but do not meet. A 'rich indirectness' pervades every aspect of language." In his final adventure in "the unsaid and the unstated," James shows, at the end, the lifelong experimentation which makes of him "one of the fathers of literary Modernism,"—a claim which Perosa cautiously does not push towards arguing for James as a specific influence on Proust, Joyce, Woolf, or Beckett, only as, if these but knew it, their fecund background.

It is to be regretted that Perosa, limiting himself to the later part of James's career, does not adequately remind us that throughout his life James was, in a less limited sense, an experimenter—first, indeed, in his earliest short stories, a Romantic—and that he was a diligent student and acute critic of the novel before ever he wrote a novel and throughout his life, passing in review the work of Sand, Balzac, Turgenev (whom he read in French) as well as Austen and Eliot and so on, to the end. He is preeminently our sole American novelist who, for a lifetime, gave to the masters of the literary art the same unremitting care that his admired painters, with the advantage of instruction in an atelier, gave to theirs.

Literary history, in the strict sense, needs, however, to be supplemented. The Master was not merely a technician, even though his own

Notebooks lend themselves to such an interpretation; for James, as Joseph Conrad wrote of him, was also "the historian of fine consciences." Though his mind may have been too fine to be violated by ideas other than aesthetic ones, his sensibility was highly and scrupulously moral; and he perfectly sensed the corruption of the English society in which, with elaborately mixed feelings, he lived. Accordingly, any specialist in James needs from time to time to turn from monographs like Perosa's to critical studies by non-specialists who, without neglecting the artistic, fill in other dimensions of James and apply other criteria—such studies as Matthiessen's *The Major Phase*, Newton Arvin's pieces in *American Pantheon* (1966), the brilliantly ecumenical 1934 "Homage" of *Hound and Horn*, Lubbock's introduction to the *Letters*, and W. H. Auden's eloquent evocation "At the Grave of Henry James."

(1979)

Appendix C:
Pater Revisited

Gerald Cornelius Monsman, *Walter Pater's Art of Autobiography.* **New Haven: Yale University Press, 1980. 173 pp.**

Let me begin this review with some intellectual autobiography of my own. Young—when I was 22—I enrolled in Irving Babbitt's course at Harvard, "Rousseau and Romanticism"; did so knowing nothing of Babbitt's classical and austere "New Humanism." Regarding myself as an idealist, and identifying Romanticism with idealism I was bewildered and shocked to find Babbitt, who so obviously stood for all that was sound and orthodox, attacking Romanticism.

I became a fervent and dogmatic convert to the New Humanism; yet the very next year, when another great teacher, less vigorous but more sensitive than Babbitt, introduced me to Walter Pater's *Marius the Epicurean*, saying, with flattering inaccuracy, that he was sure I already knew and cared for the book, I bought and read it with ardor, unaware, it seems, of any possible dichotomy between Babbitt and the aesthete, Pater. And at about the same time, meeting with the earlier books of George Santayana, I greatly admired his "Life of Reason" series, especially *Reason in Society* and *Reason in Religion*—books which appeared to me to be stating essentially the same position as Babbitt's, but giving Humanism a more subtle, sophisticated, and civilized form.

In making these identifications I was naïve. Babbitt, for whom both men would have been aesthetes, hedonists, and decadents—and naturalists in the bargain, could have tolerated neither—would have regarded their views as all the more dangerous because so refined, so gildedly corrupt. For me, however, a young "idealistic" American, all three seemed opponents of the current American world of barbarism, crudeness, and vulgarity; they represented the classics, Greek and Latin (my major in college) and philosophy and religion against the un-cultured of President Eliot's elective system; they represented the Humanities against the ever ascending sway of the natural and social sciences; they opposed technology and gadgets and industrialism; they were spokesmen for the archaic values which were everywhere being threatened. In making for the three men this broad front of affirmation and rejection I was not wholly misguided or naïve.

All three of these generalists I have revisited in my old age, pleased after professional retirement, to return to these writers of life-wisdom, and world-perspective, and general culture, these writers whom the specialized cares and concerns of middle life force us to neglect. Especially, for the length of a review, I address myself to Walter Pater (1839–1894), who, after long being out of fashion and the attention of readers, scholars, and critics, has recently been receiving heed more expert than my own.

Pater was *the* philosophical teacher of the 1890 generation of young British aesthetes—of Yeats, Lionel Johnson, Arthur Symons, A. C. Benson, and Oscar Wilde. It was Wilde who, in his "Decay of Lying" and "The Critic as Artist" (both contained in his book, *Intentions*), with aphoristic brilliance and boldness, popularized Pater's subtle and recondite critical doctrines; it was Wilde who, by his flamboyant postures and the scandal of his life, trial, and condemnation, cast shadows of suspicion on the celibate don and his first book, *Studies in the History of the Renaissance* (1873).

Pater's *Renaissance* is a collection of separately written and published essays, all little masterpieces of what their author calls "aesthetic criticism." Concerned chiefly with Italian painters of fifteenth-century Italy, but also with poetry, and with two essays on scholar-critics, Pico della Mirandola and Winckelmann, these essays take cognizance of historical scholarship and art history, yet they centrally aim at rendering in words the impressions of one perceptive observer and his search for a formula which shall express the essence of another man's work. This is literary impressionism of the highest order: delicate, subtle, meticulously and beautifully written—written slowly, and to be read slowly, attending to, bearing down upon, each word. The writing, albeit so sedulous, is yet fresher, less weary, than any of Pater's subsequent work.

What attracted prime interest to the book as it first appeared, however, was the "Conclusion" (1868), a meditative essay which begins by characterizing the solipsism in which each of us is said to live, our impressions being but those of "the individual in his isolation, each mind keeping as a solitary prisoner its own dream of a world"; and it ends with the hedonistic counsel to seize the moment. Pater is not in general an aphoristic writer, but one aphorism remembered by any who know Pater's name comes from his "Conclusion." It reads, "To burn always with this hard, gemlike flame, to maintain this ecstacy, is success in life." (The word *success* is here a jarring note: it did not then have the vulgar commercial sense it now connotes; substitute the word *end*.)

This "Conclusion," said to be immoral and quoted with appended warnings by fellow Oxford dons and ecclesiastics, Pater withdrew from the second edition of his book, not to recant its doctrine but, as he said when he reissued it, to call attention to his next book, *Marius the Epicurean*, in which he had "dealt more fully . . . with the thoughts suggested by the 'Conclusion.'"

Marius the Epicurean: His Sensations and Ideas (1885), harder to read than its predecessor, is the central achievement of his life, a masterpiece of a highly specialized sort. It is at once an historical novel, and a novel of ideas. Its titular hero is a young Roman aristocrat who is for a time a secretary to Marcus Aurelius; his purely contemplative life is traced between the ages of (approximately) 18 and 35. In the course of the book, he passes from the pagan country religion of the old Romans to Epicureanism, then considers (but finally rejects) Stoicism, and dies on the verge of the Christian and Catholic religion, indeed, a kind of martyr to the faith he had never overtly accepted. This strange book is almost without action, characters, visual description, or audible speech (the discourse is all reported)—concerned almost exclusively with "sensations" (sensuous impressions) and "ideas" (philosophies). The book is written in Pater's highly mannered style, a style anything but familiar or idiomatic and conversational, a *written style* and furthermore one in which English is written as a "learned language"; a style not matter of factly and rationally lucid but, instead, intuitive and suggestive, one for distinctions, discriminations, qualifications.

II.

After a half century of virtual oblivion, Pater is currently enjoying a revival. One of the first signs of this was an excellent chapter on him in René Wellek's judicious, and judicial, *History of Modern Criticism* (Volume II, 1965); Harold Bloom has a sympathetic essay in *Ringers in the Tower* (1967). Also in 1967 appeared fine monographs on him by Gordon MacKenzie (*The Literary Character of Walter Pater*) and Gerald Monsman (*Pater's Portraits: Mythic Pattern in the Fiction of Walter Pater*). The latter is a study of the genre to which most of Pater's work belongs—the meditative narrative in which the leading character draws his substance from Pater himself, while the description sets it in a past historical period and place. *Marius* is such a portrait; the unfinished *Gaston de Latour*, set in the France of Montaigne, is another; there is a whole volume of shorter *Imaginary Portraits*, one of them of a young Dutch aristocrat, a disciple of Spinoza's. The chief concern of Monsman's first book, however, is to trace the mythic archetypes which he sees as underlying these portraits. In this work Monsman seems to reflect, sensitive exegete that he is, the influence of Northrop Frye, whose *Anatomy of Criticism* (1957) gave rise to a vogue for mythic and archetypal criticism.

Now in 1980 Monsman has published another, actually his third, book on Pater, *Walter Pater's Art of Autobiography*, a brilliant, subtle (and, I think, partly wrongheaded) treatment of the titular theme. Monsman appears now under the influence of the French Structuralism and Deconstructionism currently vended by the literary departments of Johns Hopkins and Yale: the relevant names among the critics are Barthes, Hillis Miller, Derrida, and de Man. For me, an old New Critic, these are not hallowed names; and I have not found their works illuminating, or, for the most part, even intelligible. For me, as for my generation of critics, the center of literary study is the text; but for these others, the text is just what is to be deconstructed in order that one can center on the soul of the author; and the business of the critic is to create his own creation on the pretext of criticizing: "The Critic as Artist" was Wilde's formula for it. Yet, though highly dubious of Monsman's method, I find his use of it the most sensitive and persuasive specimen of its kind with which I have met; and, having followed up his bibliographical leads, which are rather concealed than displayed, I can attest to his mastery of all Pater's writing and the Pater "literature."

Monsman rightly sees Pater's work as a protest against any literature which tries to offer the illusion of life, against Realism and Naturalism, against even Henry James's attempt to erase the author. Pater's writing flaunts its character of being art and not life: writing and not speech; and emphasizes the presence of the author. The most striking precursor of this kind of work seems to me *Tristram Shandy*, though Sterne appears to be mentioned neither by Pater nor by Monsman. This kind of writing leads to Proust, Joyce, and Virginia Woolf, whose unacknowledged ancestor Monsman sees Pater to be: "these ultra-reflexive writers whose fictional worlds invariably lead back to the generative activity of art itself." And so, Pater's writings, "rather than attempting a veridical illusion of life, . . . affirm the autonomy of their artifice."

Of Monsman's five chapters and introduction, I recommend especially the introduction and chapter I, "Criticism as Creation." And there is certainly a sense in which criticism is, and must be, a form of autobiography: so soon as one goes beyond facts and quotations (and even both of these have to be selected, and by someone, and from some point of view), one must interpret. A sensitive critic writes about his author only what he knows not only from outside but from inside as well, by empathy, by overlap. All we can ask is that objective information and subjective insight be clearly differentiated, that the reader of the criticism can discern on what bases judgments are offered.

What I must totally reject is the attempt, in chapters 3 and 4, at a post-Freudian explanation of why Pater was never able to complete his second novel, *Gaston de Latour*—his supposed sense of guilt at having willed, somehow, the death of his father (which occurred when Pater was an infant), of his mother, who died when he was fourteen, and, much later, of his brother (and "sibling rival"), William.

Less fanciful reasons could be offered for the abandonment of *Gaston* such as the other projects which began to engage and engross Pater—for example, his *Greek Studies* of myth and sculpture, and his *Plato and Platonism* (regarded by Pater as his greatest book). And consider this: Pater had originally planned a trilogy of novels on the same pattern as *Marius*, with the protagonist in each a philosophical or at least contemplative young man, a spectator of life, a figure drawn from its author but set against differing backgrounds of time and place, the latest to be of nineteenth-century England. It is likely that he found himself, when halfway through the second of his series, already weary of the project— already aware of the obvious repetition, the unavoidable monotony.

It is hard to come to final terms with Monsman's 1980 book. I find it difficult to summarize, to state its burden, still more to criticize: it is delicate, subtle, and stimulating, but also hesitant and evasive. Denis Donoghue has called his perceptive review of it (in the *New York Review of Books* for May 14, 1981) "Hide and Seek"—though presumably applying that phrase not only to Monsman but (quite justly) also to Pater. What, finally, does Monsman think of Pater? Does he like him? or admire him? identify with him? I can't say. As for Pater, did his Marius cease being an Epicurean, and become something else, or just (as the central chapter of the novel, "Second Thoughts," suggests) refine upon his hedonism, distinguishing between lower (sensual) and higher (intellectual) pleasure? Did Pater himself, who had been, like Ruskin, one of those boys who play at being priests; who had then a period of mocking disbelief (as one can learn from Thomas Wright's 1908 life of Pater): did he then return to the Church? He did aesthetically, certainly, but did he intellectually, and in faith? What does Monsman think?

Pater's own writings, for which Monsman offers a provocative (as well as elusive) approval, have left me with very mixed and conflicting feelings. I cannot doubt, however, that he is a strangely impressive writer in his low-pitched, slow, languid insistence. For the English-speaking (or -reading) world, he remains *the* unique aesthete. His own derivations are almost entirely Continental—Winckelmann, Goethe, Heine, Baudelaire, Gautier, Hugo. Though English, Pater was extraordinarily uncompromising. If, in the latter part of his not long life (he died at 55), he softened the expression of views generally offensive, yet he never recanted. He is a hero of vocal passivity and articulate spectatorship.

(1981)

Appendix D:
Tradition and the Individual

Edward Shils, *Tradition*. Chicago: University of Chicago Press, 1981. 334 pp.

All men can, probably, be divided into those whom the word tradition is likely to attract, among whom I count myself, and those whom it is likely to repel. The word, and its derivative adjective, traditional, turn up everywhere. Yet there has, till now, existed no book dealing with tradition in general, tradition the abstraction, as distinct from the plural, traditions. Professor Edward Shils, eminent seventy-year-old sociologist, who has given twenty-five years of study, meditation, teaching, and writing to the subject, has attempted such a book, a considerable achievement, excellent in kind.

To which group does Shils belong, to the defenders or the detractors of tradition? His richly suggestive and meticulously written book, I would say, intimates divided impulses and allegiances—a division suggested by the two very different persons to whose memory the book is dedicated.

The first of these persons is T. S. Eliot, whose early and most famous essay, "Tradition and the Individual Talent," is a literary essay on the contemporary poet's assimilation of the poetic past. In 1974 Shils delivered the T. S. Eliot Memorial Lectures at the University of Kent; and prefatorily he acknowledges how much Eliot's writings—presumably (though he never mentions or quotes from them) *The Idea of a Christian Society* and *Notes Towards the Definition of Culture*, as well as the literary essays—had done to "arouse and nourish my mind on tradition." Though the Eliot Memorial Lectures are said to have been incorporated into the present book, I wish I could have read them in their original, unincorporated form.

The other author, much more quoted and cited in this book, is Max Weber, the German sociologist (d. 1920), whom Shils, a professor of sociology at the University of Chicago, obviously regards as the greatest figure in the entire repertory of sociologists. Weber, best known for his *The Protestant Ethic and the Spirit of Capitalism* (1904–1905), was a man of unusually wide intellectual range. Essentially he was an historian of ideas, a learned and candid reporter; but his own point of view, not often overtly expressed, is that of the rationalist, the man of the Enlightenment, who believes in mankind's gradual emancipation from tradition and in the gradual bureaucratic organization of the world.

Where does Shils stand? It is my guess—one which I am not in a position to substantiate—that, during his lifetime, he has moved from early identification with Weber to a partial organic conservatism nearer to Eliot's position, though never supported by Eliot's religious faith. Shils's book is sympathetic to tradition in general without ever showing acceptance of any one tradition.

Though praise is to be given Shils's book for its absolute impartiality, judiciousness, justice, and lucidity, yet these virtues prove, at some times and in some moods, irksome, irritating. The carefully written long book, set in small print hard on the eyes, cannot be speed-read, nor can it be read as I like to read a book—first piecemeal, sampled here and there to catch its quality and its drift, then taken in its prologue and conclusion, and finally, if these procedures prove the solid worth of the book, read in its entirety, *seriatim*, and closely. *Tradition* yields itself to no such method: must be read in sequence and in its entirety or not at all—at least by a conscientious reviewer. It contains no developed examples, though copious examples are briefly cited; and no dogmatic, programmatic, or propagandistic thesis emerges.

This is not a pro- or con-book (despite the author's sympathy with tradition) but a serene and ranging survey of tradition in general and traditions in particular—traditions religious, political, social, philosophical, literary, artistic, scientific. The book is bafflingly difficult to summarize, or indeed to recall either in general or in detail—this chiefly probably because it isn't, doesn't profess to be, an argument.

The very word "tradition" is slippery—hard to pin down. With this problem of terminology Shils never wrestles; reading his book, one slides from sense to sense: Tradition stands for the past in contrast to the present; the collective in contrast to the individual; the unconscious in contrast to the conscious; the felt in contrast to the thought. It is, in a sense, all that is not Reason; yet Reason itself is (as Shils points out) a traditional concept, or a concept shaped by tradition.

The opposite of tradition would appear to be Reason—and so the Enlightenment thought, regarding tradition as virtually equivalent with superstition; yet, as Shils observes, "The patterns of reason and scientific method are not acquired by each possessor who works them out for himself. They are for the most part transmitted to him." And indeed, "the program of reason and scientific knowledge could never have succeeded to the extent that it did without being overgrown by tradition. The confidence in the powers of reason and science became a tradition accepted with the same unquestioning confidence as the belief in the Judeo-Christian accounts of the origin and meaning of human existence had been earlier."

So Tradition and Reason cannot, by a philosophical mind, be as crudely (or as sharply) opposed to each other as they appear to the ordinary layman. And probably the whole never clearly defined area of Shils's book may lie in just the removal of this crude dichotomy—the removal of which strengthens the case for tradition and, more largely, for conservatism.

As for traditionality and superstition, there is "no necessary connection between them": "Superstitions are certainly common among progressivists, secularists, and rationalists, but traditionality has been made to bear the obloquy which superstition calls forth among progressivists; their own superstitions spared. The same may be said of intolerance and dogmatism. . . . Traditionality no more requires intolerance and dogmatism than do scientism, rationalism, and secularism."

Not all traditions are conservative: Shils cites books called *The Socialist Tradition, The Tradition of Modernity,* and *The Tradition of the New.* Indeed, the moral of his book might be—though Shils nowhere says so—that every thinker, whether he knows it or not, belongs to some already existing tradition—or to a mixture of existing traditions—*i.e.,* that the universe of thought affords but a finite number of modes of thinking. All the basic types of philosophical thought, to my perception, appear already in classical antiquity—idealism, materialism, scepticism, hedonism, and ethical rigorism. Heraclitus and Parmenides, Plato and Aristotle, Epicurus and Epictetus, Sextus Empiricus, Democritus: all these names represent traditions. To be a conscious individual, one might say, is to find the tradition to which, by virtue of one's innate nature and temperament, one already belongs.

To find oneself is to find one's tradition; to be original is to place oneself in one's tradition, by the act of discovering one's ancestors, and to add refinements, adjustments, modern "improvements," and variants—

to do all which is to emancipate oneself from vulgar contemporaneity. Fortunate is the man who can find his congenial tradition in that of his rearing—the country, family, political persuasion, religion in which he was born and reared. But one may have to convert to a tradition he did not inherit, or may have to supplant it.

Irving Babbitt, the great teacher at Harvard during the first half of this century, had to create for himself a syncretistic system, impressive indeed as he embodied and expounded it. Called by him the "New Humanism," it posited an ethical system of which Confucius in the Orient and Aristotle in the Occident were the exemplary sages, while on the religious level, the possible supplement to ethics, perhaps even its ultimate foundation, Buddha and Jesus were the teachers and exemplars. As Babbitt represented, in his own magisterial presence, this syncretistic fusion of East and West, it seemed, was felt to be, a tradition.

Studying under Babbitt as a youth, lonely, isolated intellectually from those around me, seeming eccentric to my fellows, I felt that I had now discovered my ancestors, a distinguished line even if distant in time and place; and this discovery gave me strength and courage. In Paul Elmer More, Babbitt's ally, I found another mentor, who, to his American and British spiritual ancestors, had added the Hindu thinkers, and Plato, and later the Greek Fathers of the Church and the Anglican divines of the seventeenth century.

Babbitt's most brilliant student, T. S. Eliot, later the friend of More also, began his intellectual career by adopting the double lineage of Sanskrit and Greek antiquities; ended up by becoming an Anglo-Catholic and a British citizen: "joining" two institutions not his by birth—ended up by adopting a far more institutional view of tradition than that of his elders—indeed, if I may so put it, he espoused a far more traditional view of tradition than either of them. When we—as men generally— speak of defending Graeco-Roman European Christian Culture, we mean defending an aristocratic state, an episcopal church, and a university founded on a liberal arts college in which the humanities occupy the central position. Tradition, in this traditional sense, emphasizes the shared inheritance as embodied in institutions—all organized, continuous, and more or less coherent expression of values and ideals.

In these last paragraphs, though I seem to have forgotten Shils, I have not. I have wanted, against the background of his wide-ranging study of traditions, in the plural, and tradition in the abstract, to single out an example of the kind of thinking and questioning which I do not find in his otherwise excellent book. Some of his chapter heads will best illustrate the kind of book it is: "The Endurance of Past Objects" (*e.g.*, in Artifacts; in Religious Knowledge; in Works of Science and Scholarship; in Literary Works); "Stability and Change in Tradition"; "Why Traditions Change: Endogenous Factors . . . Exogenous Factors"; "Tradition and the Rationalization of Societies"; "The Prospects of Tradition"; "The Permanent Task."

I keep asking, as I read and reread this book, what follows? What should we do, we who cherish much of the past and deplore how rashly it and its lessons are brushed aside? After years of study devoted to tradition, Shils should, I think, have some practical suggestions to offer for an intelligent, not uncritical, conservatism. I cannot find that he has.

(1983)

Appendix E:
Foreword to *The Courage of Judgment*

George A. Panichas, *The Courage of Judgment: Essays in Criticism, Culture, and Society*. Knoxville: University of Tennessee Press, 1982. xiii + 303 pp.

Professor George Panichas has wished me to introduce his latest book; and this I do in deference to his modesty, meanwhile reflecting that, at this midpoint in his dedicated literary career, he and his work need no sponsorship.

Panichas and I have been friends for upwards of ten years, our relation beginning when, after reading his essay on the Cambridge Platonist, Henry More, and the Greek spirit, I wrote him an appreciative letter. Our friendship, growing ever warmer, has progressed through occasional meetings and occasional telephone conversations, but most frequently, and to our mutual edification, through the exchange of letters. What I like to call, in echo of my early studies in neoclassicism, the "epistolary art," is dear to us both; and letters we both write with the same assiduous care as our essays tended for publication. I know my friend best, I think, from his meditations, couched in epistolary form.

Friendship is cardinal for us both, ranking next to adherence to principles. Loyalty to persons and loyalty to principles—sometimes these two high loyalties painfully conflict, as our letters testify; and occasionally we have differed over matters of what my old master, Irving Babbitt, might have called "mediation," over matters of practical policy, or what medieval thinkers would have called "prudence." But then we have each practiced patience with the misjudgment of the other.

In his new book Panichas demonstrates his loyalty to earlier admirations: he adds heroes without subtracting or substituting others, transcending by including; F. R. Leavis, D. H. Lawrence, and Dostoevsky stay in, while first Simone Weil and then Irving Babbitt is added, included. It is difficult to see how all these admirations, all these loyalties, can be reconciled; but it is an engaging task for the friendly critic, and critical friend, to work out the unnamed, uncommon denominator.

Panichas thinks of himself as conservative, but if "conservative" can cover Lawrence and Babbitt, or even Simone Weil and T. S. Eliot (who wrote a sympathetic preface to Weil's *The Need for Roots*), what can the term mean? That we may say, with Panichas in his introduction to the *Courage of Judgment* (1982), is just the function of the critical spirit to explore. The very word "conservative" proves as slippery, when examined, as other terms in constant use. Perhaps one thinks of it first as a political term; but, if one is a generalist, only at first thought, for subsequent thoughts show it to be of universal application—notably, however, to religion and education, to the *paideia* and culture which shape us all. A conservative, in Panichas's sense, is not a reactionary, an unmitigated finance-capitalist, else he could not approve of the Christian Socialist, Simone Weil. The conservative is not necessarily a Christian, for Lawrence, the vitalist, was no more Christian than Nietzsche, and Babbitt was a New Humanist and, unofficially, a crypto-Buddhist; but, in the deepest sense, he must be devout.

Whatever else it is, Panichas's conservatism is neither doctrinaire nor programmatic. Deeply concerned, as his anthologies and the essays in his book both show, with politics and religion, and their relation to literature, he does not proselytize for any specific ecclesiasticisms, though presumably his taste is for the more traditional and orthodox varieties; and politically he is neither a monarchist, nor, necessarily, a Republican. He stands for man's recognition of his dual citizenship in church and state, society visible and invisible, for man's recognition that all we are we owe; that we do not, and cannot, begin *ab ovo* and *de novo* but are heirs to a great inheritance of tradition and wisdom, represented in the West by our joint indebtedness to the Greek philosophers, the Hebrew prophets, and the Christian saints.

Panichas admires monolithic men who attack and expose the sins and follies, the errors and heresies, of the modern age; yet, for the most part, he does not himself appear in that role of enemy, but rather as guide and as the sympathetic expositor of the great exponents of positions he admires—preeminently Leavis, the moralist; Babbitt, the humanist; and Weil, the prophetic and spiritual seeker. In his humility he calls our attention to his own masters. Though his discipleship is selective—that is to say, discriminating and critical—he dwells not on any restrictions he may put upon his approval but upon those aspects of his heroes to which he can give reverence.

194

Foreword to *The Courage of Judgment*

Panichas's *The Reverent Discipline* (1974) is subtitled "Essays in Literary Criticism and Culture." "Literary" criticism is "reverent" because it is ancillary to imaginative literature (*i.e.*, poetry, the novel, and drama), and because its prime object is the appreciative illumination of writers and works selected by the taste of the critic. *The Courage of Judgment* represents, for Panichas, a shift of emphasis: here, the essays are in "criticism—and culture and society." In both titles, "culture" stands halfway between Arnold's use of the term, which we might now gloss or paraphrase as "high culture," and "culture" in the quasi-sociological sense the term bears in our time: the common matrix of habits and attitudes shared by a society, the matrix out of which more specialized and professional emphases develop.

Courage of Judgment is a title complementary to *Reverent Discipline*, for the critic—whether a literary critic or a critic in the readily intelligible larger sense which covers men like José Ortega y Gasset, Lewis Mumford, and Babbitt—needs both reverence and courage of judgment: reverence in the presence of persons and principles he deems higher than himself and in the presence of masterpieces of art and thought, and courage of judgment to make his own assessment of what are those higher values. Panichas praises Sir Harold Acton, an aesthete, for his "reverence for beauty"; and, since we may assume that our critic's supreme values are the so-called Platonic trinity of the Good, the True, and the Beautiful, reverence for beauty, though beauty be the least of these values, is itself a virtue.

Henry James speaks, in a phrase of which both Panichas and I are fond, of "the ceaseless wear and tear of discrimination" required by the act of judgment. It indeed takes courage to face, in one's own silent thought, in one's speech, in one's letters and in one's published writings, this ceaseless and fatiguing discrimination—never to allow oneself to slip into easy compliance with the currently accepted compromised standards of one's neighborhood, one's university (academics are not noted for their courage), one's inherited nation, one's church or religion. There can be no relaxation of the critical spirit, no unbending of the bow; and no sphere is exempt from its operation—if the critical spirit be justly joined to the spirit of reverence. It is a "vulgar error" to suppose that conservatives need accept whatever is; and Panichas's conservatism, like Babbitt's (though it often judges differently), is highly critical. Any position can be taken hastily, on grounds of temperament or tradition; but it can also be taken reflectively, after experience, observation, meditation, and judgment, as Panichas does.

Earlier I have said "All we are we owe"; but I should have added, "all save our present act of judgment and commitment." In ecclesiastical terms, we are baptized into the faith of our parents but "confirmation" awaits some degree of maturity, some time at which we are capable of ratifying the decision provisionally made for us.

It is the supreme merit of *The Courage of Judgment* that it covers almost the whole of man's basic categories—political theory, religion, and education—that its "criticism" is so unspecialized, so general and generalist. Its prime virtue will not be grasped if one reads only the essays on the subjects of one's own professional and temperamental competence. I can myself testify how such a total reading has forced me, in my old age, to reexamine, rethink, rejudge, reflect upon the range and repertory of my own intellectual positions. Panichas's book might thus be called what Coleridge called one of his, *Aids to Reflection*.

On the first page of his penultimate *Democracy and Leadership*, Irving Babbitt wrote: "When studied with any degree of thoroughness, the economic problem will be found to run into the political problem, the political problem in turn into the philosophical problem, and the philosophical problem itself to be almost indissolubly bound up at last with the religious problem"; let us add, somewhere along the line, the problem of education, to which Babbitt devoted his keenly sound first book, *Literature and the American College*. The critic, as distinct from the purely literary critic, is deeply aware of this interpenetration of values—as was Matthew Arnold, in his *Essays in Criticism* as well as in his books on culture, society, and religion, as was T. S. Eliot, in all his later books. Such is the ancestry, in the English line, to which Panichas belongs.

Like all thoughtful men, Panichas esteems knowledge as a good, but fears its substitution for wisdom (*sapientia*): indeed wisdom, and its Latinized adjective, *sapiential*, appear often in his book. Knowledge and specialized expertise are not enough without wisdom and what is inseparable from it, character, responsibility, integrity. These qualities, of which the world stands in such dire need today, cannot be acquired just by taking college courses, or just by reading whatever comes to hand:

reading as such may be an opiate, a more refined version of watching whatever emerges on the TV screen. For the development of character, the "elective system" of Harvard's President Eliot will not suffice. It is not true that any subject, any course, is as valuable as any other. There must be a rigorous selection of what is truly basic, balanced, central—one is even tempted to say: of traditional value.

We live, fifty years after Babbitt, in a time when his predictions have come true. The modern world goes on its deterministic way. Novelty, whatever its kind, is prized over continuity (a central conservative word); bigger is equated with better (though surely, "small can be beautiful"); change of whatever kind is identified with progress, or improvement, though it is often just the reverse.

The courage of judgment is the prime virtue of the critic, his *unum necessarium*. To criticize is to take a stand—it is not necessarily to damn or to deride, as popular usage would have it; much of the best criticism is considered and selective celebration. If detachment is requisite, so is empathy—each in its place. Experience and a certain degree of learning are the prerequisites to detachment; just as an unabashed openness to new experiences and further learning are to enlightened empathy. All this suggests the necessity for balance; but balance (which so easily may seem calculation and compromise) is not to be sought for as such.

The critic must work out his decisions with fear and trembling, for he must be a responsible guide, if not an actual leader, in a world which, most of all in America, but increasingly in the whole Western world, becomes quantitative. In an age given over to all manner of polls, so that one can discover the "trend" and, lest one prove eccentric, follow it, the critic must judge for himself, and then be possessed of the final courage to utter his judgment.

(1982)

197

A Bibliographical Note

"A Spiritual Chronicle" was first published in *Search for the Sacred: The New Spiritual Quest*, edited by Myron B. Bloy, Jr. (New York: Seabury Press, 1972), in two parts and originally entitled "The Crisis of the Young," 21-30, and "The Tradition of the Spiritual Life," 115-22.

"Carroll and His Alice Books" was first published in *The Sewanee Review* (Summer 1980): 331-53.

"Herrick Revisited" was first published in *The Michigan Quarterly Review* (Summer 1976): 245-67.

"Frost Revisited" was first published in *Canto: Review of the Arts* (Spring 1978): 145-56.

"The Quest for Auden" was first published in *The Sewanee Review* (Spring 1979): 229-48.

"The Poetry of Auden" was first published in *The Southern Review* (July 1981): 461-78.

"Homage to Allen Tate" was first published in *The Southern Review* (October 1973): 753-77.

"A Survivor's Tribute to T. S. Eliot" was first published in *The Southern Review* (October 1985): 1110-1117.

"Pondering Pater: Aesthete and Master" was first published in *The Sewanee Review* (Fall 1983): 643-54.

"William Law: Ascetic and Mystic" was written as the introduction to *William Law: A Serious Call to a Devout and Holy Life [and] The Spirit of Love*, edited from first editions by Paul G. Stanwood (New York: Paulist Press, 1978) 11-32, with a selected bibliography, 499-500.

"Our Colonial Heritage" [Appendix A] appeared as a review of editor Everett Emerson's *Major Writers of Early American Literature* (1972), in *American Literature* (November 1973): 453-54.

"Modern Literary History" [Appendix B] appeared as a review of Sergio Perosa's *Henry James and the Experimental Novel* (1978) in *The Henry James Review* (November 1979): 107-110.

"Pater Revisited" [Appendix C] appeared as a review of Gerald Monsman's *Walter Pater's Art of Autobiography* (1980) in *Modern Age: A Quarterly Review* (Fall 1981): 407-410.

"Tradition and the Individual" [Appendix D] appeared as a review of Edward Shils's *Tradition* (1981) in *Modern Age: A Quarterly Review* (Winter 1983): 80-82.

"The Courage of Judgment" [Appendix E] was written as the foreword to George A. Panichas's *The Courage of Judgment: Essays in Literary Criticism and Culture* (Knoxville: The University of Tennessee Press, 1982) ix-xiii.

About the Author and Editor

AUSTIN WARREN (1899–1986) was professor emeritus of English at the University of Michigan and served five years on the executive council of the Modern Language Association. In 1975, he was honored with election to membership in the National Institute of Arts and Letters. Author or editor of more than a dozen books, his best-known works include *Theory of Literature* with René Wellek, *Rage for Order*, and *The New England Conscience*.

GEORGE A. PANICHAS is the author of several books of literary criticism, including *The Critic as Conservator*. He edited *The Simone Weil Reader* and is editor-in-chief of *Modern Age: A Quarterly Review*. He holds a Ph.D. from Nottingham University and is a fellow of the Royal Society of Arts of the United Kingdom.

In Continuity: The Last Essays of Austin Warren
Introduced and edited by George A. Panichas

MERCER UNIVERSITY PRESS, Macon, Georgia 31210-3960.
ISBN 0-86554-501-4.
MUP/H393.
Page design and cover photograph by Jon Parrish Peede.
Agaramond 12 headers and footers and TimesNewRoman
Postscript 11/10/9 text via Wordperfect 5.1/5.2.
First Printing June 1996.
Printed and bound in the United States.